# EDEN UNDONE

# EDEN UNDONE

A True Story of Sex,

Murder, and Utopia at the

Dawn of World War II

## ABBOTT KAHLER

 CROWN
NEW YORK

Published in the United States by Crown, an imprint of the Crown Publishing Group, a division of Penguin Random House LLC, New York.
crownpublishing.com

Library of Congress Cataloging-in-Publication Data
Names: Kahler, Abbott, 1973– author.
Title: Eden undone: a true story of sex, murder, and utopia at the dawn of World War II / Abbott Kahler.
Description: First edition. | New York: Crown, [2024] | Includes bibliographical references and index.
Identifiers: LCCN 2024019732 | ISBN 9780451498656 (hardcover) | ISBN 9780451498670 (ebook)
Subjects: LCSH: Utopias—History—20th century. | Murder. | Sex.
Classification: LCC HX806 .K25 2024 | DDC 307.7709866/5—dc23/eng/20240527
LC record available at https://lccn.loc.gov/2024019732

Hardcover ISBN 978-0-451-49865-6
International Edition ISBN 978-0-593-80082-9
Ebook ISBN 978-0-451-49867-0

Printed in the United States of America on acid-free paper

Editor: Libby Burton
Editorial assistant: Cierra Hinckson
Production editor: Liana Faughnan
Text designer: Aubrey Khan
Production manager: Dustin Amick
Proofreaders: Robin Slutzky, Andrea C. Peabbles, Tess Rossi, and Chris Fortunato
Indexer: Stephen Callahan
Publicist: Mary Moates
Marketers: Chantelle Walker and Rachel Rodriguez

9 8 7 6 5 4 3 2 1

First Edition

Title page illustration: Shutterstock.com/Pen-Is Production
Page xi map illustration: Jeffrey L. Ward

*For S.J.W.*

*I think I would have liked you*

Nobody owns anything, but everyone is rich—for what greater wealth can there be than cheerfulness, peace of mind, and freedom from anxiety?

—Thomas More, *Utopia*

Maybe there is a beast. . . . maybe it's only us.

—William Golding, *Lord of the Flies*

# CONTENTS

# PART III · · · · · · · · · · · · · ·

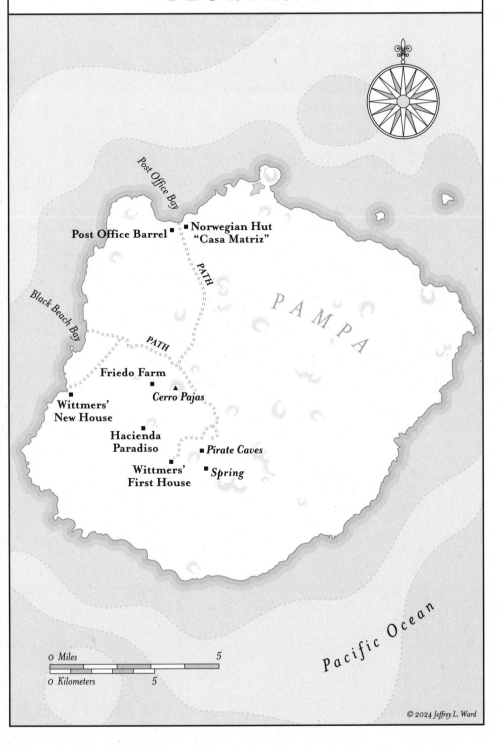

# FLOREANA

Post Office Bay

Post Office Barrel ▪

▪ Norwegian Hut
"Casa Matriz"

*PATH*

Black Beach Bay

*PATH*

P A M P A

**Friedo Farm**
▪

*Cerro Pajas* ▲

▪
**Wittmers'
New House**

**Hacienda
Paradiso**
▪

▪ *Pirate Caves*

**Wittmers'
First House**
▪

▪ *Spring*

*Pacific Ocean*

0 Miles       5

0 Kilometers     5

# AUTHOR'S NOTE

As strange as this story may seem, this is a work of nonfiction, with no invented dialogue or events. Everything that appears between quotation marks comes from an archive, diary, letter, newspaper article, book, or unpublished manuscript. Many of the characters in this story wrote first-person accounts of these events, which allowed me to accurately depict detailed scenes and entire conversations and to reveal characters' thoughts, gestures, facial expressions, personalities, and histories. A comprehensive list of notes and sources (including for each line of dialogue) appears at the end of the book.

# PROLOGUE

## Paradise Lost

*Los Angeles, November 1934*

The wire reports traveled three thousand miles across the Pacific Ocean and described a gruesome scene: On Marchena Island, a bleak and barren speck of land in the northern part of the Galápagos, passing fishermen found two bodies. Over the course of several months the tropical sun had mummified the corpses and eroded their features. Both lay on their backs. The larger one measured about six feet and had a tuft of brown hair sprouting from the skull. Parts of the body in touch with the ground were punctured with wormholes. The other, presumed to be a woman, was a foot shorter and dressed in torn scraps of clothing. The desiccated facial skin was affixed so tightly to the bones that the skull looked encased in parchment. Neither wore shoes. One of the fishermen noticed traces of faded footprints, as though the victims had paced the ground just before death came.

Hundreds of burnt matches and a pristine pile of wood suggested they had failed to start a fire. The head of a seal, the body of another, and scaly strips of iguana flesh apparently served as a final meal. The pair had died of thirst; on Marchena, covered almost entirely with lava rock, there was no freshwater. Beneath their overturned skiff lay a passport, baby clothes, several photographs, and a cache of thirty letters. The fishermen unsealed and read them all. One described the contents as "a hell of horror." Another confessed they inspired nightmares.

A few of the letters were addressed to George Allan Hancock, a Los Angeles industrialist and explorer who had made several excursions to the Galápagos. Inspired by Charles Darwin and, more recently, the American naturalist William Beebe, Hancock sailed to the islands in search of exotic wildlife but found himself equally intrigued by the humans he encountered.

Over the past five years, eight people had settled on the island of Floreana, 112 miles south of Marchena, with one common desire: to create a utopia, although each of them had different visions as to what a utopia might be. The settlers were a doctor and his patient; a war veteran, his pregnant lover, and his teenage son; and a Viennese noblewoman with two male lovers by her side and a pearl-handled revolver on her hip.

Hancock was aware of escalating tensions on the island. There had been violent disagreements, a suspicious shooting, fantasies and threats of murder. A recent letter from the doctor to Hancock hinted at further turmoil: "We will hope that you will come once more. . . . Then I must tell you what I cannot write—because I have no proof of it."

Hancock planned to answer this plea, but death was faster. As he learned when he came ashore, the Floreana community had lost yet another member.

# PART I

## Our Inner Demon
## and Its Whims

# ONE

# The Doctor and His Disciple

**A**t first the doctor terrified Dore.

It wasn't his stature that provoked this reaction; he was short and slender, with narrow shoulders and wiry muscles, wormy veins twitching beneath his skin. Nor was it his face, framed by untidy brown curls and anchored by striking blue eyes, with a wide mouth that parted, in moments of contemplation or amusement, to expose the tip of his tongue.

Rather, it was the combination of it all. What seemed prosaic—and even charming—separately fused into a disquieting whole. His body's lithe movements suggested a predator's gait; his gaze was one of harsh and final judgment; and his general disposition seemed strangely absent of any amiability or compassion, all the more unsettling given his chosen profession. She stopped just short of calling him brutal, and hoped he would never lay his hands on her.

Dore Strauch Koerwin, newly twenty-six years old in that spring of 1927, received treatment at the Hydrotherapeutic Institute in Berlin, which pioneered research on the healing powers of water. She had been diagnosed with multiple sclerosis three years prior during a long hospital stay that included a hysterectomy, but this relapse brought an odd benefit. Any time spent in the hospital meant a respite from the drudgery of life with her husband, and this savage-looking doctor, despite his demeanor, piqued her interest as he roamed throughout the ward. Her fellow patients were equally intrigued. "He is fanatic on raw food," one confided. Another said, "When he once commences to speak of raw food and vegetarianism he never stops." It was inevitable, she supposed, that as he prowled from room to room and bed to bed, he would one day stop at hers.

The doctor introduced himself as Friedrich Ritter and gave her a thorough examination.

"You are not ill," he told her.

"But the professors said I am," she countered. "They said I could never get my health back again."

"You are not ill," he insisted, "but you desire to be ill." Then he walked away.

"He can look through myself," she thought, and blushed, feeling strangely exposed. She arranged to see the doctor during his private consultation hour and confessed to all that "pressed" her soul, with one exception: she didn't mention her marriage. Yet when she finished, Friedrich delivered this acute assessment: "You are not happy in your matrimony . . . let us try to change the base of your illness."

He insisted she "need not submit to illness" if she could retrain her brain to mend her body. He did not like sick people, he admitted, and whenever he encountered a patient who resisted the "will to mend," he gave up rather than waste his energy. He recommended books about the malleability and mysteries of the mind, including the works of Prentice Mulford, an American humorist and philosopher who wrote that "to say a thing must be, is the very power that makes it." Conversely, to say a thing isn't is the very power that vanquishes it. Friedrich understood the mental stress behind her physical pain, and their daily conversations became her medicine, unburdening her mind of its darkest thoughts.

Dore had enjoyed a happy childhood in Berlin, with a schoolmaster father whose strictness in his work never affected his home, and a mother whose "instinctive understanding" enabled her to sense Dore's wishes and fears. Dore preferred animals to people, and found that creatures who growled and snapped at others would come sit quietly at her side. A part of her believed that she was not like other children, a conviction that deepened as she matured. "There was some task which I was born to fulfill," she later wrote, "although I had no notion what it could be. . . . I only knew that it was something great, and in a way I cannot describe I was always looking for it."

She tried to find it in the German Revolution of 1918 by aligning herself with "the poor and poorest," as she put it, and revolting against the elite. Upset by the proliferation of alcoholism and venereal diseases among the men she'd tried to help, she decried "low instincts and passions," finding inspiration in Friedrich Nietzsche's *Thus Spake Zarathustra* and concluding that the only true path for the development of humanity was through individual dedication to this pursuit. "If each one first would fulfill the good he demands of others," she wrote, "our earth would soon be a paradise."

When the revolution ended, she turned her energy inward, training to be a doctor. After working all day as a bank teller, she attended night school to prepare for the university entrance exam, a grueling schedule made even more challenging by her unconventional diet. "I might have stood the strain of all this better," Dore admitted, "had I not chosen that time for confining my diet exclusively to figs"—a decision based on her reading of the German philosopher Arthur Schopenhauer, who, while not a confirmed vegetarian, railed against the destruction of one life to sustain another. During moments of reflection, she acknowledged that her spirit, too, had weakened. "My soul was starving," she wrote, and she began searching for something to feed it.

•   •   •

The difficulty of this regimen led Dore to abandon her studies, but she soon found another project: Hermann Koerwin, nineteen years her senior, a family friend and high school principal whose ingrained routine and staunch convictions presented an intriguing challenge. With sufficient dedication, Dore believed she could coax him away from his fusty old habits and "thaw him out with sunshine." After they married, she realized the folly of this idea.

Hermann was excessively frugal, insisting the couple live in rented rooms instead of their own apartment. When they had sex, she found it offensive and repellent, especially when her illness set in and destroyed any chance of bearing her own child. In the end Hermann proved equally determined to change her; he wanted, in Dore's estimation, a standard housewife whose goals and opinions stayed within the confines of his own. When her illness flared again, necessitating an extended stay at the

Hydrotherapeutic Institute, she viewed it as an opportunity to reevaluate her life. And now here came this peculiar little doctor, inviting her to experience his carefully curated world.

After ten days under Friedrich's care, she felt well enough to be discharged, but still craved his company. Throughout 1927 and the following year, she walked him to work every morning through the Tiergarten as Germany stood on the precipice of drastic and devastating change. European newspapers warned of a nationalist uprising. In southern Bavaria, fascists met with members of Der Stahlhelm, or "Steel Helmet," an organization for veterans of the Great War, which served as a paramilitary wing for the conservative German National People's Party. They protested against the Weimar Republic and the international order instituted by the Treaty of Versailles. Motor Transport and Motorcycle Unions conducted mysterious military exercises, and fascists in Austria began to organize. In Berlin, the Sturmabteilung, or SA, the newly formed paramilitary wing of the rising Nazi Party, attacked communist citizens at the city's dance halls and ice cream shops and the Lichterfelde Ost train station.

This violence stood in stark contrast to the raucous pleasures and excesses of Weimar culture. On Kalckreuthstrasse in the West End, the location of Friedrich's private practice, stood Eldorado, a popular "transvestite venue," where Berlin high society and adventurous tourists reveled alongside writers and artists and the actress Marlene Dietrich, on the cusp of international fame. Occasionally the two worlds intersected, as when Ernst Röhm—co-founder of the SA, close friend of Adolf Hitler's, and openly gay man—visited Eldorado with a British journalist. The cross-dressing hostess greeted Röhm and sat down to chat with him. The journalist assumed the two had a "business relationship," but Röhm sharply corrected him: "I'm not his client. . . . He's one of my storm troopers."

It was the strangest of times, and Friedrich Ritter, as Dore learned, was the strangest of men: forty-one years old, a scholar of physics and philosophy, a fervent believer in excessive mastication. He wanted to test his theory that gums would become "horny" enough to substitute for teeth. He also sought to map the human brain. Friends and neighbors thought him a "fantastic crank." His former professor called him "someone who takes his own path, a man in whom love of people and hatred of people unite equally; a physician for whom no step is too bold to prove his method to himself, an eccentric who achieves eccentric things." He intended to live for at least 150 years and argued that a carnivorous diet incited a nervous condition that would hasten the end of European culture. He lived in a cheap, tiny one-bedroom apartment and sowed his own oats in a window box so he could make his primary food, porridge. He never wore clothes at home. He did not trust manufactured clothing and made his own garments from coarse linen. He especially did not trust the "civilized shoe" and braided his own leather sandals. In fact, he trusted nothing civilization had to offer, and had long been desperate to flee it.

·  ·  ·

In their long walks through the city, he shared with Dore the details of this desire, which had taken root decades earlier. Born in May 1886 in Wollbach to a prominent local family—his father, Johann Friedrich Ritter, was both the town's mayor and a wealthy shopkeeper—Friedrich was a small and sickly child, frequently besieged by colds, headaches, earaches, and a general, lingering malaise. His doting mother, Elisabeth, wished to delay his enrollment at school, but relented when Friedrich insisted on attending. His ailments were exacerbated by the brutal beatings of his elementary school teacher who, in Friedrich's words, was a "firm believer in the virtues of a hazel switch." Neighbors would recall him as a loner and "peculiar nature boy" who found solace in the outdoors and books. He spent long afternoons rambling through the Black Forest or rereading the *Leatherstocking Tales* and *Robinson Crusoe*, imagining himself a brave castaway on a remote island.

In seeking to abandon the civilized world, Friedrich was following the German philosophy of *Lebensreform*, or "life reform," a cultural movement that emerged in the late nineteenth century. In 1906, a German named William Pester settled in Palm Canyon, California, where he explored natural healing, practiced vegetarianism and nudism, and even made his own shoes. He cultivated a community of kindred spirits, among them a German neuropath known as the father of the detox bath and a married couple who owned Eutropheon, a vegetarian raw food restaurant. Together they practiced Eastern mysticism, lived off the land, slept outside, and wore as little clothing as possible. One member wrote a "cook-less" book that condemned the violence of a carnivorous diet and offered recipes, including "soups for the toothless."

Friedrich also studied philosophy and was particularly enthralled by the work of Friedrich Nietzsche: the notions, simply put, that all of morality is subjective; that God is a lie and death is not to be feared; that all humans are not created equal (with the *Übermensch,* or "superman," being the highest attainable form); and that humans are no better than animals. "What a great prophet Nietzsche was," Friedrich wrote. "A man is more of an ape than any ape." As a high school student, he grew obsessed with mortality. When the town gravedigger gave him a skull, he soaked it in a bucket of chlorinated lime until it was bleached bright white. Across the skull's forehead, in black ink, he sketched a Nietzschean line about the "painless state of eternal being" and set it on an altar in his bedroom.

Though he claimed that his father, an avid hunter, taught him how to use firearms, Friedrich found no pleasure in killing animals for sport. He recalled a specific incident in which his father entrapped a red-tailed bird that had been attacking his beehives. His father instructed him to carry the bird home, but on the way Friedrich unlatched the cage, allowing it to fly free—the shame of betrayal eclipsed by his pleasure in facilitating the escape.

A relative told a different story of Friedrich's interest in animals. In this version Friedrich did cultivate an affinity for hunting, a slingshot his weapon of choice. He shot trout in a local stream, and magpies as they circled the dead trout, and rabbits as they bounded through the forest, and even the occasional cat that crossed his path. After dark, he took them all to the shed behind his home where he kept a secret laboratory. He skinned and dissected each one, marveling at how the parts looked separated from the whole. One day, he burned his laboratory down, offering his mother a cryptic explanation: "It was a somewhat dangerous, but highly interesting experiment."

• • •

While enrolled at the University of Freiburg, studying chemistry, physics, and philosophy, Friedrich married an aspiring singer named Mila Clark. He seized control of her career and urged her to accept a contract with the opera house in Darmstadt as a soprano, where she sang the roles of Carmen, Mignon, and Amneris. When she confessed that she'd rather stay home, Friedrich objected. Mila's destiny was not that of a dull and docile housewife, according to Friedrich. Like he himself, Mila was destined for higher things. They had long, intense arguments that often turned violent. Once he hurled a vase against the window. Sometimes he struck her. Many times they reconciled with sex that was itself tinged with violence, Mila confided to relatives. She escaped to his mother's house in Wollbach, and their separation was extended when Friedrich left to fight in the Great War. Later, he would tell Dore that his religious views leaned toward Buddhism, and he never anticipated taking any part in the killing of others, but a "psychic experience" compelled him to volunteer.

In July 1916, Friedrich was stationed along the Somme River in northern France, where British and French Allied forces planned an offensive against the German army. The Allies discharged chlorine and phosgene gas upon the German trenches, to swift and dire effect. "Great mustard-coloured suppurating blisters, with blind eyes," one nurse wrote, "all sticky and stuck together, and always fighting for breath, with voices a mere whisper, saying that their throats are closing and they know they will choke." Friedrich lay in a ditch, flanked by dead bodies rotting in the heat, the poisonous clouds coiling around him. After several months in a hospital, where he was treated for liver damage, he was discharged and sent home.

The experience changed him irrevocably. He came to believe that war was encoded in human genes; it pulsed inside him like a second malevolent heart. At a party hosted by his sister Elisabeth, he argued with Mila and slapped her. His brother-in-law intervened, grabbing Friedrich's arms to restrain him. Friedrich left, returned with an ax, and, with a few feverish blows, chopped his sister's piano until only the keys remained. A month later, disgusted by the sight of his nephews' dachshunds rolling around in their own shit, he took his pistol from his pocket and shot both of the dogs dead.

·   ·   ·

He retreated into his studies and completed them by 1923, becoming a doctor and a dentist and a purveyor of his own philosophical ideas. After long days at his private practice and Berlin's Hydrotherapeutic Institute, he wrote essays and gave lectures about chemistry and physics and the effect of sunlight on human skin. Albert Einstein, who lived a short walk away on Haberlandstrasse, became a casual acquaintance, and by the time Friedrich met Dore, he was convinced that there would one day exist a bomb powerful enough to destroy all of civilization.

Friedrich did not have a purpose for or within a society that measured progress by the consumption of goods and commodification of people. He concluded that the world was beyond redemption; he could do nothing for it, and it could do nothing for him. Society was, in his opinion, "a huge, impersonal monster forging ever-new chains with which to shackle the free development of its members." He would withdraw not into loneliness per se but into his *own* loneliness, a solitude of his specific design.

Over the course of two years, from 1927 to 1929, Friedrich ushered Dore into his life. He did not mock her relative ignorance of philosophical matters, but rather devoted himself to leading her down the path he had so diligently carved. "I cannot have a love-sick woman full of romantic notions trailing after me into the wilderness," he told her, but she argued that she would be an ideal partner.

Dore believed he was one of the world's great geniuses, and that he sought the unforgiving wilderness not to punish the flesh but to illuminate the mind. Her leg, damaged from the effects of multiple sclerosis, would not be an impediment, she told him. She would find strength in self-denial, in taming her own ego. Eventually, Friedrich acquiesced, calling her his "fellow pilgrim on the way to a final wisdom." She suspected she was the only woman in his acquaintance whom he did not despise.

Dore confessed her love for Friedrich to her husband, Hermann. Furious, he ordered her to avoid the doctor, but she refused. Secretly she wished that Hermann had put up a fight, yelled and pleaded, betrayed even a speck of passion. "There were no scenes between my husband and myself," she lamented. "I should have respected him more if there had been." In contrast to Hermann, she sensed within Friedrich the "triumph of the masculine" and told herself not to take his harshness personally; when he demanded sacrifice of her, he required it doubly of himself.

At home, Dore still felt obliged to play the role of the housewife, accompanying Hermann to social gatherings where she mingled with dull strangers, her high heels pinching her feet and paining her bad leg. With Friedrich she could avoid what he called "the evil inventions of modern costume" and dress purely for comfort and ease. On the rooftop of Friedrich's building, he and Dore lay side by side and imagined their future— the two of them alone, isolated and safe, far away from the burgeoning madness in Germany. Right away they decided that their ideal locale should be tropical. They spent long hours at the State Library in Berlin, perusing geography books with photographs of sumptuous, far-flung islands, starting west and moving east, arriving at last on the Galápagos Islands, which, they were intrigued to discover, did not look very sumptuous at all.

What better location for their private utopia than the rocky, lava-encrusted islands, just off the western coast of South America? They wanted tropical, but not necessarily a paradise: the typical vision of a soft, abundant land with glittering sand and waving palms would not suit their Nietzschean dream of rigorous self-creation.

Charles Darwin, whose 1835 exploration of the islands informed his theory of evolution, had called the archipelago "a little world within itself" and "sterile and incapable of supporting life." Nearly a century later, in 1924, the American scientist William Beebe visited the Galápagos and wrote an internationally best-selling book, *Galápagos: World's End*, in which he reached a similar conclusion: "When I enter a tropical jungle I feel only elation . . . [b]ut here there came the feeling of despair." One of Beebe's colleagues, Dr. Charles Haskins Townsend, the first director of the New York Zoological Society's Aquarium, was even harsher in his assessment: "If his Satanic Majesty were to arrange a crawling and climbing torture for lost souls, [the Galápagos] would inspire him. The islands lie just about as Vulcan cast them down, or perhaps it was Lucifer who heaved them out."

For America, still swept up in the romance and thrills of the Roaring Twenties, Beebe's dispatches provided a glimpse into the future of exotic travel—a luxury that seemed increasingly accessible to even those of modest means. Newspaper advertisements extolled the benefits of cruising around the world—"one unbroken holiday, 133 days, the most glorious days of a lifetime," promised the American Express Travel Department. "The cost, usually the first consideration, is little more than expenses at home for the same period. And as for the necessary time—just a little planning now, a little saving on commonplace trifles, perhaps—for this Great Adventure."

For Dore and Friedrich, haunted by the Great War and facing increasing unrest in Europe, Beebe's words offered a true escape to an exotic land. A successful retreat from the world required an uninviting locale, they believed, lest the world followed. Aspiring to sublime tranquility meant an equal risk of misfortune: if they couldn't find happiness in such a place, perhaps they didn't deserve it.

# TWO

# Dying in One World

Hoping to ease the betrayal of their jilted spouses, Dore proposed a brazen scheme: she would persuade Friedrich's wife, Mila, who was currently living with Friedrich's mother, to move in with Hermann. But the plan had to remain secret. Friedrich was a well-known doctor and lecturer, and the gossip columns might sensationalize such an unorthodox arrangement, even in Berlin.

To escape detection by curious neighbors, Friedrich urged Dore to disguise herself for the meeting with his wife. Dore tried on her costume, baggy trousers and loose shirt, and Friedrich enjoyed her performance, assuring her that she passed for a boy. He would stay behind in Berlin and await her report.

One day in May 1929, she took the train to Wollbach and knocked on the door of Friedrich's childhood home, a striking Italianate mansion that stood close to the tracks. At first Mila received her coldly, but—to Dore's surprise—her anger quickly thawed. Deeper into the afternoon, Mila even became enthusiastic about the notion of joining Dore's husband and running their household. "Mrs. Ritter, very opposite of her husband, had all the qualities that my husband admired in a woman," Dore later wrote. "She is a shining example of what a housewife should be." Friedrich's mother was kind and charming, and before Dore left, they embraced each other and wept.

Dore had no trouble convincing Hermann, and he had only one condition: Dore must write a letter explaining why she was leaving him, including a declaration that he had always given her everything she wanted. To Dore, he seemed more concerned with avoiding a public scandal than with the logistics of making a life with a stranger.

She and Friedrich began to sift through their possessions, separating the luxuries from the necessities, seeking items that could serve a dual purpose. Two large wooden boxes would later make sturdy tables; two zinc bathtubs could provide roomy storage; a stainless-steel tray might double as a mirror. Mosquito netting would be vital, but they decided against lamps, believing they would be in bed by sundown. Dore bought a full set of dishes and utensils and large steel milk cans, which would make ideal larders to protect their food from ants. Friedrich packed carpenter's tools and garden equipment. Dore gathered mattresses, sheets, blankets, a hundred-yard bale of calico for making new clothes, and sewing needles, which she sealed in paraffin to prevent rusting. She gave her finest clothes to Mila but packed a few dresses made of artificial silk, thinking they'd keep her cool in the tropical heat.

They couldn't bear to leave behind their library of Greek and Latin textbooks, medical books, and Nietzsche's *Thus Spake Zarathustra*. Friedrich packed one other vestige of his old life: his medical instruments and a small stash of aspirin and digestive pills. Dore urged him to include a supply of morphine, but Friedrich grew furious at the suggestion; hadn't she yet learned that the mind was the most efficient healer of all? When he suggested taking a gun, it was Dore's turn to admonish; wouldn't a lethal weapon deny their commitment to peace toward all living things?

Dore told her family of the news. "A great melancholy" overcame them, Dore noticed, but her mother promised to do her best to comfort Mila and Hermann and to support their new, makeshift household. Her father was particularly distraught; she had always been his favorite child. At a dinner party, Dore said her final farewell to her parents, her teenage sister, and her closest cousin. "I shall see you again," Dore's mother said, and Dore didn't have the heart to say she planned to never return. Perhaps hoping to spare her family further distress, Dore did not invite Friedrich, but Mila—innocent in this odd scheme—entertained the group with her singing. One of the most popular tunes of the day was "Mit dir allein auf einer einsamen Insel," which translated means "with you alone on a lonely island."

.  .  .

At the end of June 1929, Friedrich gave up his medical practice and made his final public appearance, a lecture on the ideal amount of protein in the human diet. "He looked pale and outwardly wretched," one attendee observed, "and I had the impression that he had gone too far in his personal experiments." The few colleagues aware of his plan doubted it would work; Friedrich was imaginative, and in some ways brilliant, but also an absolute dilettante in terms of survival skills. To one more supportive friend, Friedrich wrote a final letter justifying his decision:

> I feel as if I am dying in one world in order to be reborn in another, and am thus both sparing myself from reincarnation while enjoying two lives in the same body. If we weren't going now, we would end up reincarnating after dying somewhere in the South Sea. We are simply taking a shortcut, especially as it seems to fit so perfectly. Regarding our intentions and motivations, I must strictly insist that the physical and mental by no means be mixed. Our physical desires can never be controlled by the mind, we cannot control all our drives. That is why we are going without a plan, but will rather be driven by our id—our inner demon—and its whims.

Fully committed to staying on Floreana for the rest of his life—and aware of intractable dental problems he might encounter—Friedrich also took one important preemptive measure: he had all his teeth extracted and replaced by a set of steel dentures. But in a hint of adversities to come, he neglected to account for the shrinkage of gums, and the teeth would not stay in.

.  .  .

On July 3, 1929, at nine o'clock in the evening, the SS *Boskoop* set sail from Amsterdam carrying Dore and Friedrich and fifteen other third-class passengers, all crammed inside five dank cabins. Friedrich found their fellow passengers likable, with a few exceptions. A smoker sometimes spoiled the air, a vice made all the more unpleasant given the steward's reluctance to open the hatch. Some were provincial and ill-prepared for even the most obvious challenges of the journey, such as protection from heat and sun. "Of course, overfed, alcohol-addled brains are much more susceptible," Friedrich wrote, "and our chubby young beer brewer, who is travelling with his fat preacher's daughter and bloated one-year offspring to Nicaragua—true ambassadors of European culture—quakes at the thought of the sun like a sunburnt child." He was also disgusted by a "portly farmwife" who tried to cure her seasickness by "eating as much meat and fat as often as possible."

At least, Friedrich noted, no one snored.

They passed through the narrow green arm of the English Channel and the choppy Bay of Biscay with its jagged patches of rock. He and Dore were mesmerized by the staggering coastline of the Azores, with cliff walls rising up like an ancient amphitheater and topped by a lighthouse, casting a glow on the natural stage below. Halfway through the journey, they came to the Tropic of Cancer, and days and nights became the same length of time, with dusk lasting only half an hour. Next came Curaçao, and as the outline of the island slowly revealed itself, bald cliffs gave way to bushes, and the small, white-edged Dutch houses looked to Friedrich like "colorful, geometric corpuscles."

On July 24, three weeks after their departure, they reached Panama and disembarked to explore Cristóbal, on the Atlantic side of the canal. The landscape was so arid that every shrub seemed near death. Dore watched, laughing, as a monkey climbed Friedrich and perched atop his head, parting his hair in search of lice. Then he rummaged through Friedrich's bag, stealing a business card and a fountain pen, and defended his booty by biting Friedrich's arm. He in turn grabbed its hair and shook it back and forth to show, he declared, that he was "the stronger of the two."

Back on the ship, exhausted from the frenzy of the town, Friedrich wanted nothing more than to take a walk on the "rippled glass" of the sea. He found the heave of the waves and the rock of the bow so hypnotic as to induce a psychological experience: "I was gripped by a pantheistic longing to merge with the waves below forever—objectively this must be considered an act of madness, but subjectively it could be the peak of sensuality."

•   •   •

At last, on July 31, the *Boskoop* pulled in to the deep bay of Guayaquil, Ecuador, where Dore and Friedrich would find passage to the Galápagos Islands. Pelicans, herons, ducks, and seagulls circled their ship, a reception they both found encouraging. Church towers and the domes of various government buildings soared above the harbor. Along the dock, wooden barges piled high with bananas competed for space, and the smell of roasting meat suffused the air. People darted back and forth, carrying luggage and offering help. Native Ecuadorians were commonly called *indios* at the time (a term that is now considered derogatory), and most spoke Quechua, a language developed during the pre-Columbian Inca Empire. The native Ecuadorians were helpful and friendly but incurred Friedrich's pity. Writing in his black notebook, he predicted that civilization would eventually spoil them, as it did everyone, by stirring greed and desire.

They had hoped to embark on the final leg of their journey, but the *Manuel J. Cobos*—a schooner that ran between the mainland and the islands—had just left and would not return until month's end. A plane could take them for $100 but was not a viable option because they would have to leave their baggage behind. They visited the German consulate to inquire about the logistics of settling on the islands, but no one had clear answers. From what the officials understood, Dore and Friedrich could go to any island and build a farm without government interference, yet even this wasn't guaranteed. They couldn't purchase land outright, but after ten years—if they lasted that long—they would be its rightful owners. In case of a future emergency Dore left some money with the consul, and hoped she'd never have the need to retrieve it.

To pass the time, they explored Guayaquil and the capital city of Quito, taking a ferry across the Rio Guayas to the train station, where they sat in a packed, pungent, second-class car. The train clattered and climbed high into the jungle and then climbed higher still, the landscape yielding to prickly pampa grass and parched willow trees.

Dore had grown accustomed to Friedrich's gripes about Europe and Germany, but here, too, he found fault with everyone and everything that crossed his path. The entire population seemed sick in the streets, sneezing and coughing and hydrating the air with spittle. "There are a striking number of mouth breathers here," he noted, "and people with excessive phlegm." He was also struck by a "completely intolerable cult" that revolved around shoes, with shoe shiners on every corner; each polished pair, he assumed, was supposed to represent the pinnacle of European culture. The abominable habits of smoking and drinking alcohol were considered good etiquette. He was most depressed by the scorched landscape at the city's edge: a ravaged, silty canvas meagerly populated by wilting acacia trees, where vultures circled and lurked, waiting for prey to die.

Friedrich did not spare Dore from his criticism. When, in what she called "an attack of feminine vanity," she suggested buying an iron for their clothes, his grave disappointment made her doubt her own worthiness in their mission. He had little patience for the pain in her limp leg, or her labored breathing as they climbed Mount Pichincha, or her desire to eat a larger meal than usual to combat her mountain sickness. "One should not eat even fruit," he advised, "when oxygen is scarce."

These rebukes stung, but Dore reminded herself that her love for Friedrich was "not blind" and certainly not unconditional. "I know that for the sake of his great mind and spirit I tolerated more in Dr. Ritter," she wrote. "I made more compromises in order not to hinder our great mutual quest than most women would in relation to any man, and I certainly in relation to any other." But she believed that she alone could help him realize his historic vision, and it was her life's purpose to do so. Only in denying her own strength would she become her most powerful self. She had to appreciate the moments when he would be "very human," and tolerate, as best as she could, the moments when he was not.

When the *Manuel J. Cobos* at last arrived to take them to the islands, Dore boarded with a renewed determination. As they drifted from the harbor, all of the bustle and noise and disappointments falling away, she considered how far they'd come: "We felt a oneness with each other that we had never felt before, and if we thought about the past at all, then it was with an utter absence of regret, and with a feeling of deep happiness and gratitude to the fate which had permitted us to approach our goal at last." And that goal? Nothing less than utopia.

# THREE

# The Enchanted Isles

Dore and Friedrich had fled a place on the precipice of violence for one with a history steeped in it. The Galápagos Islands are themselves vestiges of terrestrial violence—the tips of underwater volcanoes rising up more than a thousand feet from the ocean floor, formations born of eruptions over the course of several hundred thousand to millions of years. The archipelago numbers eighteen main islands and more than a hundred other named islands and islets, and a scattering of other rocky promontories that peek just a few square meters above the water, most of them rarely visited by humans. The islands' craggy, barren landscape had always been their most defining characteristic.

When Fray Tomás de Berlanga, the fourth bishop of Panama, sailed to Peru in 1535 to mediate a dispute among rival conquistadors, his ship veered off course and stumbled upon this peculiar collection of islands. As he and his crew explored the land and found no water, they grew so desperate that they tried to quench their thirst by sucking the liquid from cactus pads. Two men and ten horses died. Berlanga led the remaining crew in prayer, at last found a small stream of water, and fled, never to return. He reported the incident to King Charles I of Spain. "It seems as though some time God had showered stones," he said of the islands, "and the earth that there is, is like dross, worthless, because it has not the power of raising a little grass, but only some thistles." Berlanga didn't even bother to name or claim the territory for his king.

Subsequent visitors were likewise unimpressed, including Herman Melville, whose ironically titled novella, *The Encantadas, or Enchanted Isles*, begins with similarly foreboding words: "Take five-and-twenty heaps of cinders dumped here and there in an outside city lot; imagine some of them magnified into mountains, and the vacant lot the sea. . . . A group rather of extinct volcanoes than of isles; looking much as the world at large might, after a penal conflagration."

For their utopia, Dore and Friedrich had chosen a small island, about sixty-seven square miles, in the southern part of the archipelago. Floreana would be ideal for their purposes, since it possessed a freshwater spring and a relatively lush swath of vegetation on the highlands of its extinct volcanoes. Like all of the islands, Floreana has a complicated nomenclature. The British buccaneer William Ambrose Cowley produced the first map of the Galápagos in 1684 and called it Charles Island, after King Charles II. Its official Ecuadorian name is Isla Santa María, but Galápagos residents prefer to call it Floreana—an homage to Juan José Flores, the first president of Ecuador. Floreana, the first capital of the archipelago, also served as its first penal colony, a small compound located in the highlands near where Dore and Friedrich would build their home. As time passed, this history would seem eerily fitting, as events would transform Floreana from a wild paradise to a prison, one from which there was no easy escape.

• • •

From their studies, Dore and Friedrich knew that the penal colony represented only one chapter of Floreana's past. Throughout the late seventeenth and early eighteenth centuries, the island—with its freshwater source, abundance of tortoises, and safe anchorages—had been a convenient retreat for pirates looking to avoid the customary Spanish trade routes. A pirate of slightly later vintage, Patrick Watkins, was likely the first true inhabitant of Floreana; he was also Melville's inspiration for the character Oberlus in *The Encantadas*, a fearsome hermit and misanthrope who captured and enslaved passing sailors, forcing them to do his bidding and murdering them if they failed to comply.

The story of Watkins came to light through the journal of Captain David Porter, a U.S. naval officer who was instrumental in attacking

British commercial ships during the War of 1812. As Porter tells it, Watkins was expelled from his ship for unruly behavior in 1807 and marooned on Floreana. He built a ramshackle hut on a patch of fertile soil in the highlands where he grew potatoes and pumpkins, which he sold or exchanged for rum to passing ships. "The appearance of this man," Porter wrote, "was the most dreadful that can be imagined; ragged clothes, scarce sufficient to cover his nakedness, and covered with vermin; his red hair and beard matted, his skin much burnt, from constant exposure to the sun, and so wild and savage in his manner and appearance, that he struck every one with horror." He spent two years on Floreana getting drunk and, as Porter noted, "rolling among the rocks of the mountains," before managing to capture a few unfortunate sailors whom he forced to procure a boat. In 1809, Watkins sailed to Guayaquil after killing his captives. Dore called him a "lunatic and murderer" and could not dispel his crimes from her mind.

She was equally haunted by the provenance of the ancient schooner that was, at present, ferrying her and Friedrich from Guayaquil to Floreana. The *Manuel J. Cobos* had once belonged to a tyrant of the same name, who, in 1880, transferred the prisoners from Floreana's penal colony to Chatham Island (also known as San Cristóbal), where he enslaved them on his plantation. Manuel Cobos minted his own currency in the form of oval coins and meted ruthless punishment to his captured men: shootings, deadly beatings, banishment to barren islands. His brutal reign came to an end when his subjects revolted and murdered him.

Nearly fifty years after Cobos's reign came settlers with more prosaic ambitions: escaping the monotony of their daily lives and getting rich along the way. In 1925, a group of twenty-two Norwegians declared that they had tired of Europe and made the bold decision, in the words of one member, to "venture to a more beautiful, cheerful nation." At first they hoped to settle in the United States, but were soon dissuaded by the nation's strict immigration laws. After further research, they were seduced by the stories of fast, easy money to be found in the Galápagos Islands.

Development in the islands had all but ended with the murder of Manuel Cobos in 1904, and the Ecuadorian government was eager to revive the archipelago's economy. Ecuador's consul in Norway, August F. Christensen, had launched an ambitious settlement plan offering twenty hectares of land (fifty acres) to any Norwegian who wished to relocate to the islands. Additional incentives included a ten-year tax waiver and the permission to establish a commercial hunting, fishing, or agricultural enterprise on any colonized island. Newspaper columnists publicized the cause, offering faint assurance that "the problem of water" could be easily resolved. The Norwegian group brought with them a number of modern conveniences: a large radio set, fish nets, boilers for reducing whale and seal oil, and even ready-cut houses. From Norway they traveled to Los Angeles and set sail on a little motor schooner, the *Floreana*, named after their new island home.

Four years later, in 1929, around the time of Dore's unusual farewell party in Berlin, a man named Gifford Pinchot, the former governor of Pennsylvania and the first head of the U.S. Forest Service, set sail for the South Pacific, planning an extended exploration of several Galápagos islands. Pinchot, working with the National Museum in Washington, was one of a growing group of wealthy Americans who aimed to re-create Beebe's travels, visiting remote and unexplored islands, investigating rumors of buried treasure, and wishing, as the naturalist wrote, "for a dozen eyes, so filled was the sea with strange living things"—transparent eels, living coral, mother-of-pearl snails, unidentifiable fish with lights on their heads and others with scales like hair, a giant sea bat with a fifteen-foot wingspan, and a fish with spiky horns that to Pinchot seemed like some otherworldly, underwater demon.

Pinchot found the land equally wondrous, although he lamented that the giant tortoises that gave the archipelago its name (*galápago* is an old Spanish word for land tortoise) were long extinct on many of the islands. An examination of the logbooks of seventy-nine British and American whaling vessels between 1831 and 1868—hardly a complete survey, since whalers had been visiting the Galápagos since the late eighteenth century—revealed a total catch of 13,013 tortoises, some weighing as much as seven hundred pounds. Their meat was a prized delicacy, and they could be kept alive, unfed, for months or even longer; Pinchot heard of one tortoise that survived in storage for two years. According to legend, there had once been so many tortoises that it was possible to cross an island without stepping off their exquisitely etched shells.

Instead, Pinchot marveled at the guileless animals that continued to thrive on the archipelago, wholly unaccustomed to humans and therefore lacking the instinct of fear. A wild sea lion poked its whiskered nose into his shoulder; a four-foot-long iguana (or "lap dragon," as Pinchot called the creature) crept into and lounged across his lap; an albatross with a wingspan of eight feet was content to be picked up and nestled against his chest. So tame were the birds that they flew toward Pinchot's group rather than away and perched on their outstretched arms; a hawk even alighted upon his wife's head, and a man-o'-war bird swooped in close, bowed its long hooked beak, and accepted bits of fish from her hand.

Approaching his next stop, Floreana, Pinchot's yacht anchored at Post Office Bay—so named for the simple wooden barrel "mailbox" erected long ago by the whalers, who'd left letters for homebound ships to retrieve and deliver. He and his crew walked a wide, curvy path bordered by lava rocks and came upon a sight they least expected: a house. How strange, Pinchot thought, that this bleak, desolate spot of island would have such a dwelling—"friendly and home-like," he noted, "painted brown, with white trimmings and white doors, and with a flight of steps leading up to a broad veranda." And yet the place was undeniably eerie: no one in sight, no smoke from the chimney, no noise from behind the door, no sign of life at all. A dog barked and trotted into view; he was mangy and half-starved, and did not mean to welcome them.

After knocking on the doors and receiving no answer, they walked in. A veranda in the rear contained two clocks, numerous chairs, a rack of shotguns and rifles, a trophy of whale harpoons, and a phonograph. Shelves were filled with English and Norwegian books and magazines, and a large pile of yellowing newspapers lay stacked in a corner. Pinchot found boxes of corn and crackers and bags of sweet potatoes and two machetes and an open bottle of ink not yet gone dry. The house was even wired for electric light, with every bulb fastened in its place. Pinchot paged through a stack of abandoned diaries that carried hints of the occupants' loneliness—long entries about family back home, meandering descriptions of cricket games. The final entry in one was written only twenty-six days earlier, in June 1929. Someone had even more recently attempted a last meal; a rusty pan still contained remnants of liquid, veiled in mildew.

Watches, field glasses, and journals had all been left behind. Soiled linens were strewn about; clearly, Pinchot mused, no women had lived here for quite some time.

Pinchot knew of the Norwegian entrepreneurs in the Galápagos, but thought they'd all settled on other islands; Floreana, he'd believed, had been uninhabited for hundreds of years. Yet here was evidence to the contrary and signs that these people, whoever they were, had fled in a hurry.

•    •    •

Friedrich and Dore had heard about the Norwegian settlement during their stay in Guayaquil while awaiting transport to Floreana. These neighbors, Friedrich feared, could threaten the peaceful solitude he and Dore planned to cultivate on the island. But the schooner's owner, Captain Paul Edvard Bruun, told him not to worry. Out of the twenty-two residents who settled on Floreana during that initial immigration in 1925, only two Norwegians and one Ecuadorian remained. A few weeks earlier, those three holdouts took a fishing trip and ran into a storm. Their schooner got tossed about and drifted north to Isla Santa Cruz, where Bruun found them. He brought them back to Floreana, but this time their stay was brief. Having finally succumbed to the difficulty of the enterprise, they gave up their island dreams for good, leaving their belongings behind. Friedrich and Dore would have Floreana all to themselves.

From the deck of the schooner, Dore watched the island come into focus: the tips of the volcanic mountains protruding like the knuckles of a fist; tube-nosed petrels skulking along the water and frigate birds in the air above; the slanted foothills with their scattering of palo santo trees and their leafless branches, stark white and skeletal; the dense thickets of mangroves, florid in comparison, bristling along the lava shore; the long, bleached sand of Post Office Bay glinting beneath the late September sun.

Dore stayed on board while fellow passengers helped unload her and Friedrich's cargo. Captain Bruun introduced them to a fourteen-year-old Ecuadorian boy, Hugo. If they so desired, the boy could stay on Floreana for a while to help transport their belongings to the highlands. All around her the sea broke into white crests, the receding waves peeling back to reveal obsidian lava rocks, shot through with holes like the face of the moon.

Occasionally the tip of a shark's fin would pierce the ocean's surface, and she turned to a Norwegian passenger nearby.

"I should never dare to risk entering that shark-infested water," she said.

He assured her that the sharks weren't quite as bad as they appeared; mostly they were content with taking just an arm or a leg, and left the rest of their victims' bodies alone.

The *Manuel J. Cobos* left before dark, taking with it the mysterious Captain Bruun, rumored to have spied for German naval intelligence during the Great War. Dore and Friedrich set off to explore the Norwegians' abandoned home—the Casa Matriz, as it was known, or "Casa" for short.

She noted the large chicken coop and the lightbulbs and the impressive architecture of the building itself, yet there was something almost ornamental in its abandonment, a heavy desolation hanging from every rotten tile and warped beam. They slept on its floor that first night, surrounded by the sounds of scuttling rats and howling dogs and a thousand other unseen creatures, the ghosts of their failed predecessors all around them.

# FOUR
# Friedo

Dore rose early, eager to explore Floreana. She knew it would sound silly to admit to Friedrich, but something about Post Office Bay seemed to portend evil. The tall cactuses looming up against the sky looked, she wrote, "like weird sentinels ever on the watch for strange things about to happen. But at the same time there was something ludicrous in those imposing watchers, for impressive as they looked, I knew that the slightest push could topple them over." That was the paradox of Floreana, she concluded; the land was rich enough to bloom new life, but too shallow for that life to take deep root.

They decided to search for the freshwater spring. The Ecuadorian boy, Hugo—whom Friedrich called "our Indian Victor Hugo"—warned them to protect their seeds and foodstuffs from ants before they set off. They packed enough provisions for three days, as they didn't know how far their expedition would take them. Two wild dogs circled Hugo's legs as he hoisted an old rifle over his shoulder, and the long trek began.

The paths they walked were ancient, forged by the enormous, powerful bodies of long-gone tortoises, deepened by donkeys and cattle and other invasive species introduced by earlier settlers. As Friedrich hacked his machete through the thorny brush, they came to their first lava field. The stones tore gashes in the soles of Dore's shoes, lacerating her skin. They came to another lava field, and another, Dore's feet burning with each step.

They walked this way for an hour, mostly uphill, Hugo and the dogs bounding ahead, and came to the slope of the highest volcano on the island, long dormant. Hugo advised them to use this peak as their guide; the same route downward would bring them straight to Post Office Bay. Dore looked back and counted the five lava beds they'd crossed to reach this summit, descending in a perfect line down to the sea. Friedrich turned too, sharing the view.

"We have come here five hundred thousand years too soon," he said to Dore. "The few centuries since this volcano ceased to be active have hardly sufficed for life to take root here. These dull and leafless acacias and straw-like grass will give place some day to rich and abundant vegetation, if the water supply can in some way be made adequate."

As they climbed higher and higher, the air grew dense with a cool mist and pockets of vegetation appeared in riotous bloom. Lemon trees lined their path, fragrant and bright—the first Dore had ever seen—and the ground around them was pocked with bruised and fallen fruit. Even the trails changed, since the cattle and swine thrived best here, too, and with their hunting and prowling carved the grooves wider and deeper than in the dry planes below. From a distance Dore spotted a family of donkeys, watching as they passed.

Hugo's dogs barked and sprinted ahead, and the boy rushed to catch up with them. A moment later a gunshot cracked through the air. When Hugo returned he announced proudly that he had shot a boar. Dore told him she admired his bravery and marksmanship, but Friedrich grew silent and sullen when Hugo said it was customary to take the best cuts of meat and leave the rest. Friedrich remained unconvinced and even gave an order: if Hugo must continue with his shooting, he should in future use up one whole beast before doing away with another.

Dore did not think it wise to remind Friedrich that he himself had wished to bring a gun to the island. With great reluctance, she aided Hugo and Friedrich in cutting the flesh into long strips to be hung like laundry over a tree branch, out of reach of the feral dogs.

They continued on in silence as the sky dimmed with the last dregs of the afternoon sun. Dore could not keep her mind from replaying the tense exchange between Friedrich and Hugo; it unsettled her in ways she was afraid to name, and with each painful step the realization grew clearer until she was forced to confront it. "Friedrich was jealous," she thought. "This man of intellect, the disillusioned heir of all the centuries of civilization and culture, was jealous of [Hugo's] native skill, his oneness with the world he had been born into."

Dore had abandoned her life—indeed, the entire outside world—for a man whose grand philosophical vision was in perpetual conflict with his childish pettiness and temper. What could she do, what *would* she do, if he succumbed to his worst instincts? Yet she knew she mustn't dwell on her fears. She needed to believe that this experiment—and her role as Friedrich's helpmate and companion—were worth all the sacrifices she had made, and all the trials yet to come.

At last they reached the day's final destination: the lava pirate caves of Floreana, dark gray pockets resembling gouged-out eyes, some deeper than others, some natural and some dug by human hands. The largest was only three square yards, and with trepidation Dore followed Friedrich inside. A rat scuttled out, startling her. Two benches had been carved from the sooty walls, a hole served as a hearth, and a bed had been fashioned from a sheet of corrugated iron. As they lay side by side, an eerie wind blew across the mouth of the cave; it sounded to Dore like "a train of specters gliding past, each uttering a sigh of dark despair." She recalled the gruesome stories she'd heard about its long-ago inhabitant, the murderous pirate Patrick Watkins, and imagined him hiding in the shadows, watching her as she slept.

•   •   •

At noon the next day, after hours of roaming, the trio came to an old, rusted barbed-wire fence, surrounding an extinct volcanic crater. Friedrich estimated that the spot was five hundred feet above sea level and to the east of the island's main central mountain. Quickly they made their way down the crater and arrived at a luxuriant jungle of grasses and vines and trees bearing fruits: bananas, pineapples, oranges, lemons, papayas, guavas, and others too exotic to identify. At the center of this natural basin rose a freshwater spring, the source of a small stream that looped toward the opening in the crater and cascaded down to the sea.

"The spring," Dore said, and later recorded this moment in her diary.

She fell to her knees and cupped the water and drank greedily from her hands. She found Friedrich through the tangle of branches and knew they shared the same thought: this was home.

"This is our place, Dore," Friedrich said, "and we shall call it Friedo."

Dore immediately understood: "Friedo" was not only a nod to *Frieden*, the German word for "peace," but a combination of their two names. In the moment, any doubts about Friedrich's dedication to her and their experiment fell away. She began to cry, from relief as much as joy, and Friedrich reached for her hand. They had made the right decision in leaving their lives behind.

"We'll christen the valley and I'll honor the occasion with a ceremonial dance," she said. "That ought to make it legal enough."

She spun in circles, dancing as she once danced at home to the music of the Weimar Republic, music that had all the texture and scope of this wild landscape, tinged with the influences of American jazz. Inspired, Friedrich scooped up a handful of water and sprinkled it at their feet.

"In the name of the Ritters I take possession of thee," he said. "O lovely valley, against all comers, and with thine own pure waters I christen thee Friedo, our Garden of Peace."

After a moment she realized Hugo was standing there, watching the scene in awkward silence. He pointed his finger at a pile of lava rocks just a few feet from where she and Friedrich stood, and said it was there that the pirate Watkins had built his other house. He urged them to continue on and look elsewhere for their permanent home. Dore followed the direction of the boy's finger and then heard him mutter an addendum: Watkins had murdered someone on that very spot.

·   ·   ·

They slept against the damp, gnarled roots of a ciruela tree, and in the morning awakened to find that Hugo had already prepared tea—a different tea from what they were used to in Europe, made of some strange and delicate herb. Dore added a spoonful of sugar to her cup, and as soon as she raised it to her lips, she heard Friedrich's rebuke: "I see you haven't yet put your European ways behind you."

His words stung Dore. She quelled the impulse to toss her tea to the ground; she did not want to give Friedrich the opportunity to call her childish. Instead, she let the moment pass, and forced herself to consider his words in a different light. When they'd decided to flee civilization, he had promised to "cast out the foe" in Dore as well as in himself. She told herself he had spoken with good intentions. She reacted when she should have listened, resisted when she should have acquiesced. His admonitions only underscored his love for her.

They began the work of transporting their belongings from Post Office Bay to Friedo. Later she would describe the experience as one of "almost terrifying hideousness"—the interminable treks across the lava fields, the prickly overhanging brush batting her face, the grueling climb up the rough-hewn slopes, again and again and again, her shoes in tatters. The tropical sun seethed with heat. Friedrich declared that they should discard all of their clothing save for their high boots to shield their legs from the rocks. They were, he joked, "a toiling Adam and Eve—in boots." Hugo was un-fazed by the nudity but soon tired of the work. Sometimes he'd wander off without explanation, and when he returned, he refused to carry any of the load; they had only an aged horse to assist them. Dore called the animal El Viejo, "The Old."

Soon Dore noticed that El Viejo was suffering under the weight of their cargo. She suggested they release the animal to the pampa, but Friedrich's insistence on efficiency and practicality won out. After several more trips, Dore, unable to witness the horse's suffering any longer, kissed his nose and set him free. A few days later, near where the path forked off to the caves, she found him, dead and picked nearly to the bone.

Day after day they worked naked in the searing sun. At night, they slept in hammocks strung between the branches of their ciruela tree. Dore pushed on, remembering her commitment to their new life, the impor-tance of banishing her old self. Yet the endless walks across the rough ter-rain pained her limp leg, and she often called for Friedrich to help her. He ignored her and walked on. She begged him to stop a while, sit down, take a breath, but he failed even to turn his head. Silently she cursed him with terrible, hateful epithets, words she wouldn't dare say aloud. She vowed to herself that she would never again show weakness to Friedrich, nor expect from him any kindness or sympathy.

Their relationship established its own volatile rhythm: a brief contentment, an inevitable dispute, a silent seething, a blistering confrontation during which Friedrich's pent-up rage would release itself, his expression as menacing as his words. And when the cycle began anew, a fragile peace replacing the anger, Dore told herself that Friedrich and Floreana were her destiny: "In spite of all our differences, deep-rooted and important as some of them were, we never doubted but that we had been intended for each other, and both of us knew that we could never be parted and live."

•   •   •

By late October, work on Friedo was progressing as planned, although it was increasingly clear that the property had long been occupied, and that Dore and Friedrich were themselves the invasive species. "We had fled from the society of overcivilized man," Friedrich wrote, "but now we had for neighbors a vagrant colony of wild cattle, wild hogs, wild asses, wild dogs, and wild tabby cats. They ranged over the whole island and seemed to resent our intrusion by their preserve." He denounced them all as "perverted creatures" and fretted about the "devilish attempts" they might make to impede his plans.

The pests, at least, had not disturbed their garden, which bloomed with remarkable speed and vigor. Melville, in *The Encantadas*, had written that the Galápagos climate was unchanging—"Cut by the Equator, they know not autumn, and they know not spring"—but Dore and Friedrich realized that the islands had their own idiosyncratic cycle of seasons. Little rain fell from July to December, but the Humboldt Current, originating in Antarctica and flowing three thousand miles northward, cooled the tropical air and created the mists that now nourished their garden.

During the hot and rainy season, from January to June, the Humboldt Current reversed its course, and the islands were bathed instead with warm water that restored the tropical climate, relieving the arid lowlands and facilitating the mating season of the reptiles and birds. A drought during the rainy season, as Dore and Friedrich would learn, affected not only the lowlands but also Friedo, halting the flow of the spring.

For now, though, Dore was dazzled by her garden's "feverish fertility." The first crop of radishes were as large as any turnip she'd ever seen in Europe, and the cucumbers and tomatoes shot up from the ground as though fleeing some danger beneath. The tomatoes, Friedrich marveled, were as large "as a baby's head."

He built a primitive pressing machine to squeeze sap from the sugar-cane, which Dore could work herself by cranking a lever back and forth. With these items, and the rice and maize they'd brought from home, and the oranges, lemons, avocados, and papayas from the abandoned orchard near the caves, she made meals hearty enough to sustain herself on long journeys across the lava fields.

But still, her body and spirit both inched ever closer to breaking down. She wondered if Friedrich even noticed her malaise, for he had again become distant and cold and seemed so perturbed by her affection.

"He did not even see that I needed to be loved and treated kindly," she wrote. "If he had seen, his answer would have been that not until I had freed myself of even these so natural earthly chains could I expect to follow him into his world." And, once again, she told herself he was right.

•    •    •

What Dore lacked in physical strength she made up for in tenacity. She continued on with the trips back and forth to Post Office Bay, nearly blinded by the pain in her feet, until she could no longer stand it and allowed herself to complain. This time, surprisingly, Friedrich stopped, put down his cargo, removed her shoes, and with great concentration examined both of her feet. The deep lacerations could be blamed on the jagged shards of lava rock, but he could not explain the severity of her swelling—perhaps, he suggested, she'd stepped on some poisonous thorns?

Hugo caught up with them and gave an immediate diagnosis: Dore's feet had been attacked by niguas, vampiric Floreana sand fleas that burrow beneath the skin to lay eggs. Using his medical instruments, Friedrich performed an impromptu operation, puncturing her skin to remove thirty-two of the insects. In all her life, Dore had never felt such excruciating pain.

When Friedrich finished, he offered a supplemental treatment: Dore should erect a "defense psychology" around her feet that would warn her in advance of any impending danger—the sort of advice he'd given when they first met, one of the many revolutionary ideas that had seduced her.

While recovering at Friedo, limping about as she performed minor tasks, she focused her entire mind on her feet, firing each synapse in her brain, willing them to connect with neurons, willing those neurons to surge through her muscles and joints, replenishing their strength. To her shock she was never attacked again.

. . .

As Hugo continued to slaughter the wild cattle and boars, Friedrich insisted that they suspend if not abandon their vegetarian diet. If they were to be complicit in the suffering of animals, he argued, they were morally obligated to use every last swatch of hide and strip of flesh. Dore protested, and even invoked his service in the war—had he felt the need to eat enemy soldiers after killing them? He did not respond, and instead retreated to record his thoughts in his notebook, processing and cementing his convictions:

> If vegetarianism is to mean the creed: to eat meat under no
> condition—that is, dogma—I am then not a vegetarian. But I myself
> could neither raise cattle nor indulge in hunting or fishing: nor can I
> be okay if I induce others to do this for me. . . . However, I can answer
> to myself for eating meat when it would otherwise spoil, and I even
> feel obliged to eat meat if I am an accomplice in the murder of animals
> by any circumstance; for eating meat is not a pleasure for me, but a
> punishment and anger, in that I myself bear all the harmful
> consequences that eating meat necessarily entails. I therefore have to
> pay hard physical and mental penalties for every meal of meat.

Their bodies, unaccustomed to eating meat, soon delivered those penalties. Sores bloomed across their faces; the skin festered beneath their nails. Friedrich complained of becoming sensitive to the heat and emotionally depressed. Dore worried that her own hands were "stained with murder," and felt that each animal she encountered regarded her with loathing.

On a stunning fall day, Dore, Friedrich, and Hugo took a break from their duties and walked the island for the sheer pleasure of it, marveling at the tar-colored sand along Black Beach—so different from the golden shine of Post Office Bay—and listening to the calls of unfamiliar birds, cries that sounded like zippers through the air. They came to the fork in the path, one direction leading toward the pirate caves and the other toward Friedo, and Hugo, as he often did, wandered off into the brush. Suddenly they heard two quick shots, and the boy's voice: "¡El toro me mata! El toro me mata!"—*the bull is killing me.*

They rushed toward the direction of Hugo's screams, finding him splayed across a bed of lava rocks. Blood spattered on the earth around him. Friedrich knelt next to Hugo: the horn had slashed through his left armpit but did not penetrate his chest cavity, sparing the major arteries and nerves. Hugo whispered in soft but frenzied Spanish that the bull had fled, chased away by Hugo's loyal dogs, but it was still out there. And like all of the malevolent forces that stalked Floreana, it was certain to return.

# FIVE

# A Moment Lived
# in Paradise

When the schooner *Manuel J. Cobos* next arrived on Floreana, Hugo decided to travel back to Guayaquil to heal from his wounds. Friedrich was relieved to finally be alone. "Thank God we are rid of our meat eater Hugo," he wrote. "He always wanted to hunt and shoot 'toros' and that was very painful for us." Dore felt sorry for the boy and was surprised to realize that she missed him, although she could not shake his warning. The wounded bull was out there, roaming back and forth between the pampa and Friedo, and each time she ventured down to Post Office Bay, she listened for hooves and peered through the thickets for pairs of inhuman eyes.

She found distraction in clearing the brush around Friedo, rising with Friedrich at the first spark of sun and working until she could no longer see the glint of the blade in her hand. But she quickly became frustrated by her own physical weakness, realizing, at the end of what felt like an interminable day, that she had barely made an impression on the gnarled webs of branches while Friedrich had carved yet another stretch into a viable walking path. She gave up, and instead spent hours watching her pet donkey and chickens until Friedrich gave her a stern rebuke, reminding her that they were not like other people; they were above the human instinct to settle for mediocrity. "We have gained the better world, or at least we are well on the way to it," he said. "That is why we must have no pity for our own weaknesses, and find no excuses for them. In leaving civilization, we left behind us our excuse."

Dore wasn't satisfied. She felt the urge to press and provoke him. "Don't you believe in charity towards shortcomings? I mean for us?"

"No. For us there is only discipline. We must conquer by will."

"And by brutality, it seems."

He spoke quietly but without hesitation. "With brutality too, if it must be. You never see the animal in man, Dore. And yet, there lies the root of every evil. It is the animal in us that torments us, and drives us from the path. That is the evil spirit which we must drive out, and it is all the more difficult because it appears so often in a charming mask. You think that the outward forms of kindness and humanity—your love of animals, for instance—are good and admirable. Nothing could be more mistaken. . . . Your affection for all these wild creatures here, and for your plants and chickens, is no more or less than a flattering and cherishing of the animal in yourself."

Dore told herself she was not yet advanced enough in her enlight-enment to grasp the full meaning of Friedrich's words, to "breathe the rarefied air of his high intellectual sphere." Sometimes she felt most alone when she was by his side. She continued to dote on her donkey and stray cats and chickens, living defiantly in a world where such crea-tures mattered.

With each passing day, Dore's fear of the wounded bull only deepened. It seemed the animal was always watching her, poised to leap from the thickets at her first lapse in vigilance. On trips to Post Office Bay she sang as loudly as she could, hoping to scare it away. One afternoon, heading back to Friedo alone, she looked up to see the beast in her path. Her legs refused to move and she stood there, passively—"as in a bad dream," she thought—waiting for it to lower its head and charge her in deadly fury. Instead, it regarded her with a strange indifference. Slowly, gently, she slithered past it.

•   •   •

Friedrich had very specific ideas about the house he wished to construct, a "tropical eternal dwelling" worthy of the name Friedo. He envisioned a very "light" building made of reinforced concrete with a glass dome roof (or, even better, Nirosta, a durable, rust-resistant steel) and walls made of mosquito-proof wire mesh. But such a castle would have to wait. They needed a decent shelter as soon as possible, no matter how primitive. He decided that acacia wood would be the most appropriate roofing material but changed his mind after a downpour. The wood withstood the rain, but subsequently buckled and cracked when dried by the sun—looking, he thought, "like the skeleton of some prehistoric monster."

For once, luck intervened. A fleet of Norwegian fishermen sailing around the Galápagos stopped at Black Beach and offered three dozen sheets of corrugated iron, perfect for a roof. Dore busied herself carrying the material back to Friedo, a much easier and shorter route than the one from Post Office Bay, half an hour as opposed to three.

The house began to resemble a permanent structure and fit so perfectly in the landscape that it seemed a natural extension of it. At night, in his little black book, Friedrich sketched a detailed vision of his ideal garden, which took on the shape of an egg—the "Friedo egg," he called it—with numerous internal parts comprising the whole.

The narrower rounded tip represented the "embryo" entrance, which led downward to a barbed-wire fence ("egg shell") to the rows of figs, mangoes, and oranges ("yolk membrane"), to the vegetable garden ("yolk") to the water ditch and banana ("egg white") to the cotton "skin," and finally to the bulbous "axis" exit, facing west.

He imagined that within each plant bloomed a unique melody, and that these melodies converged to create a glorious "garden symphony"—a thought that, although fleeting, made him trust that his work was not in vain. "A moment lived in paradise," he wrote, "is not too dearly paid with death."

•   •   •

Floreana was now home, but Dore felt the island had not accepted them in turn. "Something on Floreana had changed," she wrote, "and there was a menace in the air, something sinister and frightening, the more so because there was no outward sign of anything amiss."

Hugo's dogs returned to Friedo, circling the garden, searching for evidence of their owner. Dore fed them the leftover dried meat from Hugo's kills until it was gone, but the dogs still came. Each week they looked worse than the last, their bodies gaunt and sparse of fur. Out of pity Friedrich killed them with his machete. Dore believed their deaths had atoned for Hugo's sins, but soon understood she was mistaken. Wild dogs, nine of them, found their way to Friedo, surrounding its perimeter like an advancing enemy regiment—"sinister, emaciated creatures," Dore saw, "with wolfish and despairing eyes . . . the very embodiment of Hugo's own bad conscience." Friedrich killed all of them, too, and she hoped that Hugo had at last been exorcised.

A few days later, while she was clearing the undergrowth around the trees, she heard the sound of something smashing and then a cry for help: Friedrich. She pictured him strangling to death in a ratty tangle of liana vines or crushed by a falling trunk.

She found him lying prone on the ground, his right arm trapped between the trunk of a felled tree and one of its thick, weighty branches. He whispered something about the crowbar, and she understood: if she could maneuver it correctly, she could free his arm. It was so heavy in her hand, but she worked it with painstaking anguish; if she thought even once of the many times when Friedrich ignored her pain, she did not admit it. She did not tell him to erect a "strong defense psychology," to use his mind to conquer his body, to rise above his mortal human weakness. Instead, she rejoiced to discover that his arm was not broken, although it would be two weeks before he could work again.

•   •   •

They treated Friedrich's period of recuperation as a holiday, reading and writing. He planned to turn his diary into a memoir, a project separate from his philosophical works. The downtime also forced them to assess how far they had come, and how far they had yet to go. They had been on Floreana for nearly half a year. They still had not transported all of their belongings from Post Office Bay. The second planting of the garden failed to bloom as brilliantly as the first; almonds and hazelnuts refused to sprout, and the radishes were riddled with worms.

One morning they took the long hike to Post Office Bay to drop some letters in the barrel, and afterward headed to the abandoned Casa to pick up foodstuffs and supplies. As they approached, they discovered several empty crates strewn along the beach. They ran the rest of the way and, upon reaching the Casa, found that all their belongings were gone, even a rusty old generator and a small boat left behind by a passing ship. Captain Bruun's possessions had also vanished; Dore did not trust the man, but doubted he was behind this theft.

She noticed that donkey tracks had imprinted on the damp sand, leading away into the brush. Had a marauding band come and seized possession of the island? Since Hugo had taken his gun with him, their only weapon was Friedrich's machete. How foolish they'd been, she thought, preparing for every possible challenge from nature while failing to consider the equally deadly challenges of man. They walked back to Friedo in silence.

# SIX

# The First of the
# Dollar Kings

O n the morning of January 3, 1930, broadcasting pioneer Eugene
McDonald held a press conference in Miami, announcing his imminent departure on his yacht, the *Mizpah*, for a mission to the South Seas.
The gathering was a welcome diversion from the news coming out of Wall
Street. October 29—"Black Tuesday"—had seen the loss of $14 billion in
stocks. By mid-November, the Dow Jones had lost nearly fifty percent of its
value. Fear and uncertainty gripped the country. People lost their life savings, their jobs, their security. Newspapers tallied the growing number of
suicides: a Chicago investor died by asphyxiation in his kitchen; a civil
engineer from Pennsylvania lit himself on fire; a stockbroker in St. Louis
drank a vial of poison.

Even bootleggers who had accrued tremendous wealth during the Roaring Twenties now felt the pinch. No one had money to buy smuggled liquor, even at reduced rates, so many bootleggers were "returning to the
not less exciting calling of gunmen," as one observer put it, "from which
school most of them graduated." In some circles, insolvency had become
fashionable. "I do not know what has happened," wrote one British colum-
nist, "but I am told that it is now considered vulgar to be rich in New York.
Bankruptcy gives you a social cachet."

McDonald, who harbored no such reservations about his wealth, had
selected a diverse team to accompany him on this oceanic expedition: the
president of the Michigan Archaeological Society; two Chicago actors; a

comedian; the former mayor of Syracuse, New York (his hometown); and Dr. Baker Brownell, a close confidant and professor of philosophy at Northwestern University. McDonald said that he would make stops in Cuba, Puerto Rico, Haiti, the Virgin Islands—and other locales he refused to name.

"After the stop at the Virgin Islands, I do not wish to discuss the expedition further," he said. "We have one chance in a thousand of accomplishing our objective and I do not wish to state it beforehand."

McDonald invited newspapermen on board the *Mizpah*, considered one of the finest luxury yachts in the country. Constructed in 1926 at a cost of $1.3 million (about $21 million today), the *Mizpah* measured 185 feet long and 490 gross tons, with a cruising range of seven thousand miles and twin diesel engines of 800 horsepower each. It was the twenty-third boat, from dinghy to yacht, that McDonald had owned, and he led the reporters to its new, custom feature: a specially constructed cabinet holding several high-powered rifles, revolvers, automatic pistols, and the very machine gun that was used in the St. Valentine's Day Massacre of Chicago gangsters, reportedly ordered by Al Capone. "The *Mizpah* should return to Miami in two months," McDonald added, standing in front of his display. "Then we will state the results of the expedition."

It was rumored that McDonald had also installed a modern radio detector that could identify and locate sunken pirate treasure—a claim he would neither confirm nor deny.

•  •  •

McDonald, forty-three years old, with the dark, brooding appeal of a silent film star, was accustomed to being in the spotlight. Born in 1886 in Syracuse, he dropped out of high school in his sophomore year for a factory job with the Franklin automobile company, and soon learned to assemble a complete engine in one day. A few years later, working as a car salesman in Chicago, he drove a car up the steps of the General John Logan Monument in Grant Park and paid a policeman $10 to arrest him, while a hired photographer documented the stunt for the press.

McDonald joined the Naval Intelligence Service, rising to the rank of lieutenant commander. Throughout the war he operated a telegraphone, an early recording device that could pick up German radio transmissions by utilizing a long piece of wire, an electromagnet, and a telephone. In 1923, after establishing Zenith Radio Company, he provided the renowned arctic explorer Donald MacMillan with radio equipment and, in doing so, made history. MacMillan's next arctic exploration was the first to maintain contact with civilization during the long, dark polar nights. McDonald would go on to develop the world's first portable radio. In later years, his Phonevision was a pioneering experiment in subscription television.

Pursuing his pastimes and pleasures with equal rigor, he was a man who, according to a friend, "could drink a lot and not show it. He always knew what he was doing." He ended each day with an established cocktail routine, drinking, in this order, beer, old-fashioneds, scotch and sodas, and after-dinner servings of Cointreau. On the weekends he amplified this routine, allowing himself to become spectacularly drunk, a particularly dangerous habit considering his collection of guns. Once he fired shots at his chauffeur's car. On another occasion, while the *Mizpah* was docked near the Michigan Avenue Bridge, he fired his machine gun at a passenger boat across the water.

Yet even more than alcohol or guns, McDonald was enamored with exploration, especially on the ocean. "Land," he often said, "is something to tie a boat to." He was fortunate to have sold $1 million worth of stock just before Wall Street collapsed, enabling him to continue operations and pursue his interests. His purchase of the *Mizpah* inspired him to plan the South Seas adventure he announced to the press on that January day—with an unnamed stop at the Galápagos Islands.

McDonald had followed the travels of Gifford Pinchot and other wealthy Americans who, inspired by William Beebe's work, had visited the archipelago. The actor John Barrymore had even taken his wife on a honeymoon cruise to the Galápagos and returned with more than one hundred live birds. The archipelago was no "lost world," Barrymore reported, "but merely behind the rest of the world in animal life because they got a late start."

The businessman and philanthropist William K. Vanderbilt, grandson of Cornelius, visited the islands in 1926 on his yacht *Ara*. Vanderbilt, like Pinchot, was enthralled with the tameness of the wildlife and brilliant plumage of exotic birds and a lizard that gorged on seaweed until his stomach was distended. He returned to New York with thirty ocean specimens his researcher was unable to identify (possibly "entirely new to science"), several baby sea lions (captured while their mothers were restrained by lasso), and six marine iguanas who died of malnutrition shortly after arriving at the New York Aquarium. "We gave them sliced beef meat," explained a representative, "quartered apples, hearts of lettuce, live minnows, dead herring and everything but ginger snaps, but they wouldn't eat it. It wasn't our fault."

Next came Charles Kettering, vice president of General Motors and future founder (along with Alfred Sloan) of the cancer center that bears his name; Julius Fleischmann, heir to a Cincinnati yeast fortune, who boasted of the "Noah's Ark" captured for his city's zoo; and Charles Townsend of the New York Zoological Society, which was specifically dedicated to safeguarding rare and endangered species. The expedition captured two hundred Galápagos tortoises in the mountains of Isabela (or Albemarle) and Española (Hood) Islands, where they were under threat from wild dogs and pigs. One tortoise, likely captured by the Zoological Society as a young adult and named Diego, spent twenty-five years at the San Diego Zoo before being transferred back to the Galápagos island of Santa Cruz (Indefatigable). Determined at that point to be one of only fifteen Hood Island turtles left in existence, Diego was enrolled in a captive breeding program and became famous as a Testudines lothario, fathering nine hundred offspring and almost single-handedly saving his species from extinction.

Finally, there was Huntington R. "Tack" Hardwick and Winthrop S. Brooks of the Harvard Museum. Inspired by Melville's *Moby-Dick*, the pair were intent on capturing a sperm whale. They found one along the coast of Isla Genovesa (Tower Island), about 117 miles north of Floreana. The whale, measuring thirty-five feet in length and weighing twenty tons, was traveling with a school of whales when it was harpooned at 9:30 in the morning. For six hours, members of the expedition fired bullets and bombs into the body of the whale. Even injured, the creature managed to tow the boat seventy miles during the chase. Once, during the afternoon, a bomb dislodged the harpoon and the whale disappeared in its school, only to be harpooned a second time when discovered lagging behind. It continued to fight, even when spouting blood instead of water. Defeated at last, the whale was beached on San Cristóbal Island, where the expedition's doctor performed an autopsy and removed 120 pounds of oil from its head.

• • •

At the end of January, a few weeks into his mysterious expedition, Commander Eugene McDonald steered the *Mizpah* to the rocky coast of Floreana and anchored at Post Office Bay. He had heard of the famous mailbox barrel, which looked like an old whiskey cask impaled on a pole. Out of curiosity, he reached his hand into its opening and was shocked to find a note written in German; he'd thought that the island was uninhabited. He passed it to Baker Brownell, who confessed that his command of the language was "rather shaky" but was able to translate the words. The note was addressed to the captain of any ship that might anchor at the bay and stated that two people, a Dr. Friedrich Ritter and Frau Ritter, currently lived on the island. Their food supply was running low. They lived far away from the bay, close to the highlands, where they'd found a spring. Their supplies had been stolen by a person or persons unknown. They had been injured and did not have any antiseptics. The note was dated five days earlier.

McDonald and his crew debated their next action. The sun was inching lower and the nearby spiky stretches of lava seemed too treacherous to cross. The best they could do was fire guns into the air and sweep the sky with searchlights. They waited for a response—the call of strange voices or the sound of running feet—but none came.

• • •

In the morning the group split into four search parties. One, led by Brownell, set out for the center of the island, heading toward the foothills, the lava rocks stabbing at their shoes. They marched for hours up the sparse trail, over the gray plain and barren gulches. As the path bent upward, the air grew cool and misty, suffused with the scent of citrus. The men began to wonder why the Ritters were nearly starving, for all around them lay wild sources of food: birds, goat, pigs, fish, fruits. At last they came upon a spring, and from behind the brush emerged two figures, a man and woman, so youthful in appearance that she nearly passed for a girl. "Gott sei dank, sie sind hier," the man said, and Brownell translated: "Thank God, you are here."

The man wore white duck trousers and was short, hardly taller than his companion, with wild brown hair and deep lines etched into his forehead. He weighed no more than 120 pounds, Brownell guessed; ropy muscles pressed taut against his skin. His left arm hanging limply at his side, he explained the difficulties they'd encountered during their time on the is-land. Recently he had slashed the arm with an ax while chopping wood, and life had still not returned to the fingers of his hand. As he spoke, his lips parted to reveal a set of steel dentures. Every tooth, from the incisors to the molars, gleamed in the sun.

The woman, clad in a white housedress, had short, curly blond hair and walked with a subtle limp. She, too, had been injured, having fallen di-rectly on the hot lava rocks, burning her knee to the bone. McDonald couldn't help but notice her hands, raw in spots and calloused in others, the hands of someone who spent long days working the land. Every few moments Friedrich would take her hands into his own and caress them, shaking his head in a display of sadness and pity, as if to scold nature for leaving its mark on her delicate flesh.

McDonald invited the couple aboard the *Mizpah*. Friedrich walked alongside Brownell, eager to discuss his life and philosophy—particularly with a man—in his native tongue. He spoke of his three years in the army; the wife who "understood everything" and "released" him, allowing him to implement his plan; his strict commitment to vegetarianism; his theories about teeth and gums; the brilliance of Schopenhauer and Nietzsche and the Chinese philosopher Lao-tzu; his vision for the "Friedo egg" and the work it would entail; his desire to live in perfect harmony on the island until the end of his days.

"Why don't you use one of the many wild donkeys on the island as a beast of burden?" Brownell asked.

Eager to present an ideal version of himself, Friedrich shook his head and said, "I do not think that is right."

Only Dore knew that these words were a lie.

Friedrich, with all of his talk of escaping the constraints and superficial-ity of civilization, cared what these Americans thought of him.

•    •    •

On board the *Mizpah*, Dore spoke to the men's wives in broken English, answering dozens of questions about her life. She was touched by their curiosity and kindness. "We in Europe are given a very false impression of the American women of the wealthier classes," she wrote. "They are de-scribed to us as superficial, blasé, sensation-hunting persons, without a se-rious interest or worthwhile thought in all their lives. . . . I found them, on the contrary, at least as much concerned with the serious things of life as German women." Dore was surprised by the intimacy of their exchanges. They viewed her, she realized, as someone who made an "extreme attempt to solve a certain problem of life which affects all women"—the stifling performances they were expected to give, the dreams they were forced to abandon, the opinions they had been conditioned to hide in the further-most reaches of their minds. In moving to Floreana, Dore had become not only a curiosity but also a prototype, someone who had found a way to align both her inner and outer lives.

The disparate groups and conversations converged. McDonald opened his cabinet of weaponry and retrieved his machine gun, prompting Dore to comment that she could easily believe he came from Chicago, where she'd heard that such "terribly efficient" devices were used even by ordinary citizens. Despite Friedrich's stated desire to live without any modern con-veniences, he eagerly accepted the Commander's gifts: picks and shovel and wheelbarrow; soap and a toothbrush and toothpaste (Dore's most es-sential needs); antiseptics and medical supplies (including the once-forbidden morphine); rubber shoes and a few items of spare clothing; seeds and foodstuffs to last for half a year; rat poison and floor polish; and a shotgun and fifteen hundred rounds of ammunition to guard against any intruders, man or beast. Explaining that his ax was incapable of removing the tree stumps around Friedo, Friedrich also asked for a supply of dyna-mite to blast them out. McDonald feared that Friedrich would blow him-self and Dore to bits, but Friedrich assured him that he'd had practical experience handling dynamite during the war.

"How long do you intend to remain?" Brownell asked.

"We shall stay here always," Friedrich said. "We have come down here to live our own lives. We keep a diary and we are experimenting to some extent on the effects of light and uncooked food on the human system. But we came to live a life of contemplation, of mutual love and simple work with natural things."

"Yes," Brownell replied, "the solitude that is necessary for every great research into ultimate things needs courage to endure, and that is why so few have ever made the attempt."

Dore watched Friedrich's face closely and noted the "almost mystical light" that played behind his eyes, an unspoken confirmation that he believed in this new, private world they were building, a civilization just for two. "That may be true for others," he said, "but as for me, I think that I shall go on to the end on Floreana. I know that I shall find here what I came to find, and this is where I hope to die."

The crowd went quiet. After a moment Dore broke the silence with an uneasy joke: "Oh, Friedrich, don't let us talk of dying on our island; we've hardly begun to live there yet."

Everyone laughed.

# SEVEN
# Catalyst

As soon as Commander McDonald departed on the *Mizpah*, he sent a message via radiogram to a journalist at the Associated Press, announcing his discovery of a couple living on the Galápagos island of Floreana. Newspapers across the country reported on the "German Robinson Crusoe and his female Friday" and printed the same photograph of Dore and Friedrich: he on the right, face half-obscured by his beard, clutching a book; she with her collar buttoned up and her hands crossed, leaning almost imperceptibly away. One journalist noted that they bore a striking facial resemblance to each other.

Interest in the story deepened when McDonald returned to the United States one month later, in February 1930, and spoke to the press in person, this time at Union Station in Chicago. Accompanying him was a Galápagos penguin named Charlie Chaplin—a moniker inspired by what one reporter called its "white vest and West Point bearing"—who seemed blasé and incurious about the gathering crowd. McDonald, rather than divulge the results of his secret treasure-hunting mission, spoke of his encounter with this curious couple who had chosen to leave the world behind.

"With tears in their eyes, we left them," he recalled, admitting that in the moment he'd been a bit melancholy himself. "Their arms were around each other and the expression on their faces would tell anyone who couldn't recognize love in the civilized world that there, indeed, was a pair truly in that state of mind." He spoke of the gifts he'd left them and wondered aloud what a man like Friedrich might do with floor polish on a deserted island—"unless," McDonald joked, "he expects to use it to polish his steel set of teeth."

Later, McDonald would regret starting the "avalanche of publicity" that would befall Dore and Friedrich, changing their lives in ways they could never have foreseen.

•   •   •

In the wake of McDonald's discovery, others soon traveled to Floreana, hiking the long, tortured incline to find the "Modern Adam and Eve" and their "Garden of Eden." Charles S. Howard, the San Francisco automobile magnate who, in a few years, would buy the champion racehorse Seabiscuit, arrived after a monthlong cruise along the western coast of South America. On board his 163-foot yacht, *Aras*, was a fleet of flamingos, a seldom-seen blue-footed booby bird, penguins, marine iguanas (which Darwin called "imps of darkness"), a baby monkey, a giant turtle, and a pair of blue-eyed Galápagos doves, all housed in cages or tanks, soon to be re-homed at the Steinhart Aquarium in Golden Gate Park.

"The doctor and frau were rather scantily clad when we first saw them," he later reported, "but they donned other garments to greet us." He suspected Friedrich was tiring of his stringent diet, and gave his assessment of the doctor: "Why go so far to be a nut when it's more comfortable and you can have plenty more company right in California?"

Then came the businessman and philanthropist Vincent Astor, who had inherited the bulk of an $87 million fortune (about $2.2 billion today) when his father, John Jacob Astor IV, died on the *Titanic*. The younger Astor confessed a lifelong obsession with the ocean, and his favorite pastime was, he wrote, "a game of stalking sharks, not as hunter but as observer. My father taught me how to let my boat drift upon them silently and so get a clear view of them; the mere dipping of an oar is enough to send them racing from view." Later, Astor became intrigued by Darwin's discovery of "a natural laboratory full of mysteries," marveling, "The Galapagos stands practically unchanged—still mysterious, still a life wholly confirmatory of the theory we have come to know as 'Darwinism.'"

Hoping to retrace Darwin's steps, Astor announced his own Galápagos voyage on his yacht, the USS *Nourmahal*, a 263-foot "floating hotel," as one guest put it, that would be acquired by the U.S. Navy during World War II. Although Astor's wife, Helen Dinsmore Huntington, did not share his passion for exploration, she decorated the ship's interior, favoring early American furniture and bold patterns and chintzes. Astor's guests enjoyed a fireplace in the main lounge, a meticulously appointed library paneled in Norwegian pine, a dining salon with real windows (as opposed to port-holes), a crew of fifty to ensure superior service, and operating costs amounting to $1,000 per week, approximately $22,000 today.

Astor's itinerary included stops at twelve islands in the Galápagos ar-chipelago, covering seven thousand miles. His scientific party included Kermit Roosevelt, the son of the former president. Astor, said to be as in-terested in "pleasure trips" as he was research, invited a woman compan-ion for each guest.

When, months later, Astor returned to New York City and docked at Pier 1, he boasted a particularly exotic collection: several live specimens of the "testudo porteri," which scientists had believed to be extinct; flightless cormorants, four-foot lizards, and a three-hundred-pound turtle; a fish with two backbones; several piscatorial specimens so rare that they had no names; a rookery of penguins half the size of their Arctic counterparts; and baby sea lions that approached the crew with, Astor reported, "puppy-like affection."

Before escorting the cargo to the New York Aquarium, Astor took one of the penguins, small in stature and solemn of mien, on a short tour of the city. Remarkably composed, even nonchalant, the penguin—named Paddlewing—rode in Astor's limousine through the bustle of lower Man-hattan, was carried through the crowded lobby at 217 Broadway, and then took the elevator with Astor to his office. Once there, a witness observed, "he calmly surveyed his surroundings, picked out the mirror, walked up in front of it, and started preening himself. Quite unperturbed and disposed to let anyone scratch his head, he finally arrived at the Aquarium late in the afternoon, joined the other penguins in the pool, had a bath, ate all the minnows he could hold, and went to sleep."

Over the following months, sadly, his friends died one by one. In order to compensate, aquarium officials built mirrors around Paddlewing's tank, hoping to cure his loneliness. But the penguin was not fooled; one morning, Paddlewing, too, rolled over and died. The press claimed "heartbreak" as the cause.

Yet Astor's most enduring memory from his cruise was the time spent on Floreana, where, like the others, he paid a visit to Friedo to meet the peculiar couple mentioned in all the American newspapers. Friedrich spoke of his philosophy and dietary habits, claiming that he refused to eat any food that was obtained through violence. He even refused to eat potatoes and beets because they "had to be dragged from the earth by force." Astor gave them seeds for growing coffee and cabbages and noticed that Dore was missing a few teeth; presumably Dr. Ritter had pulled them, as he had pulled his own.

•   •   •

The explorers' tales of the Galápagos idealists became welcome distractions from the compounding ills of the world. Seven months after the crash, the effects of the Great Depression grew more severe, with endless reports of "slumps": a textile slump, a cotton slump, an auto slump, a marriage slump, a canal traffic slump, a potato sale slump, a Latin America slump, and an orchid slump, in which the value of the flowers decreased by half. Three million American citizens were out of work. Rainfall was perilously low in the eastern part of the country, a precursor to the dust bowl that would soon ravage the Great Plains. In Germany, the Weimar Republic government was forced to slash wages and increase taxes in order to pay reparations for the Great War, measures that stirred social and political unrest and emboldened Adolf Hitler.

Dore and Friedrich, themselves unaware of these developments, represented an escape, a bold blueprint for a life far removed from the madness, an experiment in extreme self-isolation that suggested a madness of its own. "One can't help believing that Dr. Ritter and his companion are just as happy as they say they are," opined *The Austin Statesman*.

They may have lost a lot of the attractions that civilization has to offer, but likewise they have gained a lot—for civilization, after all, has its price. Far from the world's beaten path, they have escaped many things. They have no nosey neighbors eager to pry into their affairs, or always ready to bother by borrowing sugar or coffee; if Dr. Ritter chooses to come home slightly tipsy at night (although goodness only knows where he would be coming from) he need not worry, because there is no one to see him. . . .

[Dore] has her freedom, too. She doesn't have to worry about trying to make ends meet in running the household, washing dirty dishes, getting ready for bridge parties, remaking her last year's dress to conform with the new fall styles or entertaining boresome guests who drop in at the most inopportune times and stay much longer than they are wanted. Yes, there's a lot to be said in favor of a solitary existence on a desert island. So much so, in fact, it's liable to make one wonder when the next boat leaves for the South Seas and how much a ticket costs.

Another editorial, drawing upon the unrest in Europe, considered the case of Friedrich and Dore in the context of a burgeoning mob mentality throughout society: A "great force which draws people together in mobs is the kind of narcissism which creates artists' colonies, writers' colonies, free love colonies, religious communities, Latin quarters, Greenwich Villages and all similar gatherings of people with the same points of view," argued the *New York Herald Tribune*. "They justify their own opinions by grouping themselves with those who think as they do. . . . We cannot get away from our fellow man, a fact which was strikingly illustrated when the newspapers carried the pictures of Dr. Friedrich Ritter and a woman friend. Seeking to escape from civilization, these two had fled secretly from Berlin and taken refuge in a remote island of the Galápagos group. All to no purpose. The members of the McDonald expedition found them there, and before long their adventure was the common property of thousands of people on two continents."

•   •   •

By the spring of 1930, Dore and Friedrich, busy tending to their garden and planning the next phase of Friedo, still didn't know that their experiment had made international news. They were unaware of a plan, proposed by McDonald and supported by four hundred fellow wealthy Americans—Gifford Pinchot, Charles Kettering, and Vincent Astor among them—to buy the entire Galápagos archipelago and gift it to the U.S. government. Such a deal would foster friendliness between North and South America, the men argued, and be a boon for both continents, preserving the islands' wildlife and increasing opportunities in trade and investment. Dore and Friedrich were unaware, too, that the citizens of Ecuador considered the very idea treasonous and urged their government to lease the islands to France, Japan, or even Germany—any country, really, but the "Yankee Menace"—in order to alleviate their own financial crisis. One Ecuadorian politician argued that selling the Galápagos to the United States would lead to a takeover of the entire country. In order to protect Ecuador, he advocated for a detachment of naval forces with "seagoing launches" to patrol the fishing grounds and the appointment of a governor capable of wresting control of the islands from "foreign intrigue."

Their ignorance of all political, social, and economic affairs, and of their growing international notoriety, ended on a date that Dore would remember for the rest of her life.

It was on May 5, a Monday, that she and Friedrich ventured down to Post Office Bay. To their surprise, the *Manuel J. Cobos* was coasting in. Captain Bruun hadn't come on this trip, but they were greeted by an Ecuadorian courier who handed them a thick parcel—their first mail delivery, forty-six letters in all, along with numerous newspapers. Together they sat on the soft sand and discovered that the letters were all from strangers; not a single envelope bore a familiar name. They hurried back to Friedo, where Friedrich left Dore in the garden so she could read all of the letters and newspaper clippings alone.

The letters were full of compliments on their initiative and bravery, followed by pleas to join them. A group of German citizens eager to escape named themselves the "South American Society" and required each member to contribute 3,000 marks ($720) for the journey to the Galápagos. In Berlin another group formed a "Galápagos-Emigrant" association (with a corresponding association in the United States), motivated as much by solitude being "in vogue" as by the political and financial upheaval. Imagine how wondrous it would be, the letters urged, if they all established a community of "like-minded souls." Dore could think of nothing she and Friedrich desired less. He believed that the vast majority of those fantasizing about building a colony on the Galápagos suffered from "a flabby and hysterical sentimentality."

With apprehension she unfolded a newspaper, wondering exactly how dire the situation had become in Germany since her and Friedrich's departure. To her surprise, the headlines centered not on her tormented country but on Friedrich's scandalous flight from civilization with one of his patients. They mentioned her name, her husband's name, the dissolution of two marriages. They reported that her divorce had been finalized. Every lurid detail, both true and false, imprinted hotly on her mind.

She felt that all of the ideas and principles she and Friedrich held most sacred were being mocked, reduced to gossipy fodder by people who knew them not at all. McDonald's visit and subsequent report had breached their solitude. They would never have peace at Friedo again.

"A radio telegram had destroyed this as surely and as swiftly as a single stroke of lightning destroys a living tree," she wrote. "We had become objects of sensational publicity. People in many countries read garbled and exaggerated accounts of who we were and what our aims had been in cutting ourselves off from their world."

The sound of her sobs drew Friedrich to the garden.

"What has happened?" he asked. "Why are you crying?"

She pressed the paper into his hands and said, "This is the end of everything."

# EIGHT

# The First Intruders

They had to move forward, Friedrich urged. They could not afford to sit idle and fret about prying neighbors back in Berlin or newspaper headlines or who might next arrive on the island. Privately, though, he confided his own frustrations in his notebook: "Nothing was further from us than to 'bother' anyone—let alone the general public—with our purely personal hermit life. . . . How poor in experiences the life of civilization must be that it disturbs the beloved loneliness of two people."

He and Dore made one concession to their new and unwelcome circumstance, sending word to the German consul at Guayaquil that any visitor should "call or yodel" when approaching Friedo to give them time to dress. As an extra precaution, they erected a sign on the path leading to the house: "Knock strongly, and enter when 3 minutes have passed."

· · ·

Dore took Friedrich's advice, vowing to push the external world from her thoughts. They began work on their new house, which would stand next to their existing shelter. It would be much grander and more spacious and implement Friedrich's "egg" philosophy, with a clear view to the coast of Isabela Island seventy miles away—a reminder, Dore wrote, "of how near we were to our fellow man, and how far we were from them." The roof would extend beyond the house to form a porch, which they would furnish with a large table and five chairs. Their beds would be protected from insects by screens of wire netting. There would be a dedicated study area, where they would read and write after long days toiling in the sun, sitting on furniture they fashioned from curved sticks.

For the new house to have their desired views, it had to be set on pillars about nine feet high. They excavated blocks of lava and carted them off. The sharp lava rocks prevented them from going barefoot, and they worked in wet shoes. Bananas and papayas had to be uprooted and replanted in the limited strip of land that was watered by the spring. The invasive wild cats and dogs prowled, closing in. To protect their chickens, they built an enclosure deep within the crater walls, but several were still killed.

Dore expected the exhausting work to ravage her body, but it caused equal damage to her mind. "It is a romantic error to suppose that in the building of our house and the creation of the garden we translated drudgery into terms of spiritual significance," she wrote. "Nothing could be farther from the truth. On the contrary, the ceaseless and excessive manual toil dulled the edge of our whole spiritual life for me, and spoiled all its freshness." At night, she thought about the foolish squabbles that occupied too much of their time, and the various ways Friedrich undermined her. He never failed to voice his disappointment when she struggled, and seemed to have "eternal dissatisfaction" with everything she said and did. When she lashed out in rage, he justified his coldness by citing his "high ambition" for her. He had faith that she could be an extraordinary woman, if only she allowed him to instruct her.

The rainy season came late, after the new year, arriving in the night with a ferocity that startled Dore; the pounding of the drops on their iron roof sounded like a thousand drums. She awakened with a sense of terror and saw Friedrich in the same state, both of them wondering if a cache of uncovered dynamite had been set off by someone or something unknown. Holding an old umbrella, guided by Friedrich's lantern, they hurried outside, where Dore found a piece of tar paper she could set atop the dynamite to prevent it from getting soaked. Just as suddenly as the downpour had started, it abated, and they looked at each other, both in sodden nightclothes, Dore dragging the tar paper behind her like a bedraggled cape, and indulged an emotion they hadn't felt in quite some time, doubling over in laughter.

• • •

With the rain came a frantic burst of life in the garden, as well as a savage plague of cockroaches and mosquitoes and beetles and lice and caterpillars and ants—the last of these especially vicious and seemingly immune to extermination. Even the very idea of the ants enraged Friedrich; they lived and operated against his philosophy. "The socialism of the ants," he wrote, "is nothing more than a systematic common robbery of all other life."

The next intruder was human, and someone they already knew: Captain Bruun, who arrived on the *Manuel J. Cobos* in the spring of 1931 with an explanation about the mysterious theft at the Casa. Dore and Friedrich weren't robbed by a roving band of marauders. Bruun himself had dispatched a boat to collect his own belongings, and the crew accidentally took their possessions as well. Perhaps, Bruun suggested, they had expected Dore and Friedrich to be living at the Casa and, when no one was there, concluded that they had abandoned Floreana for Isabela Island, the largest in the archipelago.

Dore was skeptical. "It's all very well," she said, "but what about the little rowing boat?" That was a clear sign that they had not gone to Isabela, she argued. What had he done with the boat, and when might he return it?

At that, Bruun argued that the rowboat had actually been his all along and then changed the subject. He had heard, he said, about the visits from McDonald and Astor and the other rich Americans, and the many generous gifts they'd left behind. He let this statement linger in the air, a tacit suggestion that he was deserving to share in those gifts. Dore could tell that Friedrich, too, was more amused than bothered by Bruun's entitlement, but his next declaration angered both of them.

"I have decided," Bruun said, "to give up this plying between the islands. This cruise is almost my last one in the *Manuel J. Cobos*. I'm coming here to live."

Dore and Friedrich spoke at once: "What?"

"Yes, I'm going to start a fishing station. I shall live at the Casa and make it my headquarters. We shall be able to help each other. There's a very good thing to be made out of fishing." He went on to say he had a smart young partner in Guayaquil, a Dane named Knud Arends, who had very high hopes for a profitable fishing industry on Floreana. "No one's ever yet tried to fish these waters for what's in them," he said, "but I'm going to, and you'll see we'll bring some life into this island soon." Bruun sailed off.

Dore tried to put Bruun's enterprise out of her mind, making feeble arguments to Friedrich: "Until he comes, Floreana will still be ours. Let us enjoy it all the more, if our undisturbed possession is to be short"—words that sounded false as soon as she had spoken them.

Bruun soon returned with his partner. Dore had expected Arends to resemble Bruun—grizzled, middle-aged, cynical—but instead found a young man, not more than twenty-five, dark-haired and, she wrote, "of more than usual good looks." He and Bruun moved into the Casa at Post Office Bay and transformed the site into a sort of factory, with a group of native Ecuadorians standing at long tables cleaning and slicing fish, dumping the heads and entrails back into the water, drawing shivers of sharks.

Bruun was so busy he rarely ventured to Friedo, but, as Dore had expected and feared, others began to arrive. Five young German men came separately but soon banded together, sleeping in the pirate caves. Every Sunday they visited Friedo seeking camaraderie and advice. A woman from Berlin brought her husband, hoping the tropical air would cure his lung disease. She appeared at Friedo wearing a silk gown and matching stockings, bejeweled rings blinking from every finger, indignant at the reception she'd received from the cave dwellers. Surely Dore and Friedrich wouldn't mind if she and her husband moved into Friedo? She and her husband should be very happy in Dore and Friedrich's "little paradise." Could they also accommodate her three pet monkeys?

It took several hours to convince the woman that Friedo was not a hotel and she could not stay with them.

"It sounds discourteous to designate our visitors as intruders," Dore wrote, "yet pleasant as they were as human beings, most of them, we did at times resent their coming. It might be said that had we wished to seriously, we could easily have refused to talk to anybody or entertain a single stranger in our Friedo seclusion. Sometimes, indeed, we were almost tempted to do this, but when we thought of the sheer physical effort it cost to clamber up the rough hillside to us, we felt that to turn our backs on these well-meaning callers would be too churlish. So we never did."

Friedrich's account of how they treated these visitors is strangely different: "They came expecting to be treated like invited guests, and the only way we can deal with them is to make it clear in the beginning that we want to be alone and consider them intruders. We refuse to have anything to do with them."

The dichotomy of their recollections would become an enduring theme, evidence that they lived in parallel worlds instead of jointly, as a private, unified couple who answered only to themselves. As time passed, and they felt increasingly compelled to explain themselves to the outside world, neither of them ever acknowledged the discomforting truth: They escaped civilization only to become obsessed with how society might judge them.

•   •   •

For one reason or another, the intruders soon departed Floreana. The five young men deserted the pirate caves. Captain Bruun died in a drowning accident when his cruiser, the *Norge*, ran out of petrol on the way to Floreana with supplies. Stranded, he tried to make the journey back in Dore and Friedrich's rowboat but was battered by rough swells and launched against jagged rocks. To Dore and Friedrich's relief, Bruun's partner, Arends, shut down the fishing enterprise and left the island.

The woman in the silk dress departed more quietly than she came, leaving her three monkeys behind. She confessed to Dore that she'd only brought the animals to test the safety of Floreana's wild plants before her husband consumed them. How ridiculous, Dore thought, to bring your sick husband all the way to the island hoping for a cure only to leave shortly thereafter, worried that you might kill him with poison.

# NINE

# Appearances

In the wake of the failed settlers came journalists, arriving in the summer of 1931, all of them eager to investigate Dore and Friedrich's life on a remote island—a life that had become, seemingly overnight, a universal aspiration.

The journalists wrote of the long journey from Post Office Bay to Friedo, the paths of withered thorn brush, the handwritten sign pointing the way to Friedo. They wrote of the surprise of finding the lush oasis where "Adam and Eve" had made their home—the golden vibrancy of the banana grove, the tree branches heavy with fruit, the cackle of the chickens and soft rumble of the stream. They wrote of "two absolutely naked figures, beautifully tanned," running out into the clearing, staring with mouths agape, and running back again to dress in simple, loose shirts belted at the waist.

They had been warned at Guayaquil that Friedrich would allow no photographs and chase all visitors away, but instead here came this odd little man, bringing a basket of papayas and plums and tomatoes, eager for news of the outside world, of Hitler's growing prominence, of whether the visitor noticed Friedrich's uncanny resemblance to Faust—"Am I not Faust?" he always inquired. They wrote of Friedrich and Dore's intention to live for more than a hundred years. And, most graphically, they wrote of Friedrich's teeth—made not of porcelain to resemble human teeth, they noted, but of "glittering, stainless steel," teeth that he shined not with toothpaste and a brush but with a wad of steel wool.

"With these he could crack open the shell of a clam, or even an oyster, but never did, because he and Dore are vegetarians," reported a journalist for *The American Weekly*, "but he could and did sometimes tear into a piece of tough sugar cane in a way that I am sure would have impressed a gorilla. Later, when I enjoyed Eve's hospitality at dinner, Adam astonished me by removing those powerful masticators during the meal and eating without them. It seems that, after all, they were useful mostly for decoration and speech."

Hoping to address some of the more sensational reports, Friedrich wrote a series of articles and, through a friend in Germany, placed a notice in European newspapers seeking a publisher for his work. *The Atlantic Monthly* responded, publishing his dispatches in a three-part series. Friedrich wrote of everything they'd experienced, from the journey over on the *Boskoop* to the clearing of their land; to Hugo's injury and departure; to their many battles with wild insects and beasts; to their short-lived intruders and their vision for Friedo. Eager to impress readers of the *Atlantic*, he exaggerated—and even outright lied—about his progress on the house, describing a grandiose edifice with stone walls, a lavatory, and even a second floor.

"Perhaps in America people will be astonished to find such mystical religiousness, and so little sensationalism, as the motives for our endeavor," Friedrich concluded. "But it ought not to be hard to understand that whether one lives in the temperate zone, the arctic, or the tropics, paradise is not impossible of attainment. It is only a state of the soul within one's self, and it consists of love, patience, and contentment. These are truly the entrance gates of heaven; since we possess all three, we do not ask for anything more."

Friedrich did build one ingenious feature for Friedo: a contraption for running water. After hooking up a length of old pipe salvaged from Post Office Bay from their spring to a rock in the corner of the kitchen, he fashioned a tap from an old cartridge, using a slide to control the flow. Visitors to Friedo were treated to the sight of Friedrich showering gleefully, smiling as the water splashed his face, clad in nothing but a pair of loose-fitting underwear, his emaciated rib cage displaying every one of its bones, lined up like piano keys beneath his skin. They could take as many pictures as they wished.

He would never admit, not even to Dore, that he was beginning to enjoy the world's attention, and even crave it. To the contrary, in interviews and in letters to friends back in Germany, he continued to give the impression that the American visitors were an unwelcome nuisance, and that he and Dore desired nothing more than absolute solitude.

•   •   •

During these visits Dore played her part, giving tours and praising Friedrich's inventions, offering a drink made of crushed ripe banana and egg, boasting of her own personal growth and Friedrich's role in shaping it: "The doctor taught me to know myself." But when the cameras stopped flashing and the yachts sailed away, her misgivings about their relationship resurfaced. Why did Friedrich withhold any admiration for her work on Friedo when they were alone, only to sing her praises to strangers? At times their relationship seemed to be for display purposes only—a shiny trinket or a party trick, to be tucked away and forgotten when the crowds dispersed.

She maintained her belief that his occasional cruelties were a necessary tool against her own inherent weaknesses, but she felt a slight shift within: a part of her personality was rising up and asserting itself, complicating her path. She would never be the submissive woman whom Friedrich's philosophy demanded.

Tormented by her own nature and "by many queer discrepancies in Friedrich's unique character," Dore could not help but challenge his more disturbing thoughts and whims. He objected to her menagerie of animals, exhibiting a strange envy in particular to her pet donkey, Burro; he felt he alone deserved her affection and attention, and thought her continued attachment to worldly things threatened their purpose on the island. She trained her family of cats to avoid Friedo entirely. "My friendship," she wrote, "had to be carried on with them half in secret."

His resentment even extended to her flower garden, a project she'd begun with seeds sent by an American visitor. After her plot of carnations bloomed, Dore was stricken by hay fever and begged Friedrich to water them. On the first day she was well enough to step outside, she saw that her flower bed was empty, the disheveled soil betraying where Friedrich had pulled the blooms. She did not confront Friedrich, but planted more seeds. As soon as they matured he pulled them again. She planted a third, and this time he left it alone.

In another act of defiance, Dore wrote to Friedrich's wife back in Germany, asking her to come to Floreana and live with them, promising she would "not be unhappy." Perhaps Dore wanted a companion who knew Friedrich well and could help bear the weight of his moods. It was an offer that Mila Ritter, no stranger to Friedrich's brutality, never accepted.

# TEN
# Our So-Called
# Paradise

In December 1931, a couple named Margret Waldbröl and Heinz Wittmer stood in front of a haberdashery in Cologne, Germany, debating
what to do with their lives. Although both were still married to their first
spouses, Margret called Heinz her husband and claimed that, on this occasion, they were shopping after their recent wedding. Their makeshift family included Heinz's twelve-year-old son, Harry, whom Margret treated as
her own and who had been sickly and nearly blind since birth.

As Margret tells it, she urged Heinz to buy a suit.

"Yes or a rifle," Heinz replied. "I can't decide which."

"A rifle?" Margret asked. "What on earth do you want a rifle for?"

"In case we go to the Galapagos Islands," Heinz said. "Just for two or
three years, you know. It might do as Harry's sanatorium."

Margret considered this. A doctor had advised a sanatorium to address
Harry's ills, but they couldn't afford one, and a tropical climate might be
equally restorative. "Just think," she wrote. "Wild animals, the pampa, a
hut we should build ourselves. An adventurous 'Robinson' life."

Like most everyone else in the world, they had heard of Dore and Friedrich. A recent report quoted a letter Friedrich had sent to a relative.
"People are writing all sorts of silly letters to us," he wrote. "They obviously
believe that we are living an idle life like Adam and Eve in paradise, eating
delicious fruits, swimming in the ocean, or walking about admiring the

beautiful landscape. This is a pleasant delusion." He went on to complain about the sharks that swam just a few yards from the beach, of the American millionaires who came to gawk and pry and carve their names into his fruit trees, and of the many deluded admirers who dreamed of uprooting their lives to join him and Dore on Floreana. "My companion and I cannot but laugh at the 'Galapagos psychosis' which is reported to have broken out in Germany," he wrote. "It is the result of entirely wrong notions of our so-called paradise."

●   ●   ●

Margret and Heinz were not deterred by Friedrich's words, and in fact believed they were suited to such a life. They considered themselves simple, practical, solid people, disinterested in Nietzsche and other lofty intellectual pursuits, unafraid of either grueling work or extreme isolation. They were also intensely private, and never spoke publicly of how they'd met and fallen in love while still married to others.

Heinz's estranged wife, Anna, objected to his plan of taking Harry to the Galápagos. Despite the boy's poor eyesight and fragility, he had done well in school, and Anna thought he should continue his formal education rather than embark on an uncertain future in South America. Heinz's decision, she believed, had less to do with their son's medical issues than with the physical challenges of island life. "My husband could use him very well on Floreana," she wrote, "and I am sure that is the reason he took the boy with him."

Heinz, a native of Warburg, Germany, about 450 miles southeast of Berlin, was now forty years old, lanky and lithe, in possession of only half of his hair. He wore thin-framed glasses and carried a pipe that seemed perpetually suspended from his lips. As one acquaintance put it, he was happy to be perceived as "quite an ordinary person . . . a real person of flesh and blood."

Like Friedrich Ritter, Heinz was a veteran of the Great War, having served as a lieutenant in the Eighty-Third Infantry Regiment, Second Battalion, which fought on the eastern front. He suffered a minor wound in December 1914 when his regiment fought in Poland. A year later he was again admitted to the hospital, this time for syphilis, leaving one month later. After the war he became secretary to Konrad Adenauer, the mayor of Cologne and a leading politician in the Weimar Republic who staunchly opposed Adolf Hitler. With the stock market crash and ensuing recession, Heinz lost his job and, owing to inflation, most of his savings.

A dozen years had passed since the war, but the emotional scars remained. Even in moments of happiness and calm, his voice and hands still shook. He was often besieged by worry: for his ailing son; for his 27-year-old lover, Margret, who yearned for a child; and for the future of his homeland.

In Germany six million people were out of work, members of the Nazi Party and the communists were murdering each other, and Hitler was preparing to run in the upcoming presidential election. He'd recently held a rally in Cologne with twenty thousand followers marching through the streets not far from Heinz's home. "[Hitler] began to talk quietly enough, using few gesticulations," according to one witness. "But when he started to enumerate the Fatherland's ills and to designate those whom he denounced as the authors of Germany's woes, the little man of a few minutes before seemed transformed into a classical thundergod."

With the Galápagos Islands in mind, Margret and Heinz sold their Cologne flat and invested in equipment and supplies, including tools and an abundance of provisions: rice, beans, flour, coffee, Quaker oats, washing soap, matches, tinned oil, yellow fabric to make clothing, potatoes and onions for planting, three bottles of brandy, and, finally, a typewriter, should either of them decide that their adventures on Floreana were worth recording. Their two Alsatian dogs, Hertha and Lump, would travel with them.

Margret thought of the hard work ahead of them and couldn't help but grasp Heinz's hands. "I know they are good hands, and strong," she wrote. "I trust those hands . . . and Heinz trusts me. The trust in one another is everything. The whole world lies enclosed therein. I will not disappoint this man whose hands I hold. I want to help—dig in with him." Embarrassed by her own sentimentality, she added, "But perhaps that is beginning to sound a bit pathetic."

Margret's mother had died when she was just ten years old, a tragedy that strengthened her bond with her father and sister. Still, she kept her plans secret even from them. On the eve of their departure, a Saturday night, her sister visited and gave her usual farewell—"Good night, see you tomorrow"—and Margret could only offer a strained "good night" in response, aware that she would miss her sister's company not only the next day but likely the following year and the year after that and, should unforeseen troubles arise, maybe for a very long time to come.

# ELEVEN
# Mr. Hancock of
# Los Angeles

On January 3, 1932, just as Margret and Heinz decided to flee Germany for the Galápagos Islands, the American millionaire George Allan Hancock anchored his yacht at Post Office Bay, took a small boat to Black Beach, and immediately began the long, grueling hike to Friedo to meet the famous Dore Strauch and Friedrich Ritter.

On the shore Hancock and his crew found a small table made of sticks, sturdy enough to support any gifts for the settlers that might be left in passing. A well-carved donkey trail pointed the way to the interior, layered with hoofprints and manure and long scraps of sawed timber, clearly discarded on the way inland, a reminder of the Norwegians' failed attempt to live on Floreana. Here and there, too, lay shards of pottery with a pink willow pattern, and bits of leather and scraps of iron, and, a bit farther, a set of rimless wheels that had never traveled anywhere.

Though the islands were on the cusp of the warm, wet season, rain had not yet fallen. Hancock and his colleagues trudged through thick volcanic dust and saw cacti with fluted columns. As the trail narrowed to the width of a wagon, it was clear where Friedrich's machete had done its work. They passed thorny acacia trees, delicate spirals of mollusk shells, towering lollipops of wild cotton. They climbed higher until they came upon a makeshift ramp of rocks, which carried them over a particularly rough stretch. Then, at last, they found themselves at a clearing. Before them sprawled a broad, open path decorated by green banana trees, and behind them was an unobstructed view of the sea. They approached a barbed-wire fence that led to a gate and finally glimpsed Friedo: small, but beautifully maintained. To the right stood a small pen holding a donkey with a stripe running along one shoulder. "He looked over at us appraisingly," noted one visitor, "and proceeded to give forth a long and vigorous bray. No better watch dog could be imagined."

At the sound of Burro's warning, Friedrich appeared.

•   •   •

Friedrich would find much to admire in George Allan Hancock, called Allan by friends and family. The captain, too, had been born into privilege, the son of the lawyer, surveyor, and California forty-niner Henry Hancock and Ida Haraszthy, an American-born fellow pioneer with an impressive European pedigree. Her mother was a noblewoman of Polish descent, and her father a flamboyant Hungarian count who had been exiled from his homeland. When Count Haraszthy returned to Hungary in 1842 to collect his family and move to America, they made history as the first Hungarian immigrants to become U.S. citizens.

Born on July 26, 1875, in San Francisco, along with a twin brother who died in infancy, Allan Hancock grew up on Rancho La Brea. His father had purchased 4,439 acres of the tar-rich Mexican land grant (paying just $2.50 an acre), located in present-day Los Angeles. When Hancock's father died in 1883, his widow, Ida, discovered that the ranch was deep in debt. Squatters descended upon the property, a problem Ida confronted in two ways, filing a lawsuit to evict them and chasing them off with a shotgun.

Every morning, Hancock and his younger brother, Bertram, walked three miles from their modest ranch home to a one-room schoolhouse on a dirt road, which is now Wilshire Boulevard in the neighborhood of Hancock Park. As young adults, Hancock and his brother worked under Ida's direction, picking and shoveling tar to sell for fuel, raising and plowing grain crops, and tending to the livestock. When Bertram died in 1893 from typhoid fever, Hancock resolved to never leave his mother.

Their fortunes changed in 1900, when they granted a twenty-year lease on a thousand acres of La Brea to the Salt Lake Oil Company. For more than a year, one single well flowed 1,100 barrels a day, and in 1910, a banner year, La Brea's wells produced more than 3.8 million barrels. Overnight millionaires, Ida built a mansion on what would become the corner of Wilshire Boulevard and Vermont Avenue. The following year, as workers drilled a water well on the property, they brought to the surface a number of large bones belonging to extinct Ice Age mammals, among them the skulls of a dire wolf, a saber-toothed cat, and a giant ground sloth. The former president Theodore Roosevelt, himself an avid explorer, visited La Brea and declared it "the most extraordinary storehouse of fossils in the world." Museums around the country clamored to study and house the specimens, but Hancock was adamant they remain in his city: "They belong to Los Angeles and must stay here."

Hancock was outwardly gregarious but intensely private, occasionally paranoid and prone to shutting himself off from the world. His second wife, in pursuing a divorce, testified that her husband "would be away for days at a time and then for weeks at a time"; she learned of his location only when he thought to mail her a letter. A friend added that Hancock was "very indifferent, and wasn't at home a great deal—and when he was at home he kept himself in his room or in the basement." He had an intense fear of being kidnapped and purposely made his mansion look uninhabited: the grass remained wild and uncut; the blinds perpetually drawn; and, as an extra precaution, the mailbox bore his butler's name. Hancock never even used the front entrance, always slipping in and out of the back.

Over the years Hancock collected a repertoire of hobbies, titles, and accomplishments: farmer, oilman, banker, manufacturer, inventor, railroader, aviator, food packer, philanthropist, educator, scientist, sea captain, and musician, even playing as a first chair cellist of the Los Angeles Symphony Orchestra. "Jumping from one thing to another," he explained, "keeps me young in spirit." After passing an exam for a master mariner's license, Hancock commissioned a naval architect to build him a series of yachts for cruises along the western coasts of Central and South America, the newest and most advanced of which was the *Velero III*.

Hancock billed the cruiser, which cost nearly $1 million to build (more than $13 million in today's money), as a "floating laboratory" with numerous features to enhance scientific exploration: thousands of glass vials for specimens, instruments for dredging the bottom of the sea, electrically heated and irrigated fish tanks, underwater electric lights, and cameras designed to take pictures far beneath the ocean's surface. What the interior lacked in aesthetics it made up for in safety and comfort. A thick cork insulation kept rats and vermin away. Two systems of freshwater, one for drinking and cooking and the other for lavatory and shower purposes, were constructed to run separately, avoiding the risk of contamination. A state-of-the-art ventilation system circulated fresh air to all crew quarters and guest rooms. A "doctor's room," stocked with various medicines, was sufficiently equipped for major surgery. Hancock insisted upon just one grand flourish: an elegant spiral staircase connecting his and the guest quarters. "The ship rides like a swan," one crew member said, "and if the sea comes over her bow one would have to be on the bridge to know of it."

For the *Velero*'s inaugural expedition, Hancock assembled a group of distinguished scientists from various institutions, among them San Francisco's Steinhart Aquarium, the San Diego Zoo, the California Academy of Sciences, the University of Southern California, and Harvard University. Many of his chosen colleagues also happened to be gifted musicians: a cameraman played the violin; a fossil collector, the flute; and the entomologist and ornithologist sat nightly behind the ship's grand piano for concerts in the Social Hall. During the course of the three-month expedition, the *Velero* made various stops in Central America, collecting twenty-seven iguanas, unidentifiable lizard-like creatures, a white seal (one of the few ever captured), hermit crabs and five-hundred-pound tortoises, sea elephants and booby birds, boa constrictors and ringtail monkeys, flying fish and microscopic insects. The Galápagos Islands were their final stop, and here Hancock and his crew were especially interested in the human inhabitants of Floreana, suspecting they might be the most exotic specimens of all.

• • •

The *Velero* crew took in the sight of Friedrich. "A little energetic man," noted Chief Officer W. Charles Swett, "with flaxen hair and a short beard." Friedrich was bare-legged and barefoot and wore only a filmy nightshirt that draped to his knees. He met them halfway and smiled as they introduced themselves, speaking only German in response. A representative from the San Diego Zoo, Karl Koch, acted as interpreter and related that Friedrich wanted to give them a tour of his home. They followed him, dirtying their shoes with the pulp of rotten fruits that had spilled over the path.

Dore appeared, equally enthusiastic, wearing a filthy smock dress trimmed with white. She, too, was barefoot, and had "direct manners," Swett thought, "friendly like a boy." She was tiny, five feet tall and barely a hundred pounds. Her hair was cut into a rough, uneven bob, and her smile was marred by two gold crowned teeth and a gaping cavity where another had been pulled. Nothing about her seemed capable of pausing or staying still: her face was a kaleidoscope of expressions; her fingers fiddled with any object within their grasp; she alternately burst into laughter or fell into somber silence. She showed them the crude stove Friedrich had made from scraps of iron, and Friedrich demonstrated his water pump and shower. As the afternoon meandered on, Dore grew more comfortable with the visitors and began speaking English—"almost fluent," Swett wrote, "with a quaintness of accent and pronunciation which was quite charming."

The following day, at Hancock's invitation, Dore and Friedrich came aboard the *Velero* for lunch. The captain watched as Dore stopped in the ocean to scrub her feet before donning rolled socks and white Keds sneakers (the best, Friedrich had decided, at withstanding sharp lava stones). She was eager to meet everyone and seemed remarkably at ease, and she truly was, according to her own words: "No one who came cruising to the island showed such sympathetic or intelligent interest in our purpose and ideas as Captain Hancock. In him we found that openness of mind and freedom from prejudice and preconceived ideas, as well as that respect for other people's sincerities, which are among the most likable traits of the Americans. These men, we felt, did not regard us as something escaped from a psychological zoo."

Hancock and his ensemble performed a concert, choosing the works of Beethoven and Schumann and others that Dore and Friedrich might recognize. "Music is the alcohol of the soul," Friedrich mused, and everyone agreed. During a rendition of "Still wie die Nacht" (Calm as the Night) he sang along, faltering and off-key: "Calm as the night, deep as the sea, should be thy love for me."

Dore, so sweet in her dress and tennis shoes, so charming with her accented English and skittering gestures, shocked everyone by laughing with great fervor at Friedrich's broken voice, ridiculing him so pointedly that he was put on the defensive. "I do not sing," he admitted, "but I have trained choruses and conducted somewhat."

This tense moment passed quickly, and Dore and Friedrich resumed their customary displays of affection, caressing each other's hands and exchanging glances, a performance of "mutuality and happiness," Swett observed, "which could hardly be classed as common in mere matrimony."

Friedrich then focused his attention on Hancock, sharing his ideas about how mankind might realize its full and true potential. What did Hancock think, for example, about the establishment of a "Reform Warehouse" for "healthy and harmonious living" in which everything for practical and economical use should be constructed after Friedrich's own principle, a principle he believed to be shared by American men? "Beauty is fitness and nothing else," would be one example of the principle; another might be "The best form for a desk is that of a kidney." And while they were on the subject of aesthetics and design, Friedrich had an idea: someone should build a house based on his drawings and exhibit it at the upcoming World's Fair in Chicago. Hancock, Friedrich thought, had a "very, very interesting view of the world," and he hoped that the captain would continue to share it.

At 1:00 p.m. they adjourned to the *Velero*'s dining room, paneled in rich, glossy wood, where they feasted on a simple meal of bread, sliced ham, sausage, pudding, pickles, and an array of beverages and desserts. Dore chose ice-cold milk and chocolate ice cream and couldn't believe, after two years of bananas and papayas and eggs, how miraculous the treats tasted on her tongue. "It seemed to me as though I were enchanted," she wrote. "The ordinary Dore suddenly in the circle of American dollar kings—and our simple hermitage and this luxurious yacht. But I would not exchange with these rich Americans. They are so alone and longing. All of them on board felt how rich we are."

Hancock asked what they needed most in the way of provisions. Friedrich suggested oil and lamps; Dore, when pressed, requested soap and flour. Friedrich scoffed at the idea of flour, but Dore insisted, and also ignored his objections to coffee. Hancock gave them these things and more: copies of *Vogue* magazine (Dore laughed at the long, flared hemlines and extreme high heels); a real cast-iron stove to replace her makeshift model; and, for Friedrich, a Winchester repeating rifle of .25 caliber and several boxes of shells.

"It is too much," Friedrich protested. "You must let me pay."

Hancock refused, and left them with these words: "When I first heard of you over two years ago, I had pictured you to myself, and I have found you just as I'd imagined." He urged them to write to him often about their problems and ideas.

As the *Velero* pulled away from Black Beach, Dore and Friedrich watched from the shore, delighted when they heard three blasts of its whistle in their honor. On board the cruiser, Swett recorded his thoughts about the enigmatic couple and their mercurial moods, their sudden shifts from contentment to rancor and back again. "Life grows drab in the security of the commonplace," he wrote. "Also man seems to need the conquest of his mate. To be too sure is to become stale. It apparently is more interesting to live with your neighbor's wife than with your own. There is a real basis in psychology here which can be critically analyzed." In other words, Dore and Friedrich's bright and happy facade masked a complicated tension—a tension that, paradoxically, seemed a vital component of their union.

# TWELVE
# And Then There
# Were Five

On August 28, 1932, Margret and Heinz stood on the gritty sand of Black Beach, watching the fishing boat that had delivered them to Floreana disappear. Harry ran along the shore, chasing their dogs, Hertha and Lump. It had rained overnight and a veil of steam drifted up from the lava rocks, evaporating to reveal the rows of thorny brush and, just beyond, a curtain of trees of varying heights and shapes and shades of green—looking, Margret thought, "like theater props arranged one behind the other."

It had been an arduous two months' journey from Amsterdam to Guayaquil, especially now that Margret was five months pregnant. A fellow German passenger had been astounded by their plan. "Tell me—are you people crazy?" he'd asked. "Going to Galapagos to live? Has this Dr. Ritter fooled you too with the stuff he writes? Don't make me laugh! He likes his roasts as much as any other German—only he eats it oftener. You'll find heaps of American tin cans at Dr. Ritter's place. And he doesn't lack liquor either! Don't be taken in by him." Margret tried to protest, but futilely; the man kept talking over her until she decided to stop listening.

She had endured seasickness and freezing rain and a long layover on Chatham Island (the captain of the fishing boat had declared, without explanation, that he could "go no further"), during which she had the realization that things were done differently in South America. But now, she told herself, she was at last in Floreana, and the island customs would become her customs, and the Spanish language would become a familiar tongue, and her "excitable Rhinelander" persona would yield to the relaxed attitudes of the locals, as much as she might be able and willing to let her old self go.

"How about getting us something to eat?" Heinz asked. "After that we'll pay our social call."

"Social call?" Margret asked, and then she remembered: "Oh yes, Dr. Ritter."

In Guayaquil, they had learned a bit more about their new neighbors—in particular, Dore and Friedrich's penchant for nudity and their disdain for unannounced visitors. Whether these details were true did not much concern Margret; she and Heinz would call on them only out of politeness, rather than to intrude upon their lives.

Margret set about unpacking their belongings onto the black sand. "Gray and brown are the dominating colors," she observed. "The grass is dried up and the bushes leafy and thorny. Loamy soil, dry as powder." A pelican, resting in its nest, watched curiously as Heinz erected a tarp and Margret used crates of books to make a table, laying a cloth over the top. She served rice pudding as their first Galápagos meal. To celebrate, they took a swim in the ocean, a brisk sixty-six degrees in the midst of the cool season. Afterward, Margret and Harry rested on the beach while Heinz went to greet Friedrich and Dore.

•  •  •

From Friedo, gazing down the clear path that led to Black Beach, Dore and Friedrich noticed that a small rowing boat had made several busy trips back and forth to the shore and now idled in the water. They had been warned about newcomers from a passing ship, and now the family had arrived. Friedrich started down toward Black Bay to meet them while Dore stayed behind. She considered herself the host of Floreana, ready to dispense advice, give warnings about the animals and pests, share her knowledge of the island. Before long she heard a shuffle of steps through the thickets.

She met Friedrich halfway, expecting to see her potential new woman friend, but instead saw a bald, bespectacled man of middle age whose general appearance, Dore thought, was "odd to the point of eccentricity." Sure, Friedrich was eccentric, but he did not run about with his spindly legs protruding from too-short shorts and bare feet thrust into a decrepit pair of felt bedroom slippers and a canvas bag slung over one shoulder in the manner of a tramp. At once she gave up hope that this man's wife would be worthy of her time, although, after a moment, she acknowledged silently that it was unfair to judge a wife by her husband, presuming they were married at all.

"Do you have any mail for us?" Friedrich asked.

Heinz replied that he had stopped by the barrel at Post Office Bay and pressed a packet of letters into Friedrich's hand. Friedrich was thankful, Dore could tell, but had other questions. Did Heinz have some connection with a newspaper or other publication? Did he intend to do any writing? Heinz answered no to these queries. Dore believed she and Friedrich were as polite as could be, but Heinz soon understood: his first impression had failed to win their sympathy, and he had overstayed his welcome. He left.

Dore assumed that was the end of it, but an hour later Heinz reappeared at Friedo's gate, this time with his wife and young son. Now Heinz looked perfectly presentable. Having "changed his absurd costume," she observed, he "came back dressed like a sane human being." Noting her surprise, Heinz explained that he had chosen his original attire based on the newspaper reports of Dore's and Friedrich's own appearances, thinking that an unfussy, bohemian style would appeal to them. Dore had no response, but decided this reasoning "threw a certain light" upon Heinz's character and attitude. She did not like him.

• • •

Despite all Margret had heard and read about Friedrich, she found herself stunned by his appearance. The dentures, she noticed, made his "whole jaw and head sag." Then there were his eyes, which "shifted uneasily" as he appraised her and "had a gleam in them which suggested the fanatic." In general he looked rather frightening, she concluded, and if she had visited on her own, she might have fled.

At least Friedrich had greeted her politely. Dore, however, took Margret's hand and handled it as though her fingers were contaminated. Her first words to Margret: "Aren't you a bit too well dressed for the Galapagos, Frau Wittmer?"

Quickly Margret appraised her own outfit: white skirt, pink shirt, brand-new Panama hat. She had hoped to make herself as presentable as possible and did not appreciate Dore's snide comment—nor her failure to offer a simple word of welcome. She forced herself to smile at Dore and respond in a light, friendly tone: "Oh well. I like to put on something decent when I go visiting, even here! But I promise you for work I'll wear an overall."

To this Dore had no response.

Margret walked toward the sound of the men's voices; Friedrich was giving Heinz a tour of Friedo and the garden. She found it all wonderful: the ingenious shower contraption, the chickens strutting about in their coop, the dazzling variety of fruits that they, too, would be able to enjoy in abundance. If Friedrich and Dore had suffered any hardship on the island, he made no mention of it. Instead, he boasted that "one can live on nothing but figs." He then turned abruptly to Heinz and asked, "How do things look? In Germany, for instance? Ever been in Berlin?"

His voice carried a note of melancholy, Margret thought, a longing for the world from which he'd severed himself. Heinz had plenty of news to report. There were the recent Reichstag elections, in which Hitler's Nazi Party received 37 percent of the vote; the party's campaign for the upcoming elections in November; and in Cologne, the discovery of a large cache of firearms and bombs smuggled in from Belgium and intended for distribution among Nazi storm troopers. The Depression had ravaged the country, and the Nazis were gaining ground with workers and small-business men by promising protection and relief.

In the midst of this conversation, Dore wandered over with her pained, limping gait. Privately, she was intrigued by her new neighbor and thought Margret "very touching" in her vulnerable condition. She wondered what would motivate a woman to leave behind her friends and family and embark on such a risky venture while preparing to bring a child into the world—was she, Dore wondered, "a heroine, a victim, or an idiot"? Nor did she understand why Heinz would bring his young son here, where he would have no peers or regular schooling or any of the comforts a teenage boy might crave or need. Since she couldn't voice any of these musings, she instead sought to prove her own erudition.

"What do you think of Nietzsche?" she asked.

Heinz responded, discussing the philosopher's works, while Margret silently scoffed. Why would anyone think they had come to Floreana to converse about Nietzsche? They merely wanted to be settlers, to live as simply and privately as possible. "Our equipment," Margret later wrote, "was not Nietzsche and Lao-tse [sic], but willingness to labor and persevere."

After Heinz and Margret said good night and departed, Dore once again felt a sense of unease. As would occur so often on Floreana, between all of the islands' settlers, there was a great discrepancy about the words exchanged, the favors requested, the motives divined.

According to Margret, she and Heinz never intended to trouble Friedrich for medical care; according to Dore, they absolutely did, and made no secret about it. "Friedrich was anything but pleased," Dore wrote. "He thought it both inconsiderate and impertinent of these utter strangers to saddle us with the moral responsibility for their having come so far, and then to bank so casually upon the conscience of a medical man, and place him in a position where he could not refuse his services."

The whole episode made them resentful of the Wittmers. Dore believed that the Wittmers would never truly belong to Floreana as she and Friedrich did, because the reasons for their coming were all wrong. She worried that these people, indirectly or directly, would bring harm to her and Friedrich, and one way or another force them off the island.

# THIRTEEN

# A Direct Order
# from God

In the 12th arrondissement of Paris, not far from the spot where the courtesan and spy Mata Hari was executed by gunfire, Baroness Antonia Wagner von Wehrborn Bosquet had a dream in which she saw cool, clear water flowing from a rock and heard a voice she recognized, irrefutably, as belonging to God. The voice told her that she must take possession of the Galápagos Islands, where he would send water gushing from the earth for her animals, her plants, and her own body and mouth. He would speak to and provide for her as he had done for the shepherds in biblical times.

To heed this call would require a great upheaval of her current life, but she relished this idea. Her adopted city—she was proudly Austrian by birth but Parisian by choice—was in a state of disarray. At first Paris seemed relatively immune to the ravages of the Depression, but now, three years in, the City of Light was catching up to the rest of the world. Exports suffered, since fewer Americans could afford fashion by Coco Chanel and the House of Worth. Neither could they afford to travel abroad; tourism had dipped 25 percent every year since the Depression began. Crowds in shops and cafés and bars were now sparse, and prices had to shift from exorbitant to reasonable. "Champagne bottles are going begging at about $10 each," one report lamented. "No more 'American coffee' at 40 cents a cup." And Parisians, like all Europeans, felt apprehensive over the elections in Germany. "Hitler is not yet master," wrote *Le Journal*, "but only strong and clever coalitions can prevent him from playing a capital role in German politics."

Yet Paris was Paris, and those who sought a bit of debauchery had no difficulty finding it and each other, usually at the Ritz or a tucked-away bar in Montparnasse or a cabaret in Montmartre, where they drank their discounted champagne and danced and blunted the sense of impending doom. "Those who lived it still dream of it," wrote the author Georges Simenon, "night clubs, dancers, Black musicians, without mentioning other types of unsettling characters. There was madness in the air."

On these nights Simenon encountered a boisterous roster of characters—all united, he said, "by the same orgy culture," who spoke all languages and sold rare-edition books and climbed through each other's windows when the concierge wouldn't let them in. There was an Italian countess who might just have been a "fantasy countess," known for spending her mornings drunk and her afternoons at the police station; a proud demimondaine who became an authentic Balkan princess; a wealthy English gentleman who, after a few drinks, invariably invited the entire party to go hunting in Scotland; and, at the center of it all, Baroness Antonia Wagner von Wehrborn Bosquet. The thirty-nine-year-old baroness—called Antoinette or Toni by family and friends—staunchly asserted her nobility, ran a lingerie and trinket shop on the Avenue Daumesnil, claimed to be an intimate of Hitler's, and believed the world should know her name.

•   •   •

The Baroness always had a new tale to tell, braiding the improbable with the likely, facts with fantastic invention. When she chose to share the truth, the story went like this: Antonia Henrika Jole Wagner-Wehrborn was born May 3, 1893, in the town of Zell am See, Austria, near Salzburg, a region made famous to Americans decades later by *The Sound of Music.* Her mother was an actress; her father, a supervisor with the Baghdad Railway. She had three younger brothers, one of whom, Gustav, was a skilled actor who became a Nazi loyalist, serving as a financier for the party as

well as leader of the Nazi Motor Corps, a paramilitary group that trained
members as drivers and mechanics. They were a well-to-do family but not
obscenely wealthy, with a roster of distinguished and noble ancestors:
high-ranking military and political officials; German princes of the house
of Glücksburg (a European dynasty that counts King Charles and Princes
William and Harry among its members); and a grandmother who belonged
to the famously inbred Habsburg monarchy. Despite speculation and
claims to the contrary, Toni was indeed an authentic baroness by virtue of
her grandfather, Major General Rudolph Wagner, who received the nobility with the title "Wehrborn" and officially became a baron in 1866, a trib-
ute to his bravery during the Austro-Prussian War.

When Toni was ten years old, her parents sent her to Vienna, where she
enrolled in a boarding school that catered exclusively to the daughters of
army officials and civil servants. The school aimed to "grant a higher general education corresponding to the female character," which meant producing elementary school teachers and governesses. While Toni became
neither, she did become a polyglot, mastering both French and English,
and later learning Hungarian, Czech, Polish, and a bit of Russian and Italian. The headmistress, an avid painter, reportedly required her young
charges to pose naked so that she might achieve the perfect lines. "The girl
was very gifted, very imaginative, maybe too imaginative," the headmistress said of Toni. "But she learned well and we had no reason to gossip
about her."

In 1913, Toni graduated with good grades (although she told people
she'd "escaped") and made her way through Europe, staying for an extended period in Budapest before taking the Orient Express to Constantinople. There she worked as a secretary for the Baghdad Railway and made
friends who told her she was beautiful and hot-blooded; one described her
as a "male-murdering Austrian" who "ate her way through the hearts and
wallets of her admirers." She began assembling a cache of anecdotes that
she played like magic tricks, pulling them out at opportune moments, each
one burnishing her mystique.

False: Her entire family had been massacred during a revolt in the
early years of the Great War; Toni miraculously survived by rolling
herself up into a heavy rug and playing dead.

Possibly true: A British officer proposed marriage, and when she refused, he shot himself in the mouth. Two Russian aristocrats, both in love with Toni, fought a fierce duel that ended when one of them suffered a saber slash across his cheek. A third Russian aristocrat was so distraught by the end of their affair that he attacked her with a dagger.

Likely true: Both parents dead, her inheritance squandered, Toni took a job as a waitress in a Turkish restaurant, seducing the owner and the occasional guest, surviving on strangers' generosity for as long as she could.

Definitely true: In 1920, she met a French war hero who instantly fell in love and begged her to marry him.

Roger Pierre Armand Bosquet was twenty-six, one year her junior, blue-eyed and flaxen-haired and standing only five feet five. During aerial combat in northern France he suffered a gunshot wound to the stomach, and yet, the military reported, he "kept a cold-blooded attitude, his usual demeanor, and he continued until the end to attack his enemies." Before the war he'd been a successful businessman in France, and could provide Toni with a lifestyle worthy of an authentic baroness. She agreed to marry him so long as he understood one thing: she would never "belong to any man."

They were married August 25, 1921, in Toulouse, France, by the city's mayor, an old family friend of the Bosquets, but Toni soon bored of being a housewife. At her urging, the couple moved to Paris, where Toni began calling herself Baroness Wagner and found her crowd of libertines, seducing men and women alike. That she seemed forever on the verge of neurasthenia—a vague condition characterized by irritability, anxiety, depression, and both insomnia and lethargy—somehow only heightened her allure.

Those who met the Baroness were initially confounded by her popularity. "The Baroness is small," one acquaintance wrote. "On the other hand, it cannot be said she is pretty. Her body is angulate, her body is thin, and in her collar bone cavities a large amount of the salt of the ocean could be kept. She uses strong eyeglasses in front of swollen eyelids, and even if her mouth is large it cannot close around the long, yellow, horse teeth. . . . Her straggling hair is kept against the head by means of a pink chemise ribbon. She is dressed like a baby in the kind of rompers used by chorus girls when they are exercising. She moves along in the jumpy manner of walking which jockeys call a canter."

And yet, by brute charisma, she enthralled nearly everyone she met. In the apartment she shared with her husband in the 12th arrondissement, at 9 Rue Cannebière, she hosted wild parties, smoking and drinking until sunrise, debating politics and film and literature, laughing her audacious laugh, her lips peeled up and jaw hinged wide as a marionette's, a smile that revealed every one of her lupine teeth. But her gaiety was both conditional and ephemeral, turning to violence in moments of anger. She developed a habit of wounding people, only to then overwhelm them with attention and affection, believing that when the vortex of emotion settled, they would be loyal to her forever.

•    •    •

The years passed, the debauchery continued, and the Baroness collected more admirers, two of whom seemed determined to plant themselves permanently into her life. Robert Philippson was thirteen years her junior, dark-haired and impressively muscled, a Berlin-born Jewish merchant who had fallen penniless. Robert looked, said one observer, "as though he might have been a gigolo in a very cheap place in the western part of Berlin." By contrast, Rudolph Lorenz was very fair-haired and thin and eight years her junior, a Dresden-born Protestant who had arrived in Paris more than a decade earlier. Rudolph joined the Baroness's household in February 1930, with Robert moving in soon after. Fortunately, the Baroness's husband traveled frequently and did not closely monitor her roving roster of guests.

Robert was content to do nothing but perform as the Baroness's lover, while Rudolph took on the role of assistant, catering to her every whim. A few years earlier he'd opened up a bazaar selling Parisian souvenirs and miscellaneous trinkets, and she persuaded him to close his shop and instead partner with her. He invested all of his money into the Baroness's lingerie shop, which she named Antoinette in her own honor. She insisted on controlling the finances and books and did not allow Rudolph to interfere.

By now the Baroness had heard of the brilliant Dr. Ritter and his grand experiment on Floreana. She read reports of the wealthy Americans who visited, one after another after another, lavishing the doctor and his Frau with gifts, giving flattering reports to the press.

She wondered what might happen if she settled there, too, not to conduct experiments with raw food and contemplate philosophy but to open a luxury hotel. "These islands," she confessed to a friend, "are destined to be a new Deauville or Miami on the west coast of South America." To her brother Gustav, the Nazi, she sent a letter with less mercenary sentiments: "Nothing can keep me in this civilization anymore. I yearn for a freedom only nature can give. So I have to leave Europe." And then, she claimed, came the dream and command from God himself.

As for her real reasons for fleeing Paris, rumors abounded. Some speculated that her mother-in-law, tired of her antics and indiscretions, had paid her to abandon the city for good. Others claimed she had murdered someone. Yet everyone agreed upon one accusation, confirmed to be true: she had been falsifying the books for the lingerie shop, recording the expenditures but never the income, and the time had come to shut it down.

Robert had nothing to do but accompany her. Rudolph, now broke, his reputation as a businessman ruined, his fervor for the Baroness nevertheless intact, also decided to join her. She rebranded the two men as her "engineers" and recruited a third: an Ecuadorian named Manuel Valdivieso who had been living in Paris for a few years and working as a builder. Valdivieso, she determined, would serve as her contractor on the island, designing her hotel from scratch.

"Real travelers are those who go away in order not to come back," one friend encouraged her. "With a light heart, like balloons, who don't think about their destination and without knowing why, they always just say, 'Forward!'"

In July 1932, the Baroness and her three cohorts boarded the steamship *Bodegraven*, setting sail from Amsterdam. She brought her three dogs, a swarm of bees, four crates, twenty-one packages and trunks, as many cigarettes as would fit, and her most cherished possession: a copy of the novel *The Picture of Dorian Gray*, by Oscar Wilde, the tale of a man who sells his soul in exchange for eternal beauty and youth. It wasn't just the novel itself she treasured. Over the years her particular copy had become a sort of talisman, a guarantee that no matter where she was in the world, fate would bless her with adventure and luck.

During the voyage, the Baroness experienced another religious vision. This time, the voice she heard was not God's but her own. She possessed a higher power, the voice proclaimed, and the ability to perform miracles: if she struck a hand against a rock, then water would surely flow.

# FOURTEEN
# A Pity That They Should
# Be So Unpleasant

Despite the awkwardness of their first meeting, Friedrich did Heinz the favor of showing him the pirate caves—the same ones where he and Dore had stayed when they'd first arrived on the island, the ones said to be haunted by the ghost of Patrick Watkins. Heinz and his family could live there while building a more comfortable home.

"You must have a look at it all yourself," Heinz told Margret when he and Harry had returned to Black Beach. "I've found a wonderful spring, and three caves near it will do splendidly for our temporary residence."

The following morning, Margret made coffee and did the dishes in the ocean. She found herself disoriented by the sun's schedule along the equator, twelve hours day and twelve hours night no matter what time of the year. Although she'd enjoyed an excellent night's sleep, questions lined up in her mind: Would they be able to provide for themselves here? Would Floreana be welcoming to them, or hostile?

She had no time to fret about the answers; the darkening sky told her rain was imminent, and they needed to move straightaway. They stuffed their backpacks with essentials—nightclothes, pottery, utensils, rations—leaving the large crates and boxes behind. Heinz and Harry also carried their rooster and two hens, thinking it cruel to leave the animals alone.

They began the hike, following the dry, ashy trails, cactus branches stabbing Margret's arms as she passed. At the midway point, the braying of the donkeys along the coast was overcome by the dull grumbling of the wild cows, and the clouds plummeted in the sky, misting the air, seeming to skim the tops of the trees. At least the view offered a reprieve—the brilliant hues of the lemon and orange trees—but as they continued on, the scenery seemed to repeat itself, the same batches of fruits confronting them again and again, the same worn paths of dark soil sinking beneath their feet.

"I must have a rest," Margret said, and dropped to the ground.

Heinz glanced at his watch; she noted his confused expression.

"We've been going three hours already," he said.

"Oh dear, I thought we must be almost there."

Heinz replied that he thought so, too. Somewhere they had made a wrong turn and began walking in circles. Margret's fears were resurrected; maybe this was Floreana's way of marking them as intruders. But she was practical, and couldn't very well sit on the soil indefinitely, with her dog sniffing at her feet and Heinz and Harry waiting expectantly, so on they went, up and up, walking through the heavy rain, slipping in their rubber soles, until finally they came upon the three caves, huddled close together beneath the slope of a hill.

"Our house," Heinz said.

Margret did not like the look of the caves, with their wide black openings like hungry mouths. "You forgot to close the doors yesterday," she said to Heinz, masking her unease with a joke. He didn't respond, and she forced herself to look inside the largest cave. It was about the size of a bank vault, and someone a century earlier—perhaps Patrick Watkins—finished the walls by hand and even crafted a fireplace and chimney. Toward the back of the cave she found furniture discarded by previous inhabitants, a table fashioned by crates and a couple of unsteady stools. She took solace in the nearby spring, encircled by a garland of sweet-smelling trees, the water silver and cool.

"This really is like paradise," she told Heinz. "Didn't Dr. Ritter tell us there were boars up here?"

"Say no more." He picked up his rifle. "Let's see if I can get a little joint to celebrate our house-warming."

By the time he returned, the boar's bloody body slung over his shoulder, she and Harry had swept out the cave and plucked oranges and lemons and cooked beans in a saucepan. Heinz sliced the boar with a machete, cleaned the meat, and dropped it into the simmering soup. A pristine white tablecloth draped over the crates, and a candle cast shadows against the wall of the cave.

"Happy?" Heinz asked, half-hopeful, half-anxious.

"Yes," she reassured him. "Very happy."

That evening she found a bit of stray, yellowed newspaper drifting near the spring. To her shock, it was a German newspaper—from Cologne, no less—and even contained an obituary of one of her parents' friends. Heinz speculated that it had come from a journalist he knew back home, someone who had been dispatched to report on Friedrich and Dore. But to Margret, the newspaper was a lucky sign, even a talisman: whatever happened on Floreana, she and her family would survive. "I felt," she wrote, "as if I had discovered a meadow of four-leafed clover on the Equator."

Heinz saved the head of the boar and part of its body for Friedrich, per the doctor's request, although he'd thought it strange that an ardent vegetarian would want the meat.

•   •   •

In the morning Heinz took Harry along to Friedo to deliver parts of the boar. Friedrich thanked him, explaining that he needed "meat for my chickens."

When Heinz returned to the caves, he told Margret of a disturbing incident. He'd gone down to Black Beach and discovered Dore picking through their crates and boxes. She offered no reasonable excuse when confronted.

Margret was furious, but Heinz urged her to forget it: "Live and let live . . . after all, she won't do us much harm if we keep out of her way—and that's what we're going to do, aren't we?"

"All right," she said. She would try, for him. "But it seems a pity when we happen to be five Germans, the only inhabitants of Floreana, that they should be so unpleasant."

Heinz spent hours transporting their belongings, and stopped by Friedo to ask if he might borrow Dore's donkey to help carry the loads. Back at home, he told Margret of the visit, which she recorded in her diary: "He was met by Dore, who told him they were always needing the donkey, it would be very inconvenient for them to lend it. . . . We were hurt by the woman's unfriendly attitude, which confirmed my hunch that we were not going to find this couple easy neighbors."

Dore, however, told a different story. The Wittmers, she wrote, "seemed to appreciate our good intentions towards them. . . . The severest strain put upon my hospitality was when I had to lend them our Burro for their transport. I could not forget that the predecessors of these people had been the authors of all his woes until we found him, and I had often vowed a vow that he should never under any circumstances fall into other hands than ours, as long as he lived. It was therefore with sad reluctance that I lent him, and the way he raced back home that night after his hated journey to the caves of evil memory told an eloquent tale."

This pattern of discrepancies between Margret's and Dore's memories would only escalate.

•   •   •

Margret soon learned that life on a remote island could be as unpredictable as it was in civilization. Friedrich made a surprise visit to the caves, bringing gifts: eggs, bananas, papayas, seeds. He was cordial, even kind, which pleased Margret but also aroused her suspicions: Had Dore encouraged him to be more neighborly after she'd been caught rifling through the luggage at Black Beach?

Nonetheless, they began to settle into a routine: arise at 5:15 in the morning and drink coffee; clear some land and tidy up; eat lunch at noon and retrieve more belongings; tend to the newly planted garden of kohlrabi, radishes, tomatoes, and celery; relax together before bedtime. One evening, as they rested by the fire, she and Heinz glimpsed the faint outline of a dog, poised on the summit of a nearby cliff. They were alarmed; since their arrival, wild dogs—huge, snarling yellow beasts—had been roaming around the property, digging up their plants and soiling their spring and even cornering Margret in the cave. Heinz found his shotgun and crept to the cliff and fired, sending the dog soaring over the edge.

In the morning, repeated calls for their own beloved Alsatian, Hertha, went unanswered. They realized their fatal mistake.

# FIFTEEN
## Before the Storm

On the last day of August 1932, after a journey of six weeks, the *Bode-graven*, carrying the Baroness and her entourage, approached the shore of Guayaquil. The Baroness had expected Ecuador to be a beautiful and tranquil paradise, but instead found a country in the midst of a civil war. As in Germany, the Depression had stirred political upheaval, leading to the resignation of President Isidro Ayora. His successor, Neptalí Bonifaz, won the subsequent election, but opponents challenged his legitimacy, arguing that he was a Peruvian citizen and therefore not eligible to hold office in Ecuador. By a narrow majority, Ecuador's Congress decided to disqualify him, and now Bonifaz's civilian supporters, many armed with machine guns, revolted in the streets.

The Baroness kept a hard eye on both her men and her possessions. When customs agents tried to wrench her bags from her hands, she resisted. "I defended myself like a tigress," she declared, "and cursed and shouted in Italian and French." Despite the language barrier, her antics worked; the agents handled her twenty-one crates and trunks delicately and brought them to shore. Once there she, Robert, and Rudolph smoked cigarettes and waited for the cargo to be examined. When the head of customs approached, she was prepared: "I pull out my most gracious smile. . . . I have two guns and undeclared munitions in my trunk and I did not want them to be discovered. I must have succeeded in seducing the official." The Baroness pressed further. She knew that the revolution had

caused a shortage of supplies for the armed forces, but nevertheless asked
the official if she and her fellow travelers might have some guns to defend
themselves.

The governor of the Galápagos, Luis Paredes, also received her "with
full Castilian gallantry," waiving the exorbitant storage fees and even
granting her twenty hectares of land on any island of her choosing. "All
this," she boasted, "without me having to do anything at all."

·     ·     ·

With such a cordial reception, the Baroness allowed herself to relax as she
waited for transport to Floreana. The temperature was lovely, she noted, just
a few degrees hotter than France, and the mosquitoes were bearable, and
the mice so tame they played at her feet when she lounged on her terrace.

But the city also held inescapable poverty and suffering. The old man
beneath their window ate the very insects that gnawed on him; a toddler
girl rummaged through garbage bins, unearthed an old bag of charcoal,
and carried it away on her head. "The idea came to me to do something for
these poor beings," the Baroness wrote, "but then, like a coward, I went
back to the hotel. I have lived too long amongst men, and now my heart
has hardened."

She agreed to an interview for El Telégrafo, Guayaquil's main newspaper,
meeting with its editor in the lobby of the Hillman Hotel. Her three
companions came too, with Valdivieso, the Ecuadorian, acting as her
interpreter—although, she insisted, she would soon add Spanish to her
impressive list of mastered languages.

"The purpose of your trip, Mrs. Baroness?" the editor inquired.

"Nothing can compare with them," she said, referring to the Galápagos
Islands. She explained that the "lack of comforts" on the islands deterred
American tourists from vacationing there—and what a pity, since the islands had the potential to become a paragon of civilization, industry, and
commerce. "And the art!" the Baroness added. "Oh! The art so fundamental to human civilization would find a place here." The peaceful solitude of
the islands, she knew, would lure those in search of "new horizons, more
varied landscapes, new sensations, and surprising vitality." Would Ecuador
respond to her enthusiasm and help her promote "the happiness of its

women and the manliness of its men"? She wanted nothing more than to "serve as a sincere and honest bond between this country and those of Europe and North America."

She took a moment to highlight the talents of her partners: Both Robert Philippson and Rudolph Lorenz were skilled engineers, agriculturalists, poultry farmers, and beekeepers. And Valdivieso, as a native of Ecuador and expert contractor, was familiar with the islands and could guide her project to success. The editor jotted down notes, calling her eyes "pure crystals" and her face "sensitive, sweet in expression, but resolved in her purposes." He posed another question: "Have you thought, madam, of an immediate and effective communication system between the mainland and the islands?"

"I have thought of a communication system," she said, "and I hope that it will be developed as tourism increases. I count for this on the ties of valuable friendships that I have in the United States, especially in Hollywood." Also, she expected *El Telégrafo* to publicize her endeavor on an international scale, reaching American investors who would see the potential profit to be made.

The editor, in conclusion, suggested that the Baroness embodied every contradictory archetype of women throughout history: Mary of Nazareth and Jezebel; Cleopatra and Magdalene; Lucrezia Borgia and Saint Teresa of Avila. "The woman is capable of everything," he wrote, "of verifying everything and understanding everything, from the highest to the lowest. And, above all, for heroism she is bigger and more determined than the male."

· · ·

The Baroness did not have to wait for transport very long, owing to the efforts and hospitality of M. Bertini of the Continental Society, whom she "got to know." She learned that an Italian political official was due to visit the Galápagos Islands, and she would persuade him to bring them all to Floreana.

"I have a conviction," she told her new friends, "that God has put me in his holy guard, and I will take my little troupe to the promised land."

# SIXTEEN
# Dead Sun

Each morning, as Heinz and Harry cleared the ground around the caves, hacking at bushes and trees with machetes, Margret sewed clothing for the baby, due at the end of the year. She cursed her knitting needles for rusting and wished for her sewing machine, one of many modern comforts she regretted leaving back in Germany. Why not, she thought, write a letter to her sister asking her to mail the machine to the island. It would take some time to arrive, of course, but the convenience would be worth the wait.

She shared her idea with Friedrich, who had come to ask for more meat. In Margret's recollection, he started to laugh; it could take as long as six months for her sister even to receive the letter, let alone for a sewing machine to arrive on Floreana.

"But I've read about Post Office Bay," Margret said. "Surely mail arrives there pretty regularly."

Friedrich laughed again. "My dear Frau Wittmer, it's not as regular as that. You ask your husband."

When Heinz returned to the caves, he confirmed Friedrich's warning. "I suppose mail isn't quite such a long-term business as it was in the days of the whalers, but even these days ships don't come here that often in the winter, I imagine."

Without her machine, Margret sewed six vests for the baby and a pillowcase; Heinz promised to shoot one of the seabirds to collect its feathers for stuffing. Weeks passed, and although she kept busy, sewing and cleaning and teaching Harry about the history of the island, a dull, persistent fear drummed inside her. Was her decision to give birth on a remote island foolish? Had she really considered the risks? What would happen if something went wrong?

"We've at least got a qualified doctor on the island," Heinz said. "So nothing much can go wrong."

The next time Friedrich visited, dropping off seeds and vegetables in exchange for more meat, Margret asked if he would help her when the time came.

"I'm afraid not," he said. She noted that his tone was flat, matter of fact. "I didn't come to Floreana to practice as a doctor."

Margret said nothing.

"You mustn't take it all so seriously," he said. "Children are born every minute of the day—it's nothing to be frightened of. As you work hard and keep moving all the time, you'll find everything will go off smoothly."

His attempt at comforting Margret only sharpened her anxiety.

She and Heinz began seeing Friedrich and Dore more often, perhaps in the hope of changing the doctor's mind. Together they hiked to Post Office Bay, checking for mail, discussing all the aspiring settlers who had come before them and failed. Dore always had something to say about philosophy; her latest obsession centered on the ideal relationship between man and woman. The husband, she argued, should never assist or relieve the wife of a task.

They let Friedrich expound without interruption on Nietzsche and architecture and nutrition. One could live a long and healthy life, the doctor insisted, eating only papayas and oranges for breakfast, two beaten eggs and six bananas at noon, and a few papayas at night. (His previous declaration that figs alone made a sufficient diet was apparently forgotten.) Then Friedrich would invariably ask Heinz for another cut of freshly killed boar.

•　　•　　•

Margret did, however, take comfort in the progress Heinz and Harry had made on the house. The design was simple but solid: a log cabin measuring

twenty-two by twelve feet, made from the wood of lechosa trees—
nicknamed Milky Way in English for the color and consistency of its sap. It
would be a tiny patch of Germany in South America, neat and orderly,
everything serving a purpose, everything in its place.

To celebrate Harry's birthday, Margret made his favorite island meal,
banana foam egg, squashing bananas with raw eggs and whisking it into a
pudding. "One would have to watch Harry's face while eating it," Margret
wrote, "to truly appreciate the creation." The tropical climate and salty air
seemed to be doing the boy some good.

They were simple people, stoic and proud. They did not feel alone in
their solitude. "Our day, the short tropical day," Margret wrote, "was so full
we had no time for brooding." They did not miss theater or film. Who
needed it when they had a sky and land and sea teeming with exotic magic?
And, on the night of September 18, an unexpected and exquisite sight
from somewhere northwest of Floreana—a cluster of bright, bold flames
shooting up and licking the sky, turning it red. All three of them held their
breath as they realized what it was: a massive volcanic eruption, so powerful it seemed fire and ashes would rain on their cave.

Dore sensed the eruption before it even happened. All the signs were
there: the sky had been suffused with an otherworldly blood-orange glow,
obscuring the sun. She waited for the tremors beneath her feet and felt
sure that Friedo would be swept away. In that moment she felt a renewed
closeness with Friedrich: "If fate willed that we go down thus in the midst
of our experiment, then we were willing and ready to do so, and to bow to
a greater wisdom than our own."

In that moment, Friedrich's main thought was not of his everlasting
bond with Dore but of the donkeys: "The asses were undisturbed in their
disgusting braying by the unwonted light in the heavens."

For the next three days, Dore watched the clouds thrash and roil, covering the sky like a black velvet curtain. When the sun was visible, it reflected a strange and pallid glow—a "dead sun," she thought, too sickly to
even cast a shadow.

• • • • • • • • • • • • •

# PART II
## It Does Them Good to
## Know Who Is Their Master

• • • • • • • • • • • •

# SEVENTEEN
# And Then There Were Nine

On October 15, just after lunch, Margret heard her surviving dog, Lump, bark anxiously. Then came a rustling in the brush, the sound of footsteps, and a familiar face: Wolfgang von Hagen, an Austrian whom she and Heinz had met on San Cristóbal Island before settling on Floreana. Behind him came a woman straddling a donkey. Aged about forty, she wore men's overalls and sandals, with a beret perched askew on her platinum hair. Bright red lipstick showcased a wide mouth and large teeth. Her eyes were obscured by dark glasses; she could see out, but no one could peer in.

Accompanying them was a young man in his late twenties, thin and blond. Von Hagen introduced the strangers as "Herr Lorenz" and "Baroness Bosquet of Paris."

The Baroness dismounted from her donkey and asked, "Where's the spring?"

Margret could only point and reply, "Just over there." She watched the Baroness walk to the spring, followed closely by Lorenz, who removed her shoes and proceeded to wash her feet in the water. Margret was appalled—that was their *drinking* water—but she watched in silence. When Lorenz finished, the Baroness yawned and complained of her exhaustion.

"Perhaps you would care to rest for a bit," Margret said, indicating the cave.

With a mumble of gratitude, the Baroness accepted the offer. Lorenz followed and helped her undress.

"What an extraordinary couple," Margret thought, and when Heinz returned from a hunting trip, she related the encounter.

"Well, I don't suppose they're staying long," Heinz said.

"I'm afraid they might be," von Hagen said. "They've brought a whole heap of stuff with them, not to mention cows and calves and two donkeys." He added a disturbing aside: "There's something not quite right about her. I'd be a bit careful if I were you."

"Oh dear," Margret said. "That doesn't sound too good."

They gave von Hagen a tour of their half-built house, feeling pretty pleased with themselves until their guest pointed out a serious construction error: they had been thatching the sugarcane section of their roof the wrong way, allowing rain to fall in. He advised them to tear the section down and restart from scratch, thatching from the ground up.

The Baroness reappeared. She explained that she would stay at the Casa while transporting her belongings, but would soon need a more permanent arrangement. "You won't mind, will you," she said, "if we lived quite near you to start with?"

Margret and Heinz looked at each other and exchanged silent thoughts: yes, actually, they minded very much. Margret was seven months pregnant and resented the imposition. But if this woman planned to settle here, it would be wise not to make an enemy of her.

"All right," Heinz said. "You can live in our orange grove. Near the little spring."

Von Hagen asked if Margret and Heinz might like to purchase some rice he'd brought from the mainland, which he'd left down at Post Office Bay. They offered 11 sucres (about 70 cents) for a hundred pounds, but it was too late for Heinz to walk down to shore to pick it up.

The Baroness offered to keep it for them in the meantime. "In return for your kind hospitality," she said. "And you can fetch it on Sunday." With a flourish, she pulled two packets of mail from her bag: one for Heinz and Margret, and one for Dore and Friedrich. "You'll take Dr. Ritter his, won't you?" she asked. "I must be getting back to Post Office Bay."

•   •   •

The Baroness had either lied or changed her mind, for she did not travel back to Post Office Bay. Instead, she arrived at Friedo, a journey of three hours, following the cattle trails through the shrubbery and lemon trees and withered bramble bushes. Dore heard voices and the soft pounding of hooves and went out to investigate. She took in the beret, the overalls, the rapacious smile, the regal bearing, and had to admit that this woman, whoever she was, possessed a "certain artificial charm." Her young blond companion helped her dismount and dragged one of Dore's deck chairs across the dirt for her to sit. After introductions, the Baroness turned to Dore and held out her hand, clearly expecting it to be kissed.

"If this was a mere Baroness," Dore thought, "she certainly behaved as though she were at least a queen."

Dore took the proffered hand and shook it, noting, with some pleasure, the flicker of annoyance across the Baroness's face. A duel between them had begun, Dore thought. She believed that Floreana belonged to her and Friedrich—a spiritual rather than physical possession. And now here came this stranger, this "baroness" (Dore did not believe the legitimacy of this title for one moment), descending upon the island and immediately laying claim to it.

Even so, Dore had to admire the woman's audacity: "At least she was no little bourgeois Hausfrau nor yet a foolish romanticist nor an imitation 'seeker of the light.' Whatever hidden elements in her nature would come to light in the course of her sojourn on Floreana, I felt that at last, even as an enemy, as she undoubtedly was destined to become, she was a person worthy of one's steel."

Dore asked if she and Friedrich might offer the Baroness a tour of Friedo. As the aristocrat wandered from room to room, glancing at the kitchen and study and Friedrich's water pump, Dore observed that her attitude was that of "a distinguished visitor at the Zulu section of the World's Fair," offering a condescending smile and occasional comment about the "cunning contraptions" and "marvelous" grounds. One glance at Friedrich told Dore that he, too, was annoyed by the Baroness and her supercilious attitude, a reaction that pleased Dore.

She observed how the Baroness kept her boyfriend, or manservant, or whatever he was, on a short leash—permitting him to be, at most, a few yards away from her at all times. When she sensed him straying too far, she

called him back to render one service or another: "Rudi! Take off my glasses
for me!" and "Oh, Rudi darling, there's a stone in my sandal—get it out for
me!" and "Oh, Rudi, come and show me how this thing works!" With each
command, Rudolph sprang up and did exactly as the Baroness requested.

While the Baroness chatted with Friedrich and von Hagen, Dore managed to exchange a few words with Rudolph alone. He told her he was
thirty years old, although Dore had guessed he was no more than twenty-
one. His skin was unlined, and his striking blue eyes gave the impression of
both candor and naïveté. His voice was soft, and from his choice of words
and cadence of speech Dore guessed he was of modest background and
means, with a basic education.

She could only imagine that the Baroness "must have caught him early,
drawn to him perhaps by his good looks, and trained him for the drawing
room." Toward the end of the conversation, when the subject of the Baroness came up, Dore noticed that she shot Rudolph a "menacing inquiry."
In response he shook his head, almost imperceptibly, to reassure her that
her secrets would not be divulged.

•    •    •

By now the sky was black, and it was too late for anyone to make the
treacherous journey to Post Office Bay, so Dore and Friedrich had little
choice but to invite the visitors to stay overnight. For the men, Dore offered blankets and a homemade mattress stuffed with banana leaves. Such
accommodations, however, would not suffice for the Baroness, so Friedrich
strung up a hammock for her, covering it with a sheath of muslin Dore had
brought from Germany. She and Friedrich had no blankets left for themselves and resigned to a sleepless night.

How right they were. The Baroness coughed loudly and persistently,
nearly barking, and did not let up. Dore remained unconvinced: "It was no
cough, only a hysterical imitation of one." Friedrich, disgusted, went to the
study and composed a letter to a friend in Germany:

> It is now 1 o'clock in the morning—a glorious full moon night . . .
> outside the Baroness is sleeping in a hammock . . . now there are
> suddenly two families again, a total of seven people (apart from us) on

the island, and in December there will be eight, because then the first native will be born here—instead of in Cologne. You see, we went to a desert island because we longed for solitude. Nobody wants to disturb us—but it would be difficult for everyone to hold out without our bananas and other temporary helpers until they saw how stupid they were to come here. . . . I consider every attempt at settlement here to be intrusive. Let's hope that the current settlers are here no longer than the first.

The Baroness tossed and turned and wheezed and hacked. Friedrich ignored her and kept writing:

You could perhaps blame me: one time I encourage emigration and the other time I advise against it. . . . The baroness, imported from Paris, coughs from the cold and hysteria and wants hot water—but she has to hold out until morning—the rooster is already crowing.

After breakfast, which the Baroness did not touch, the party at last assembled to leave. Von Hagen turned to Friedrich and said how pleased he was to have seen and spoken with him again. In fact, visiting Friedo was a priority. "To come to Floreana without seeing Dr. Ritter," he said, "would be like going to Rome without seeing the Pope."

Dore watched the Baroness during this exchange; she seemed incensed that Friedrich had been complimented in this way. It was this reaction, even more so than the earlier rude behavior, that convinced Dore that the Baroness was a member of the nobility only in her dreams—"so little trace was there in her behavior," Dore thought, "of her having been even moderately well brought up." She even voiced her suspicion to von Hagen, who laughed. "Oh," he said, "none of us believe the title's genuine."

If the Baroness overheard the conversation, she did not bother to correct them.

• • •

That morning, Heinz gathered the mail packet intended for Dore and Friedrich and set off for Friedo. As soon as he arrived, he began describing the new arrivals and Friedrich held up a hand, stopping him. Later Heinz recounted the visit to Margret, who recorded it in her diary.

"I know that lot already," Friedrich said. "They were up here yesterday, in fact they spent the night with me—some of it anyhow." He laughed, and added, "In the end she went off to Post Office Bay, highly offended, breathing fire and slaughter against us."

"Well anyhow," Heinz said. "Here's a packet of mail she asked to bring you."

Friedrich sifted through the stack.

"That's funny," he said to Heinz. "Why didn't she bring it herself when she came here?" He took a closer look and saw that someone had unsealed the envelopes. "Damn it all," he said. "They've been opened."

"Not by me," Heinz said.

"No, of course it wasn't you." He skimmed through the letters and stopped to take his time when he saw one from Captain Hancock in Los Angeles. He and his crew were planning another expedition to the Galápagos at the end of the year. "She's even taken photos out of some of them, the dirty bitch."

"I see," Heinz said. "That's why she left your mail with us, so that you should think we'd opened it. Perhaps she wants to have us at loggerheads for her own good reasons. As far as I'm concerned, the less we have to do with them the better."

"Goes for me too," Friedrich said. "I'm not very fond of my fellow men and women, as I think you know." It's a sentiment he repeated privately in a letter to a friend. "It could be so beautiful on earth," he wrote, "if humans weren't animals."

# EIGHTEEN
## Dentist and
## Doctor Indeed

Two days after the Baroness and her entourage arrived, Rudolph Lorenz appeared in Dore's garden. He looked exhausted and red-faced from the heat. She saw that he had brought along two cows, a calf, and several donkeys struggling under the weight of heavy bags. He said that he was transporting the items up to the caves near the Wittmers, where the Baroness had decided to build her permanent home. He was so sorry for intruding upon Dore's time and property, but he'd somehow lost his way, and he would be so grateful if she could set him on the right path. She did, and was relieved that the subject of the Baroness did not come up at all.

· · ·

A few days later, on October 24, Heinz and Harry went to Post Office Bay to retrieve the rice that the Baroness had allowed them to store at the abandoned Casa. She was on the beach and, as Heinz would later report, "dressed to kill": a heavily painted face, a coquettish riding outfit, a whip in her hand, and a revolver in her belt. She invited them inside and offered Heinz a seat, ignoring Harry entirely. Reclining on a chaise longue, she pointed to a man standing across the room and introduced him as Robert Philippson, her husband.

He was, she boasted, "very much engaged in literary labors." They both wore rings on their fingers—wedding rings, presumably. Heinz appraised

Robert: handsome, with dark curly hair, years younger than the Baroness. He offered Heinz a terse, distracted greeting: "So sorry. I'm just in the middle of an article I'm writing, and I simply must get it finished so that I can send it off at once."

Heinz suppressed a laugh. Wasn't Robert aware that, depending on the ships' schedules, he wouldn't be able to post his article for at least a few weeks, or even months?

"You know my plans, don't you?" the Baroness asked.

Heinz shook his head.

"Oh, but haven't I told you about them?" She smiled and handed him the El Telégrafo article about her hopes for an opulent hotel on Floreana. Heinz scanned the page, increasingly alarmed as he read; he and Margret had not come to Floreana to live among hordes of tourists. A list of questions queued in his mind, but the Baroness changed the subject to Dore and Friedrich. "Dentist and doctor indeed!" she said. "Dental mechanic at most, more likely a male nurse."

For a moment, Heinz listened to her ramble about Friedrich and then decided he'd had enough. He asked if she could fetch his rice, and he'd be on his way.

"Oh yes, of course, the rice," she said, and smiled. "That will be twenty-eight sucres."

Heinz stared at her, confused. He argued that he had already paid Captain von Hagen 11 sucres for the rice; she had merely been storing it for him.

"It costs twenty-eight sucres," she said. "If you want it, that is."

"I should be obliged, Baroness," he said, "if you would look for somewhere else to stay. You will *not* be welcome in our orange grove."

"I wouldn't dream of looking for anywhere else, there's no other suitable place here. Not till my hotel is up. I shall be staying in the orange grove as long as I like—or were you thinking of throwing me out, by any chance?"

Heinz said nothing.

"We have three men, you know," she continued, "and I can count as a fourth man in some respects." With that, she settled a hand on her revolver.

Heinz and Harry left without the rice.

• • •

After a few days of peace, with no word from the Baroness or any of the other settlers, Heinz appeared at Friedo one morning. He was "in a fury," Dore noted. The Baroness was supervising the transport of thousands of pounds of cement from the Casa to the caves. Had Dore and Friedrich seen the newspaper article detailing her plans for a luxury hotel?

Even so, Heinz stressed that he did not believe she'd actually succeed in building anything, and when she and her crew finally fled the island, he'd take the cement and use it himself.

Dore did not share his optimism.

Heinz wanted to know if he could count on their support as "older settlers on Floreana," should the Baroness become too domineering. Friedrich said that while they wished to assure Heinz of their "neighborly sentiments," they would never be roped into any altercations or disputes. As Heinz well knew, they had come to Floreana to escape that sort of drama, and they would be willing to battle solely for their own cherished privacy and seclusion.

Heinz, disappointed, left them alone.

Friedrich, perhaps more bothered by Heinz's visit than he cared to admit aloud, retreated to his study to respond to Hancock's most recent letter:

Dear Captain Mr. Hancock,

Since September of the current year, we have again trouble with newcomers. Surely they live hours away from us—but we are no more alone on the island, and now and then they come down for vegetables, fruits and talking, and we are disturbed in our working. This German brought with him a pregnant woman and every day we expect the first "inmate" of Floreana—but we can hardly think of this as a happy incident.

Outside, just beyond Friedo's fence, the nonhuman inhabitants of Floreana conducted their nightly symphony: the sullen grunt of the wild pigs, the staccato shrieks of various birds, the excruciating bray of the donkeys, the furtive rustling of hungry dogs.

He continued:

Yet worse than that, we consider the coming here of another woman (Austria) with three young men from PARIS. There was published in the "Telegrafo of Guayaquil" on 18 September a great article concerning her very mad idea to erect here a great international hotel for millionaires and travelers. I cannot but think about that matter as a bad joke, made by the chauvinistic journalists with this foolish woman. At her visit, she presented herself as an Austrian Baroness who had lived the past years in PARIS—but at first she behaved herself like a servant, acting the part of a capricious princess in tyrannizing dull young men. It seems she always cuts any figure, and for that purpose she never can speak the truth. . . . If we were not fastened here with every inch of that desert earth, in cultivating it by our hard—but satisfying—work, we would go on to a more lonesome place. That is however impossible, because I cannot do the same work once more and so we finish our fate here.

He concluded by requesting, with some professed embarrassment and regret, several items that Hancock might bring to him on his next visit to Floreana. Dore wanted a stainless-steel watering can; a large pot for washing clothes and another for making preserves; glasses with rubber rings for preserving fruit; and some linen suitable for clothes. Friedrich himself could really use some corrugated plates; planks; stainless wire mesh to ward off mosquitoes and to use as sieves to sift through the soil; watertight boxes to hold all his supplies; carbon paper and thin copy typewriter paper; insect poison; and an air gun and pellets for shooting sparrows.

Fearing that Hancock might not receive this letter before he set sail for the islands, Friedrich sent the same list of items to Commander Eugene McDonald, the American millionaire who had publicized their experiment to the world. In his various writings, Friedrich never once acknowledged the contradiction, or perhaps full reversal, in his opinion of visitors to Floreana. Where he once called them intruders who breached his solitude, he now curried their favor and even depended on their charity to survive.

. . .

A few days later, as Heinz worked on his house, he heard a sharp whisper coming from the brush. It was Rudolph Lorenz, crouched down, beckoning him to come closer. Heinz followed him.

"Nobody can hear us?" Rudolph asked. He glanced behind his shoulders, to his sides, into the distance.

"I don't think so, not just here," Heinz said. "What on earth is it?"

Rudolph explained that the Baroness had forbidden him to speak to Heinz or Margret. But after imploring Heinz to keep his confidence, Rudolph gossiped freely about her and Robert: "They're not really married, you know, that business about 'my husband' is just for show." He spoke of her actual husband, the pilot and businessman Roger Pierre Armand Bosquet; about her wild days as a dancer in Constantinople; about the rumors of her spying for the French during the Great War. "Don't know if it's true," Rudolph said, "but when you know her you wouldn't put it past her. She's not divorced from Bosquet either, but I think he's glad to be rid of her."

"Really?" Heinz asked. Recalling the mail he'd delivered to Friedrich at the Baroness's behest, he asked, "Did anyone open Dr. Ritter's letters?"

Rudolph paused for a moment and then said, "Yes, the Baroness did, she wanted to know the sort of people he was in touch with. I think she opened some of yours too."

Heinz was surprised to hear this. He supposed they'd been so excited to receive mail that they hadn't noticed any tampering. He recounted the conversation to Margret, who recorded it in her diary and interpreted Rudolph's words as a warning. "There was a spy living very near us," she wrote, "perhaps a former professional spy." She was disturbed by the possibility that her words and actions might be monitored by a woman who seemed intent on doing harm.

# NINETEEN
# Ready for All Crimes

On the evening of November 9, 1932, a thirty-two-year-old Norwegian man named Arthur Estampa steered his fishing boat, the *Falcon*, to Post Office Bay. Estampa, who lived on the Galápagos island of Santa Cruz, was a good friend of Vincent Astor's, having served as his guide during past expeditions to the Galápagos. In between Astor's visits, the two men stayed in touch.

On this visit to Floreana, Estampa brought with him two Ecuadorians and a German scientist and writer named Paul Franke. Estampa was eager to hunt on the pampa, and Franke hoped to do some writing and explore the wildlife. By then the island had settled into its late-fall rhythms: the brown noddy female seabirds had laid their single eggs; the sea turtles mounted each other and let the waves topple them over; curious sea lion pups, now three months old, were at last strong enough to take their first bumbling swim.

As the *Falcon* approached Post Office Bay, Estampa noticed three people—two men and a woman—standing along the shore, as though guarding it from invaders. A third man stood nearby. He was Ecuadorian, Estampa assumed, and stood about six foot three. Estampa himself was six inches shorter, with a slender build and thick glasses and a mouth missing most of its front teeth. The woman had a revolver on her hip and a whip in her hand. In a booming voice, she called out a warning: "Do not come ashore."

Estampa ignored her, anchoring his boat. The woman came closer. She asked Estampa his nationality and demanded packs of matches; Estampa and his party gave her all they had. She then asked Estampa the purpose of his visit. Accustomed to the eccentric settlers who had come and gone on the island, Estampa humored the woman: he intended to hunt on the island, as was his legal right.

At this the woman ordered Estampa to leave immediately. He laughed.

The woman took a step closer and erupted in a fury that shocked the men. The island was now hers, she proclaimed, along with everything on it—the plants and fruits and animals and anything Estampa might wish to hunt.

Estampa did not know what to do. This woman was clearly mad. So far, her three male guards had remained silent. She had taken over the abandoned Casa, and he would not be able to stay overnight there, as planned. He made a quick decision: he and Franke would return to his boat, and the Ecuadorians would hike to Friedo.

· · ·

A chorus of frantic shouts pulled Dore from her sleep. Alarmed, she roused Friedrich and lit the lantern, its slim ribbon of light guiding their way under the moonless sky. Two men stood at the entrance to Friedo, wide-eyed and panting. Dore recognized them as employees of the fisherman Arthur Estampa, who traveled often to Floreana from Santa Cruz Island. She was surprised to see them; every indigenous Ecuadorian she'd met believed that Floreana was haunted, and did not visit willingly after dark.

For several moments they labored to catch their breath, and then related the encounter with the woman at Post Office Bay. The story was almost too strange to be true, but Dore believed the Baroness was "a person whose love of sensation would stop at nothing."

It was nearly dawn, but Dore insisted they stay over and rest for a few hours. In the morning, after breakfast, the visitors set off to reunite with Estampa and Franke on the pampa. Dore bade them goodbye with trepidation. She expected Estampa to bring the entire party to Friedo later.

Friedrich tried to soothe her, saying that the Baroness was merely a "far-gone case of hysteria," and nothing to worry about in the long run. He added that if she'd had a "single proper man with her, instead of a lot of servile gigolos, she could be kept in order without trouble."

Lunch and dinner came and went, and yet Estampa and his friends still had not arrived.

• • •

While Dore and Friedrich waited, Estampa's party spent the day hunting, shooting and skinning two calves near the edge of the plains. Leaving the hides behind, they carried the carcasses down to the shore. As they approached, the Baroness emerged from the Casa flanked by her loyal guards, a rifle slung over her shoulder.

"I am the sole master of this island by the fact that I bought it from the Ecuadorian government," she said. "I forbid anyone from hunting without my permission." They must show her the hides to prove they were not from her calves, or pay her for shooting the animals.

Estampa told her to go to hell.

The Baroness trained her rifle on him. She demanded his gun, and he handed it over. He needed to buy time, and told her that he would do as she requested and fetch the skins, returning as quickly as possible.

She agreed. Estampa started off, checking over his shoulder every few steps.

As he approached the first lava field, he observed, from the corner of his eye, one of her guards lifting his gun and taking aim.

• • •

The next morning Dore and Friedrich were woken again by shouts. Dore realized they were coming not from the main path, where visitors usually called, but from the pathless southern stretch of the garden. She and Friedrich rushed outside and saw Estampa staggering toward the house, his clothes tattered, deep scratches blooming blood across his skin.

"Why did you not wait till daybreak?" Dore asked. She knew how treacherous that journey was, especially all alone in the dark.

He said he feared the woman had an entire army at her disposal, with soldiers stationed at strategic points all across the island. He'd been forced to make his escape in the hours when no one could see him.

The sight of Estampa, bloody and terrified, rattled even Friedrich. He knew Estampa was eager to leave, but asked if he might stay just long enough to recount the incident once again, in detail. Friedrich wanted to write a formal report to the Galápagos governor, Luis Paredes, which Estampa could deliver.

The report read:

Highly esteemed Mr. Governor—

A woman came to visit us three weeks ago, accompanied by three men. She introduced herself as "The Baroness." They stayed overnight at my house, during which I observed that the lady's conduct does not correspond to that of a Baroness but more to that of a woman of inferior status. In other words, she is nothing but an imaginary Princess.

A week later she sent me a copy of El Telegrafo. Translating the article regarding the Baroness and her men, I perceived that the newspapermen have been victims of a terrible joke played on them by a woman in the early stages of paralysis cerebri.

I have not scientifically examined the woman, but all that I have heard of her confirms my suspicion that she is spiritually unbalanced. This translates into a megalomaniac condition. Mr. Estampa's adventure will prove to you that she is ready for all crimes.

But at this point the joke ends, and the responsibility of the magistrate begins. It would be an ineradicable disgrace to the Ecuadorian government not to realize the crimes of which the woman is capable, who in her megalomania may take seriously her illusion that the whole island is her own property.

Therefore I ask you to take the proper measures to put this crazy woman under observation in a sanitarium.

# TWENTY
## And Then There Were Ten

In the weeks after the incident with Estampa, Dore took care to avoid the Baroness, but nevertheless felt her presence. She and Friedrich learned from Heinz—who began visiting Friedo every Sunday afternoon—that two American ships had anchored at Post Office Bay. Since none of the travelers had ventured to Friedo, they could only surmise that the Baroness had greeted the Americans on the coast and told lies about Dore and Friedrich, quashing any plans to meet Floreana's most famous settlers.

The possibility of the Baroness directing visitors away from Friedo so disturbed Friedrich he immediately drafted a letter to Captain Hancock: "If you hear any sort of eccentricities or sensations or the like about us, you can be sure that these are lies circulated from this woman. It may be, too, that she holds back letters deposited for us in the Post Office Bay. We hope that she cannot stay here very long—but she can do damage enough in a few months."

• • •

During his visits, Heinz described the growing tensions at the Baroness's place. The Baroness had become more demanding of her three subjects, threatening them if they failed to comply. It seemed Rudolph Lorenz—the Baroness's smaller blond companion—had suffered a demotion. Eager to open her hotel, she gave Rudolph a series of exhausting tasks, and any perceived slacking was met with swift violence.

Rudolph began to appear regularly at Friedo, often seeming flustered and depressed, flopping down in a deck chair and staring into the distance. Sometimes Dore wondered if he were ill, but he insisted he was in perfect health. She found him unfailingly pleasant, but over the course of these visits she noticed that his smile had disappeared. She made him cakes made of a root vegetable called *otoy*, his favorite treat, and listened as he confided about life with the Baroness.

"You don't know what I have to endure," he told Dore. "I have no great pretensions, but no man with an ounce of decency would put up with what she expects of me. She knows that I am beginning to rebel, and so she's put that fellow Valdivieso to watch me. . . . He's terrified of her, and carries on as if I were a convict. . . . He bosses me around, so that it's all I can do not to take whatever tool I'm working with and brain him."

He spoke also of Robert Philippson—the muscular, dark-haired German whom the Baroness now favored. She had an array of nicknames just for him: Kiddy; Mein Bubi, meaning "my baby"; Mousie; and the standard "darling," a moniker Rudolph himself once enjoyed. As her main lover, Robert worked only when he wished. And when he did, the Baroness treated him with excessive praise, holding him up as an example, while mocking Rudolph for being weak and inferior.

"I want to go," he said. "I don't care where to—anywhere will do. But what is there for me elsewhere?"

Dore didn't know how to answer him. He looked so young and sounded almost childlike in his complaints. Nothing in his past life as a wealthy shopkeeper in Paris had prepared him for this strange and unsettling situation. She could tell his hands had once been manicured and well kept. He spoke of that time in Paris when he'd enjoyed an entirely different life, with nightclubs and parties and foolish certainty that his relationship with the Baroness would endure.

When Dore expressed doubt about the Baroness's claim to nobility, Rudolph did not correct her, and when she asked where she'd honed her "superficial good manners," he did not mention her privileged upbringing. Instead, he explained that she simply mimicked actors she admired in theater and movies, practicing her "roles." She had ruined him in Paris, he said, and now she seemed intent on ruining him here.

At the end of one of their conversations, Dore observed a change in his demeanor, his dejection sliding into a fury, his fingers making and unmaking fists. This was an aspect of Rudolph, she later wrote, "which the Baroness herself had probably never seen."

•   •   •

Rudolph also began making surprise visits to Margret. He had a habit, she noticed, of "creeping through the bush followed by sudden jack-in-the-box appearances." He told Margret that he had already tired of island life and was contemplating leaving Floreana as soon as possible.

"I was up at Friedo yesterday with Dr. Ritter," he said, "trying to find out about getting away from here." He took a sip of the hot coffee Margret had made for him. "Do you know the Baroness can't eat any rice without milk, so every day I have to go down to the hut on the coast with fresh milk for her ladyship. She only gives me the bare necessities to eat."

Margret had sympathy, but only to an extent. There was nothing she could do to help him. "It is very moving the way the poor fellow tells about it," she wrote, "but he is German, and can change things if only he makes up his mind to it."

In those final weeks of 1932, she and Heinz had their own set of troubles. She was hugely pregnant and unable to move much. It took all her strength to dig out sand fleas that had embedded in Heinz's and Harry's feet. Her greatest kill, she reported, was seventy-five in one day. Their new rooster had inexplicably stopped crowing, and the hens couldn't lay eggs. Worms embedded in their tomatoes, and cattle invaded their garden each night. Eventually they had no choice but to take turns guarding the crops: Harry took the first shift, from eight until midnight; Margret took over until three in the morning; and Heinz until dawn.

Holding a torch in one hand and her gun in the other, with her dog, Lump, by her side, Margret found these patrols to be haunting—even though, unlike Dore, she did not dwell on the ghost of Patrick Watkins. Instead, she was unsettled by a "strange, nocturnal concert": the scuttling of rats across her feet; the low, belch-like calls of the petrels; and the squeaks of the pigs and the rustling of other unseen beasts in the brush—all of this beneath a starless sky. When she did find a cow scavenging through their row of runner beans, she raised her rifle and killed it with one shot.

At least the new house was nearly complete. It was a true log cabin, with a lava stone foundation and thick tree trunks supporting its four corners. Harry had been a tremendous help to Heinz; the boy, once so frail and weak, could now easily lift one hundred pounds. In the kitchen, Heinz had constructed a proper stone fireplace and a wide chimney to eliminate smoke and odors. He'd also built a full dining set, with sideboards and a large table, and a chair upholstered in raw cowhide. The bed had four posts with crossbars strong enough to support a straw-filled mattress, covered in bright cloth. The sugarcane roof—woven properly, this time— covered the kitchen and one bedroom, and reminded her of the thatched cottages back home. Although they had no glass for windows, wire mesh made a fine substitute. Their bedroom door led into the living room, which wouldn't be finished until after the baby was born.

She passed the time by monitoring the construction of the Baroness's hotel. In the orange grove adjacent to the springs they'd built a square log wall, stretched a canvas over its top, and covered the entire structure with corrugated tin. The hotel stood about sixteen hundred feet from Margret's house, just far enough that entire days passed without hearing anything from them, although sometimes the Baroness sent Robert as an emissary. On his most recent visit, he informed Margret that if she so desired, the Baroness would be willing to put in a good word for her with Friedrich, perhaps changing his mind about delivering her baby.

But the doctor remained noncommittal. "Don't call me until it is really necessary," he told Margret during one visit, "for I don't care to sit a whole long day at your house." When her labor pains began on December 30, she did not think to alert Friedrich. She did not even want to bother Heinz and Harry, as there was still much to do outside the house. She hid her pains and carried on, making her own preparations.

She had stocked up on supplies: fresh linen, bandages, scissors, diapers, cotton wool, a tin of talcum powder. Her mind spun in a feverish panic. "Would it be enough?" she asked herself. "I ought to have bought two, even three—but it was too late to think of that now." At least her bed was ready for the delivery, sheathed in thick wads of paper and a piece of linen, sterilized by boiling. "Dear God," she prayed, "let it all go well."

Half a day passed. The pains were violent now, seizing her entire body, turning it scalding hot and freezing cold and back again. Heinz made a support for her back so she could sit up. Sleep eluded her. In the morning, after a cup of strong coffee, the pains subsided enough for her to prepare meals for the days ahead and bake a New Year's cake. The pains returned at night when Heinz and Harry were asleep. She bit into her pillow to smother her screams. All the next day and night, she kept control, and then came New Year's Eve. She was desperate for it to be over. She could do nothing but lie in bed and drink and drink, hoping to extinguish the fire in her throat. The pain, she thought, was "more than flesh and blood could stand."

That night none of them slept. She heard Heinz and Harry get up and go out while it was still dark. She didn't know why they left, and she wished they hadn't. She couldn't breathe any longer. She pulled herself up, dizzy with terror.

"Heinz!" she called. She couldn't hear her own voice. She wondered if they'd gone out by the caves. She staggered in that direction and half-fainted. She tried to shout Heinz's name again but could manage only a squeak. All around her everything looked the same. How far had she walked? She saw a bed of straw on the ground and remembered that she had a real bed back at her house, a bed with clean linen and a roof over it. She felt herself drop, her body going immobile. She called for Heinz again, twice in a row. No one responded. No one came.

Her vision darkened. She couldn't see, but she could plainly hear a rustling at the entrance to the cave. She heard the hooting of an owl and the bellowing of a bull. A cold sheen of sweat glazed her body. She was too weak to call for Heinz again.

Then the moment came. "I heard a cry," she later recalled. "A short, shrill, squeaky, penetrating cry. It didn't come from me, nor from Heinz—it was the first cry of our newborn child. The child was there. I couldn't realize it, I was too weak, too helpless. I didn't hear the steps of people hurrying up to me, I didn't see my husband standing by me. I was past seeing and hearing."

Harry and Heinz helped Margret up from the straw bed and guided her and the baby back to the house. She heard a voice say, "It's a boy," but didn't know whose voice it was. Heinz bathed the baby and wrapped him in a blanket and placed him in Margret's arms. He was a New Year's baby, born at three in the morning. At last, his mother slept.

. . .

When she awakened, as she marveled at her son's pink fists, the pains returned. "It was over for the little creature that lay near me," she realized, "but not for me." She knew that the afterbirth had not been completely expelled. Her life was in danger, a danger that grew with each passing minute. She turned to Heinz and said, "Dr. Ritter. Get Dr. Ritter."

Their home was three miles from Friedo. Heinz was about to send Harry, but Margret objected. Given the boy's poor eyesight, he might get lost, or never make it to Friedo at all. Heinz agreed and went alone while Harry sat with her and the baby. "For the first time I had a good look at our new islander," she later wrote. "He had very fair hair and brown eyes. To judge from his crying his lungs were quite in order."

Within three hours Heinz returned with Friedrich. He had brought a medical bag and was acting as a doctor now, not as neighbor or friend. His professional demeanor reassured Margret as he examined her.

"Have you still got pains?" he asked.

"Yes. Very bad ones."

"I must operate," he said, but then changed his mind. "No, I'll try first with quinine, and hot and cold compresses." He told her to apply the compresses herself; he had to go off and speak to the Baroness. He did not offer any explanation for this sudden departure.

He returned in an hour. She watched him wash his hands a dozen times with antiseptic soap. He removed the placenta with neither gloves nor an anesthetic. She forced herself to remain silent as his hands did their work. When it was over, he smiled and congratulated her on her son. "You've been very brave," he said. "I congratulate you on that, too."

She smiled back, regretting that she had once called him a "heartless brute." At the same time, she wondered if he would have felt any moral responsibility had something gone terribly wrong.

He appraised the baby: "A fine strapping boy. Well built. Don't go feather-bedding him. The harder his mattress the better. That's the way to get worthwhile characters."

Margret didn't agree that a mattress would have much to do with the development of a baby's character, but figured the advice was part of Friedrich's "special philosophy."

"We do appreciate your coming very much," Heinz said. "May I ask what we owe you?"

"Money—you want to give me money?" Friedrich shook his head. "What can one do here with money? It's no good to one at all. And besides, I want to live without money, live only off what nature offers us. But I'd be pleased if you could bring down a pig some time. And my chickens are extremely fond of your dried meat. If you'd let me have a sackful every fortnight . . ."

Margret turned her face so Friedrich couldn't see her laughing. There he goes again, she thought, the vegetarian asking for pork.

She and Heinz let Harry pick the name for his new baby brother. He suggested Rolf, which they all liked—nice and short, and it paired well with "Wittmer." He would also sometimes be called Prince Charles, in honor of Charles Island, the English name for Floreana.

•  •  •

When Heinz had come to Friedo, proclaiming the birth of his son and asking for help, Dore noticed Friedrich's expression: "I have seldom seen such spontaneous pleasure light up Friedrich's face as when this news was brought. It touched me, but caused me a pang as well, for I should clearly have loved to have a child too, Friedrich's child." She was reminded of the hysterectomy she'd had years ago, before she and Friedrich had ever met.

As he rushed off with Heinz, she tried to quell her envy, even though she knew Friedrich had never wanted children. She wasn't bitter, she told herself—she was truly happy for Margret—but felt empathy and sorrow for all of the women in the world, like herself, who desperately desired but couldn't bear children. Hours later, when Friedrich returned, she felt calm enough to inquire about both the baby and its mother.

After the arrival of baby Rolf, a convivial mood settled over Floreana, touching all ten of its inhabitants. Quarrels were forgotten and grudges dismissed; everyone seemed willing, even just for a time, to think the best of one another.

When Friedrich told Dore that he had visited the Baroness's hotel and had a "long and pleasant" chat with her, Dore told herself there was nothing strange about this at all, even though the hotel was three miles away from Friedo and separated by the Cerro Pajas mountain slope.

Photographs taken around this time, however, suggest that Dore might indeed have had reason to worry. One image in particular hints that Friedrich and the Baroness had developed a clandestine intimacy. Side by side, their bodies tilted toward each other, she wears a greedy smile and gazes at him with adoration. His shirt unbuttoned halfway down his chest, his tongue pinched between his steel teeth and resting on his lip, he looks at her with the same longing expression, and snakes an arm around her back.

# TWENTY-ONE
# The Man Isn't Born
# Who Can Resist Me

Friedrich's kind words toward the Baroness inspired Dore to reconsider her own animosity. Through Friedrich, the Baroness had even given Dore a gift—flower seeds, the one luxury she did not fault herself for wanting. She had the urge to rush to the Baroness as fast as her bad leg would allow and thank her in person. She was grateful, too, for Friedrich's current mood, so "soft and gentle" that he did not once object to Dore's care and cultivation of the flowers, and even praised her ingenuity in fashioning pots from banana leaves.

When Friedrich suggested that they accept the Baroness's invitation to visit for lunch, Dore agreed. It would be the perfect opportunity to patch up differences. She admitted that, for all of the Baroness's bombast, there was something about the woman that "pleased and attracted" Dore—perhaps their mutual disdain for conventional lifestyles, and all the stifling mores women were conditioned to follow.

Dore went so far as to tell herself that she had done the Baroness an injustice by thinking so uncharitably of her, and that from that day forward she would view her neighbor as a potential ally and friend, united in their desire for a utopia, no matter how each of them defined that word.

•　•　•

Four days after baby Rolf's birth, Margret had tired of "this lazy lying around," as she confessed to her diary, and forced herself to stand up and test her own strength. In the midst of this exercise she heard footsteps—strange footsteps, she realized, that did not belong to either Harry or Heinz. Lump barked, and to Margret's surprise she turned to find the Baroness, Rudolph Lorenz, and Robert Philippson. Margret noted that the Baroness's belt, for once, did not hold her pistol, and she seemed to be in an exceptionally pleasant mood.

"Congratulations on your son," the Baroness said. She gripped both of Margret's hands, shook them hard, and then dropped them to hand over gifts: a tin of oats and some baby clothes she claimed were from her shop in Paris. Margret was wary of the Baroness's "grande dame benevolence," but thanked her for the presents. She hoped her visitors would not stay long, but the Baroness went on and on about her plans for her hotel. At last, she noticed Margret's waning attention, and the trio took their leave.

Dore and Friedrich arrived soon thereafter. They also brought gifts for Margret: a date palm tree, two other palms, and fruits and vegetables. Dore was impressed with the Wittmers' house; with its tidy carpentry and intricate roof—half sugarcane, half cowhide—it looked like something out of a Bavarian fairy tale. The interior was equally well constructed and orderly; clearly Margret "had the talent of a born housewife." She reminded herself that while Margret's home was picturesque, Friedo was a literary and philosophical salon—a place, as some visitors remarked, where "you can talk."

Dore praised baby Rolf as "a very promising specimen of new-born human being" and marveled at the homemade cradle Heinz had carved for him, but couldn't refrain from criticizing Margret: "I am afraid she forfeited all my sympathy with her one remark that she was resolved not to nurse the baby but to bring it up by hand, so as not to lose her girlish figure. This on Floreana!" (The accusation was as catty as it was false: Margret recorded that she nursed Rolf for six months, and weaned him only because it made her "too weak.")

The conversation that afternoon inevitably focused on the Baroness. Heinz told the story of how the Baroness had stolen from him, demanding money for rice he'd already bought. Dore grew concerned: "I was surprised to see how intense their dislike of the Baroness had become, and shuddered to think what open hatred might lead to in a place like this island, if it were allowed to grow."

Hoping to broker peace, she offered to be a mediator between the two parties. As a symbol of new beginnings, they planted the date palm tree together. The ceremony concluded, Dore mentioned that they were on their way to the Baroness's place for lunch.

At this, Margret had some petty thoughts of her own: "When they left, they went straight to the Wigwam of the Baroness. . . . A woman who was living with three men, who announced and exchanged favorites, and who shamelessly invited to her place every man she met!"

When Heinz questioned why they'd go out of their way to visit the Baroness, Friedrich explained that he, as a student of Lao-tzu and Buddha, felt it his duty to treat all people and animals with equal love.

•     •     •

Dore had to admit that the Baroness looked enchanting. Dressed in a black-and-white-checkered silk frock that accentuated her figure and a cravat made of pigskin, she offered Dore and Friedrich a tour of her garden. This, too, impressed Dore, who thought the lush tangle of fruit trees and flora looked straight from an illustrated garden book. The Baroness showed them the source of her water supply: a stream tumbling down the side of a cliff densely covered with ferns and vines. Often in the dark of night, the Baroness confided, cattle would stumble over the fifty-foot cliff and plunge to their deaths, scattering blood and remains uncomfortably close to her hotel.

The exterior of Hacienda Paradiso, as the Baroness had named the place, was done plainly in corrugated iron, but Dore found the interior nothing short of astonishing: Brightly colored carpets adorned the walls; two broad divans were upholstered in exquisite silk and stacked with cushions; the fireplace was flanked by drapes that shimmered in the light of the flames—all of this done in refined taste. The divans doubled as beds for the Baroness and her entourage, which, Dore noted, "told a great deal of the intimacies of the Baroness's household." The Baroness pointed out the section of wooden planks, all filched from the Casa down at Post Office Bay, that served as a dance floor. A rustic door divided the main room from a small storage area where the Baroness's Ecuadorian contractor, Valdivieso, slept—or so the Baroness claimed.

She led Dore and Friedrich back outside, where Rudolph and Robert were waiting. Lunch was served. The Baroness monopolized the conversation, speaking mainly of herself, bouncing from subject to subject with a vivacious and natural ease that reminded Dore of a precocious child. "She had a most attractive way of bragging," Dore observed, "and if one had believed her, one must have thought her an absolute phenomenon." Among her many talents, the Baroness claimed, were excellence in arts and crafts, gardening, medicine, painting, teaching, and literary endeavors. Somehow she aimed her attention and words at Friedrich while not exactly excluding Dore, a feat even Dore had to admire: "For the first time in my rather retiring life, I watched the woman's game played at close quarters, and though I found it somewhat despicable, I could not deny that, well played, it was full of charm."

●    ●    ●

After lunch, Friedrich, Rudolph Lorenz, and Robert Philippson walked around the garden and grounds. At last Dore had the Baroness's full attention, and she welcomed it—until the Baroness began talking about sex with a prurient glee that Dore had never before witnessed: "It did not take me long to discover that this woman was completely sex-mad, and I had as little desire to hear her confidences in this respect as to satisfy her burning curiosity as to my conjugal relations with my own man."

Dore sat silent and red-faced as the Baroness boasted about her sexual prowess. "The man isn't born who can resist me," she said, "and I'm free to confess that I find variety the spice of life. I don't know how long I'll manage with Philippson alone, and I'm pretty tired of Lorenz. Still, something else will probably turn up."

Dore didn't respond.

"I suppose you think I'm very Parisian in my point of view," the Baroness continued, "but I happen to believe in making the most of the things you can do best. Of course in Paris, a lot of men fall for one's title, you know, but if that is what lures them first, it's something else that keeps them."

In the light of day, Dore thought the Baroness looked every bit her forty years and then some, despite—or perhaps because of—her coquettish gestures. Beneath the smooth patter and garish charm Dore sensed a challenge, as though the Baroness's true message was this: better look out, because Friedrich is also just a man.

# TWENTY-TWO
# A Hunter Since His
# Kitten Days

For George Allan Hancock's latest expedition, he invited representatives from the San Diego Zoological Society, the University of Southern California, and the Smithsonian Institution, all of them with varying areas of expertise on birds, amphibians, fish, flora and fauna, marine invertebrates, and decapod crustaceans. Hancock's stated goal was to prepare, at the behest of the Ecuadorian government, a comprehensive report detailing the zoological life on the islands that would assist in the establishment of an animal sanctuary. He also told the press of his plans to visit Friedrich Ritter and Dore Strauch on Floreana, but didn't mention the island's newest residents. Perhaps Hancock, well versed in the sensational reports about Dore and Friedrich, hoped to investigate the situation himself before word got out about trouble in paradise.

He had kept Friedrich's letters, written in the fall of 1932, about the Baroness and her many transgressions: discouraging tourists from visiting Friedo; stealing and opening his mail from Post Office Bay; giving interviews about her absurd plans to build a luxury hotel. In his most recent missives, however, Friedrich focused on other topics, including his improving command of English, his hope that more of his writings would appear in U.S. publications, and his thoughts about *The Journal of a Recluse,* a book by an anonymous French author that Hancock had sent for him to read. (Little did Friedrich—and likely Hancock himself—know that the author was not an obscure French intellectual but an American high school teacher named Mary Fisher.) "I have had in my life some similar psychical happenings like the 'General Recluse,'" Friedrich confided. "I know that to become happy and self-content, this [sic] infernal psychical roots must be trained. . . . This 'Training' of his own mind, I think, is the most important, most earnest, and highest purpose of a man's life generally."

And—perhaps because of their recent truce, or a clandestine love affair—not one word about the Baroness.

In Dore's letters to Hancock, she, too, avoided mentioning the Baroness—at least directly. Instead, she had taken to sending Hancock short stories, some featuring a protagonist named Gertrud (an obvious stand-in for Dore herself), and others featuring animals in situations that strangely mirrored events on Floreana. One such story was titled "The Cat" and suggests that Dore, subconsciously or not, harbored fears about the Baroness's attraction to Friedrich, and how he might act upon it.

Peter Charles is a huge tomcat—a native of the Galapagos Islands—a hunter since his kitten days, and lord of his particular corner of the island.

Dimly, in the family saga of his ancestors, there remains a memory of pre-historic days when his forbears were pets of creatures called humans—lovingly caressed and protected. Finally, one day, he discovers intruders on his island, two creatures who must be humans, and with beating heart he approaches. He finds that these intruders have a lady cat with them—very attractive, with three little kittens, and he loses no time in introducing himself.

From her he hears how she came to the settlement, and they chat quite awhile about various subjects interesting to cats; but the lady soon bores Peter Charles, as she can find no subjects so enchanting as her three little kittens—and he is a man whose chief interests do not lie in the nursery.

So, although he is curious about these humans, and although his new acquaintance is very charming, he decides that he will not become a house cat, but will remain a true native of the Galapagos, a hunter and wild creature of the brush.

•   •   •

Despite the Baroness's crude behavior at her luncheon, Dore—perhaps wishing to keep her enemy close—extended an invitation to the Baroness and her companions for a reciprocal meal. She began intensive preparations at Friedo, taking special care with the menu: rice soup and kohlrabi stuffed with a puree of peas; a salad made of her prized cucumbers (which, she boasted, "grew like weeds and had an unusually fine flavor"); a cake made with ingredients from their garden, save for flour; a cocktail of sugar-cane juice and pineapple; and, especially for Rudolph Lorenz, an *otoy* dish with peanut butter, his favorite. She told herself that such an elaborate display was not a point of rivalry with the Baroness but a desire to show off what their garden could produce.

Her guests arrived just as she was placing the final garnish on her dishes. With great disappointment she noticed that only the Baroness and her favorite, Robert Philippson, had taken seats at the table. Rudolph was nowhere to be found.

The poor boy was sick, the Baroness explained. She dropped her voice into a rich contralto. Rudolph was suffering from a peculiar, undiagnosable ailment, she said, a tropical island something-or-other that came on very suddenly. "It was all terribly alarming," Dore wrote, paraphrasing the Baroness, "and for fear it might take a rapid, fatal turn, she had put him down at the Casa, though of course it was most dreadful that the wretched house was so far away, and one almost perished of alarm lest the next time one went down to see the patient, one would find him dead."

Wasn't it strange, Dore thought, that the Baroness had taken the time to transport a gravely ill man all the way down to Post Office Bay, yet had failed to alert the only doctor on the island? Dore waited for Friedrich to ask questions—what treatment is Rudolph receiving? Is anyone checking on him?—but he said nothing at all, and instead merely regarded the Baroness with an almost imperceptible smile.

As the Baroness continued to speak in somber tones about Rudolph—eating greedily all the while—Dore took a good look at Robert Philippson. She noticed the "mask-like absence of expression" on his face and was chilled by his absolute calm. Her mind churned a rush of terrible thoughts: "I knew that these two men were rivals, that [Rudolph], the ex-favorite, had been deposed in favor of this other, and that, while both were slaves to this woman, even to the extent of sleeping with her together in one bed when she commanded them to do so, a deadly hatred existed between them."

Floreana, small though it was, seemed at that moment permeated by hate: Heinz and Margret's for the Baroness; Rudolph's for Robert; Robert's for Rudolph. Moreover, Dore wondered, where was Valdivieso, the Baroness's Ecuadorian contractor? Was he busy working on the hotel, or did he inhabit some other, nefarious role? She recalled one of Heinz's Sunday afternoon visits, during which he described bouts of "violent quarreling" coming from the Hacienda Paradiso—so loud he and Margret could hear it from inside their own home.

At that moment Dore's donkey, Burro, let out a long bray, and she was grateful for the distraction. She excused herself to let him into the corral, and when she returned the Baroness began to lecture on the latest Parisian fashions; lately, she said, the biggest trend was white lace. "You know," she explained to Dore, "the kind of thing they put all the virgins into for their first communion." Her salacious tone unnerved Dore, but she was saved again by Burro's call, and she excused herself to tend to him. When she returned, the Baroness said, "If you treat your husband as well as you do your donkey, what a happy man he must be."

The Baroness then spoke of her hunting prowess and expeditions on the island. She would accept nothing other than the best cuts of meat, and she hunted animal after animal until she found them. She hoped to capture one or two of the island's wild dogs for pets, but so far they'd managed to elude her.

"Men and dogs are all alike," she said. "If they won't come willingly, you bring them down by force, and then you make them well again. They will stay then, and it does them good to know who is their master." To Dore's horror, the Baroness elaborated: She had ventured out onto the pampa and shot two wild dogs in the gut, wounding but not killing them. She took them home and nursed them. One remained very loyal to her, although he'd been permanently maimed.

For Dore, that was enough. Here she was in Friedo, a place of peace (or so she told herself), where animals could visit without fear and all humans received a warm welcome—what, exactly, was the Baroness doing here? For Dore, the woman's very presence made a mockery of Friedo, and she felt "as Eve must have felt on learning that the serpent was the Evil One."

The Baroness turned to Friedrich. "Dr. Ritter," she said, "do tell me. Is it true that milk's the antidote for arsenic poisoning?"

•   •   •

After the visitors left, Friedrich dropped all politesse.

"Such a waste of time," he said, "chattering with a woman all afternoon."

Dore was astonished. "You must be blind! Can't you see the woman's a criminal?"

"My dear child," Friedrich said. "Don't tell me you're becoming theatrical too."

Dore's disbelief turned to fury—and a sudden sharp fear. Rudolph could be dead and no one would know it. They could be living with a murderer. What might the Baroness do next? Whom else might she kill? Go down to Post Office Bay at once, Dore ordered Friedrich, to see if Rudolph was alive or dead. They had to get a message to the Ecuadorian authorities. No one was safe on this island until the Baroness was gone.

Friedrich responded with maddening calm: "Listen, my dear, you are much too excited not to resent it if I tell you that I think you take this woman far too seriously. I think she's just an actress. But even supposing she was everything you suspect—what would be her advantage at present if she murdered this young man? Murders of such a kind always have a motive, and the Baroness, though hysterical, is shrewd enough."

Dore stayed silent, letting him continue.

"There would be inquiries. That would be very embarrassing to her, for I am qualified to make a post-mortem. . . . As for leaving Lorenz quite alone down at the Casa, where any moment people might land and take him off the island and put him into a hospital where he could talk unchecked, that is even less likely. So you see, this is obviously a scheme of sheer intimidation. The woman is undoubtedly a person who would stop at nothing, but it isn't in her interest to do what you suspect."

•     •     •

Dore and Friedrich didn't have much time to dwell on the incident. As they awaited Hancock's arrival, another cruise ship docked at Post Office Bay: the *Stella Polaris*, carrying wealthy American tourists eager to visit Friedo. The Norwegian ship, built shortly before the onset of the Depression (and seized by German forces in 1940), was billed as one of the first cruise ships devoted solely to luxury travel, with 130 crew members to attend to every guest's whim and an unprecedented array of features: a Smoking Room, Music Salon, Social Hall, Reading and Writing Room; a beauty salon and barbershop; a fully equipped hospital complete with waiting room; a state-of-the-art gymnasium and a deck for outdoor exercising; deluxe cabins each paneled in different types of wood; and special gala events boasting exotic menus of beluga caviar *malossol* and clear turtle soup (the latter now illegal under the Endangered Species Act in most parts of the world). The *Stella Polaris* allowed only 198 passengers at a time, and half this number on around-the-world excursions. One such fortunate traveler in 1929 was the English writer Evelyn Waugh, who, in exchange for a free trip, promised extensive coverage of the journey and published his first travel book, *Labels*, about the experience.

On this trip, which commenced in New York on January 14, 1933, the *Stella Polaris* planned stops at numerous South Sea locales, including Floreana. One passenger was Carl Block of Peoria, Illinois, president of the Block & Kuhl company, which owned the preeminent department store downtown.

As soon as the ship anchored at Post Office Bay, Block made his way to Friedo. Friedrich gave him a tour and insisted that Floreana's inhabitants wished to be wholly self-sufficient (this, as he waited for Hancock to deliver items from a lengthy wish list). Next, Block made his way to the Wittmers' home and met the family. From there, for the grand finale, he walked the short distance to the Hacienda Paradiso, where the Baroness invited him inside.

For half an hour she spoke with Block intimately, confiding that there was turmoil within her own home. "A cook-pot had mysteriously disappeared," Block later recalled, "and a catastrophe of much less consequence to her was the disappearance of one of her subjects, 'only a gardener.'" But that wasn't even the worst of it, the Baroness confessed: one of her companions, Rudolph Lorenz, had tried to escape, and she would not abide it.

"The next time that rascal tries to run away from this Utopia," she said, "I'll shoot him. The idea, when he is number two in my favor."

Block believed her.

# TWENTY-THREE
# What a Girl

For Hancock and his crew, this journey to the Galápagos was their most eventful yet. They found a crocodile sunning himself on a rock and hunted him, fruitlessly, with spears. They hooked an eight-foot tiger shark and dragged it over the stern; "the gaping jaws, dissected and dried," wrote Waldo Schmitt of the Smithsonian, "draped easily over a man's shoulders." They launched harpoons at turtles until a doctor with the San Diego Zoological Society asked them to stop. They captured a seal lion pup and hand fed it with a bottle of milk: "more pets every day," quipped one crew member.

A female sea lion, caged on the *Velero*'s deck, spent too many hours in the hot sun and began to vomit. After she died, they put her on ice, ready for transport to the New York Zoological Society. They slaughtered more seals on the beach. They took an albatross from a rookery and carried it to the beach, only to have it die. They shot finches and mockingbirds and hawks. They filched four eggs from the nest of a red-faced booby. They got close enough to the birds, tame and unafraid, to pet their feathered backs—and also to quickly strike them dead by hitting their heads with the butt of a gun.

At 4:00 p.m. on January 26, the *Velero* at last arrived at Post Office Bay and prepared to drop anchor, only to find that the *Stella Polaris* was already there. Hancock anchored instead at Black Beach Bay and noticed a heliograph message coming from the direction of the highlands. He at once understood this to be a signal sent by Friedrich, using a mirror to refract the sun's rays. Hancock and Chief Officer Charles Swett began the hike to Friedo, returning at dusk to report their conversation with Dore and Friedrich. "It was a wild tale of a baroness with three husbands and a machine gun," wrote Waldo Schmitt. They also heard how Vincent Astor's friend Arthur Estampa had come to Friedo terrified and seeking protection, "his clothes half torn from his body."

·  ·  ·

The following day, at Hancock's invitation, Dore and Friedrich boarded the *Velero*. They had washed themselves and wore clean clothes, but Dore was embarrassed by the gaps in her smile. Friedrich, blaming her fondness for sugar, had pulled more of her rotted teeth. In the presence of company, she sometimes borrowed his now-infamous set of steel dentures even though they were too large for her mouth and competed with her remaining teeth. The couple traded them back and forth depending upon who was speaking at the moment. For long stretches of time, when Friedrich monopolized the dentures, Dore refused to speak at all.

Friedrich, at least, had adapted well to his toothless state. "I am happy every day that I have run out of teeth," he confided to his notebook. "I never suspected how superfluous these things are in the mouth until I found out about it here. At most I need teeth for the visit, but when eating they are terribly troublesome and greatly diminish the taste sensation."

They ate lunch (Friedrich, presumably, sans dentures), listened to a concert by the *Velero*'s ensemble, and then were treated to a surprise: home movies of the couple taken during Hancock's trip the prior year. After the viewing party, Hancock led Dore and Friedrich to the deck, where a stockpile of presents awaited them: shovels, a spade saw, a cleaver, a case of milk, half a dozen milk cans filled with beans, jars of jelly and honey and cocoa and sugar, writing paper, and clothes—especially clothes. "Dore got quite an outlay of clothing from Hollywood's best shops," noted one crew member, but Friedrich was finicky with his loot, rejecting some of the very items he'd requested. "It would not be bad," mused the scientist Fred Ziesenhenne, "if one were to live here and have a Good Samaritan like the captain come annually and leave several hundred dollars' worth of stuff."

The next bit of business was far less pleasant: the *Velero*'s doctor, H. M. Wegeforth, examined a lump on Dore's finger and determined that it was a cancerous sarcoma. Immediately Friedrich agreed with this diagnosis and said he was well aware of the seriousness of the situation, but had not treated it himself. The entire crew gathered to watch Dr. Wegeforth operate. "Dore felt no pain during the cauterization and kept up rapid-fire conversation under the knife," said one witness. "She is a Spartaness."

At Schmitt's request, Friedrich made a census of the ten current residents of Floreana: he and Dore; Heinz, Margret, Harry, and Rolf; the Baroness, Rudolph Lorenz, Robert Philippson, and Manuel Valdivieso. The tensions on the island so intrigued Hancock and the crew that they made a unanimous decision to stay and visit all three homes.

•   •   •

At 8:30 in the morning, right on schedule, Friedrich appeared at Black Beach, riding a donkey and wearing only a loincloth. Some in Hancock's crew assisted in hauling Friedrich's gifts and others ran ahead of the caravan, shooting olive and vermillion flycatchers, yellow warblers, and finches. They followed a path thick with donkey turds and passed two barbed-wire fences before arriving at Friedo.

The crew was impressed with the property's improvements since their last visit. The house seemed less slapdash, and was now a sturdy structure that worked in harmony with its wild surroundings. The bananas and papayas had a remarkable growth spurt in a year's time, and more ground had been cultivated for peas, cabbage, and kohlrabi. Friedrich gave an enthusiastic demonstration of his irrigation system, showing the pipe he'd made to transport water from the mountain foothills to his garden. He took a shower and smiled for the cameras. The overall effect, thought Waldo Schmitt, was one of prosperity achieved at considerable physical cost. Even Friedrich's machetes had, from constant usage, been whittled to half their size.

The party bade goodbye to Dore and, with Friedrich leading the way, started off for the Hacienda Paradiso. They climbed over the barren trail, spackled with cotton plants, acacia trees, and hibernating land snails; one zoologist in the party filled four vials with the mollusks. Higher up, they entered the green zone, where the scrubby terrain turned luxuriant, and a misty rain began to fall. They followed the pig and mule and cow tracks, catching butterflies and shooting birds. On the way they encountered a man who identified himself as Rudolph Lorenz. The sight of Rudolph would torment Charles Swett for years:

A pitiful figure he made as he sat for a moment and rested by the side of the trail. His great sunken blue eyes seem to haunt me yet. Five feet in height and so wasted in frame that I doubt he would have moved the scale to an even hundred pounds. His clothes were in rags, he was hatless, and burned by the sun to the shade of a native, his skin contrasted strangely with his light blonde hair. Over his shoulder was a pack which in the tropics would have sorely puzzled me to carry. Where he was going, where he was from, I asked him in Spanish, only to be met with a dumb uncomprehending stare. . . . Why I had tried my halting, stammering German on him, I do not know, but at once he became the most voluble of persons. . . .

I stood for a new hope, a chance to escape the drudgery of his everyday life, and the constant reminders of the days when he was well and strong and still the favorite of the Queen. Would we take him away? He wanted to leave so badly. Was there not room for one more? How much would it cost to get back to Paris? Once there he would not have to work so hard, and soon he would be well again. His eyes glowed as he thought of some scenes so far away, the pinkish spots on his cheeks became brighter, he coughed a little, slumped over, and in a hopeless, listless tone, said: "I think I am not as strong as I was. Won't you come up the trail with me? I know that the Baroness will be glad to see you."

He led them the rest of the way to the Hacienda Paradiso. Along the path roamed wild donkeys and pigs and cows and cats. Some tree trunks were splashed with red paint, marking the route. Clusters of butterflies disbanded, escaping the swinging nets. The rain came harder, and at last they arrived at what Fred Ziesenhenne sardonically called "the mansion." Rattan chairs in the yard, he joked, "convinced us that some royalty must be living there." Lingerie of various colors and fabrics draped across a clothesline. As the crew came closer, they spotted thick clouds of flies feasting on long, stringy strips of rotting meat, the smell so thick they could taste it on their tongues.

Still, the surrounding scene was idyllic, with water trickling through the crevasses of the moss-covered cliffs, creating miniature waterfalls that tumbled down into troughs and buckets, waiting for collection.

In the garden they met Robert Philippson, who spoke perfect English. He unlatched the fence and ushered them into the yard. The Baroness rushed out to meet them, full of questions, clad only in underwear—a testament to her nickname among island neighbors: Crazy Panties. Were they exhausted from their walk? They must be thirsty—what a pity she had run out of tea. Had they brought mail for her from Post Office Bay? They must excuse her appearance; she hadn't had time to dress properly. Won't they come inside and tour the Hacienda Paradiso? She even had a few kind words for Friedrich; he, too, was more than welcome in her home.

In the few weeks since the Baroness's luncheon, the interior of her home had become dingy and disheveled. True, the cots still boasted crisp white linens—a rarity for the country—but otherwise the place was a mess. Stacks of clothing and supplies filled the rooms, threatening collapse. The air seemed damp and fetid, drawing more flies. The zoologist John Garth in particular was disgusted. The Baroness, he wrote, had "no good ideas of housekeeping nor sanitation and we shuddered at the filth in which they lived."

If the Baroness noticed the party's collective distaste, she chose not to acknowledge it. Instead, she took the opportunity to advertise herself. She spoke eight languages, had lived in Vienna, Paris, and Constantinople, and—despite never setting foot in the United States—had excellent connections in Hollywood. Had they heard that she was the grandniece of Richard Wagner, the famous composer? And that another ancestor had been an intimate confidant of the late Franz Joseph, emperor of Austria?

Had they noticed the bold white streak running through her blond hair? It had gone that way in one single night, if they could believe it. "It happened during the war," she explained, when the village where she was living had been occupied by Russian soldiers. A group of them broke into her home. Thinking quickly, she rolled herself inside a rug and hid there all night, listening to the soldiers boast about what they'd do once they finally found her.

She was "very jolly and witty," thought Waldo Schmitt, and she proved she could take a joke. When she turned to one of the crew's field collectors and asked, "Haven't I seen you somewhere before?" he served a fast response: "I heard that gag before someplace, but I'm too much of a gentleman to say where it was." The Baroness did not object.

Before the party left, she showed them around the garden and her menagerie of pets: rabbits, a poodle, ducks, chickens, a cow, two donkeys, the only pair of turkeys on the island, and her favorite cats. She had caught them all in the wild, she said, and now they were as tame as any domesticated pet. At that, she sipped from a can of milk, warmed the liquid by swishing it around her mouth, and then regurgitated it directly into her cats' waiting mouths.

•  •  •

With Friedrich once again leading the way, the party made the short walk to the Wittmers' home—an impressive structure, the crew agreed, especially the roof partially made of cowhide. The sharp bark of a dog lured Margret from the house. As Friedrich made the introductions, she realized the significance of this visit. "Besides having the prestige that goes with great fortune," Margret wrote, "Hancock is endowed with intellectual, spiritual, and physical qualities such as few men possess. . . . There is much happy relating and a quick trust in one another so that we are able to forget that it has to do with one of the great ones of American finance. It is truly a big day for us." She insisted that Harry do no chores so that he could enjoy this momentous occasion.

Fred Ziesenhenne was immediately taken with Margret: "She was the most beautiful of the three women on the island—blonde, blue eyes, and beautifully built. Insect bites on her legs was the only mar of her beauty." Heinz gave a tour of the pirate caves where they used to live, now used as workshops and storage rooms. Next stop was his large water spring, which came from the same fern-covered cliff as the Baroness's water supply. The scope of his land was most impressive; it had taken him four short months to clear as much acreage as Friedrich had in three years.

Inside the Wittmers' immaculate home, a phalanx of dried jerk meat hung across a taut wire, not one fly buzzing nearby. Hancock was astonished by baby Rolf, so rosy and plump despite the difficult living conditions. Turning to Margret, he asked, "And you had that baby here?" He was less impressed by her brood of hens, who ate most of the eggs they were supposed to hatch.

"Oh, so you keep chickens?" Hancock asked.

"Do you?" Margret responded.

"Well I've got a bit of a chicken farm," he said. "Brings me in about twenty thousand eggs a day."

"Twenty thousand!" Margret said, and gasped. "I'd be glad if I got twenty. Still, I suppose you have to start in a small way."

He gave her advice on her "cannibal hens," and Waldo presented a gift of jarred figs. Margret already considered the crew "old friends" and was sorry to see them go. "Naturally, we feel highly honored at having Captain Hancock and his party with us," she wrote, "and it makes us happy when Dr. Schmitt presents us with a glass of preserved figs. We have no figs as yet and so it is an especial treat for us."

Over the next year, while Margret awaited the *Velero*'s next visit, she and Waldo would develop a close friendship. "Waldo's interest in the Galapagos," joked a colleague, "seems to have been 75 percent in the Crustacea, 24 percent in Mrs. Wittmer, and one percent in everything else."

•   •   •

The group, including the Baroness and Robert, headed back to Friedo, where they planned to rest a bit before dinner on the *Velero*. Dore served a cold drink made of coconut juice and lemons, and Robert unwrapped a pork shank from a sheath of greasy brown paper and passed it around. Everyone felt obliged to partake save for John Garth, who, having investigated the method of preparation, "felt equally bound to refuse."

During the festivities, Dore kept a close watch on the Baroness. Dore noticed that she had a "sharp gleam of resentment" in her eyes as she surveyed the pile of gifts from Hancock. Within the hour other members of Hancock's crew arrived at Friedo, bringing Rudolph with them. When he saw the Baroness, he flinched—a subtle reaction, but one that caught Dore's attention. She watched, too, as the Baroness just as subtly flicked her hand, bringing Rudolph rushing to her side. The image reminded Dore of "the unhallowed mutual understanding of a wild animal and its circus trainer."

Recalling the luncheon she'd hosted a few weeks prior, when the Baroness described a deathly ill Rudolph being banished to Post Office Bay, Dore took charge of the conversation. "We are glad to see you up here again," she told Rudolph. "Are you better? We heard that you'd been ill."

The Baroness spoke before Rudolph had a chance to respond: "Herr Lorenz has quite recovered, thank you. If another doctor had been necessary, I should, of course, have consulted Dr. Ritter."

A crew member, standing nearby, joined the conversation. "Another doctor?"

"Oh, yes," the Baroness said, smiling. "I'm practically that as well, though I know I don't look much like such a blue-stocking! Just think, this place affected our poor Lorenz so queerly he fell most frightfully ill. I even thought we might lose him, but I pulled him through all right. Didn't I?" She turned to Rudolph.

Dore assessed him carefully. Indeed, he still looked frightfully ill, his once-fresh skin turned sallow, his body sunken and gaunt. It was hard to believe he was the same person who had arrived on Floreana just a few months earlier. Yet he agreed with the Baroness, insisting that he was much better now, and quickly changed the subject.

As Hancock's party said their goodbyes, Dore had the urge to take the captain aside and tell him never to bring the Baroness to Friedo again. When the opportunity came, she lost her nerve.

•    •    •

On board the *Velero*, Hancock's ensemble once again picked up their instruments. The Baroness reiterated her kinship to Richard Wagner, and added that she was also related to the Hungarian composer Franz Liszt. John Garth, on piano, played a solo especially for the Baroness, Liszt's "Liebestraum in A-flat." At this, the Baroness was ecstatic and exclaimed, "Oh, that's just the way my great-uncle would have liked to have heard it played." After the concert, she and Garth discussed Sanskrit, which she hoped to add to her ever-growing list of mastered languages. In fact, she asked, would he mind bringing her a textbook on Sanskrit the next time the *Velero* stopped by Floreana? And, before she forgot, it would be so kind if the crew might give her some cans of milk, as much as they could spare. Margret Wittmer needed some for her baby, and the Baroness would happily deliver the gift.

In the morning, the Baroness went fishing for three hours with two members of the crew: Karl Koch of the San Diego Zoo, and student zoologist Raymond Elliott. She invited both men to visit her at the Hacienda Paradiso—alone. Fred Ziesenhenne, upon hearing of this invitation, spoke for the entire crew when he remarked, "What a girl!"

His assessment echoed that of another visitor, who concluded that the Hacienda Paradiso was not so much a hotel as a "festering sex complex."

•   •   •

The following day, before they prepared to depart Floreana, Hancock and a few others escorted the Baroness back to her home. Once there, Manuel Valdivieso appeared and began arguing with the Baroness about his contract. He claimed that it had commenced officially as soon as they left Paris and was now completed; she argued that the contract had commenced only when they'd arrived on Floreana, and he still owed her his labor. They shouted, circling each other, until Valdivieso fled the room, only to return moments later brandishing a gun. "But the Baroness," Hancock witnessed, "quick as a flash, produced her small revolver, which she usually held in her hand, and the Ecuadorian dashed out of the house like a scared rabbit and hid himself in the bush."

Later, Valdivieso pulled Hancock aside. "I have to get away from here before something happens," he said. "This woman is completely out of her mind."

The captain agreed to take Valdivieso as far as Chatham Island, where he spoke more diplomatically about his former boss. "Notwithstanding her aristocratic culture, enlightenment, and refinement in her social interactions," he said, "her character at home was authoritarian and impulsive. . . . She was used to imposing her own will at all times."

And then there were nine.

# TWENTY-FOUR
# The Empress of Floreana

Once the *Velero* departed Floreana, Dore attempted to have a serious conversation with Friedrich about the Baroness. As she had come to expect, Friedrich dismissed her, calling the situation "women's bickerings" and urging her to stay on pleasant terms for the sake of everyone on the island.

"She is not harmless," he admitted, "but she is not so very dangerous either. Only one thing you must remember—she has come here to make her fortune by fair means or foul, and she is a determined person. She will sooner push us off this island than we her, because we are less ruthless than she. Open war could only mean our leaving. The choice lies entirely with ourselves—in fact with you, Dore. Is Friedo worth this effort of self-control to you?"

"How can you ask?" Dore said.

"Very well then, we must act accordingly. And I don't believe that she will be here longer than about another year at the very outside. We can well afford to wait."

Privately, though, Friedrich was equally troubled by the Baroness; if the two had once engaged in a love affair, it was by now certainly over. But he did not share his concerns with Dore. Perhaps he believed that such a confession—to a woman, no less—would be perceived as weakness. Instead he disclosed his fears in a letter to Hancock, whom he had come to view as his closest confidant:

My dear Captain Hancock:

You know I can bad [*sic*] express my thoughts and feeling with
speaking, therefore I must do it in writing—to show you my reaction
to physical events. . . . I think it is evident enough that I searched
really for solitude. The fate let me not find it. My own "karma" seems
to be too "Faustian" to find the quiet I searched for. Surely I had
here my happiest days. But fate approached. Supported by the
Ecuadorians, the Baroness came to drive me away here and to take
the place. First I hoped she would fail, because I thought that the
Americans would slightly see through her intention—but now I see
that she is very successful, and the island itself is too "small" for her
purposes and my world. . . . I know I would never be victorious
against somebody whose instinct and experience in handling men and
circumstances is so routine.

After a Nietzschean digression about following a higher law, his personal ego and impersonal self, and his subconscious desire to abandon the
"material disorder" that currently afflicted his life, Friedrich got to the
main point of his letter:

I hope you know you understand me better than anyone else in the
world. To everyone who understands me I can open my "heart"—but it
is a shame to prostitute his soul to all people.

In Friedrich's obtuse, circuitous manner, he was sending Caption Hancock a private and desperate signal for help.

•     •     •

On Sunday, February 5, four days after Friedrich wrote his letter, the Baroness and Robert Philippson arrived at Friedo unannounced, a visit Dore
would recount in her memoir. The Baroness made small talk, refusing to
expose the purpose of her visit, but she soon sliced through the pretense.
"Too kind of you to have sent fodder to my donkeys at the Bay," she said.

"I suppose that Captain Hancock thinks your kindness to animals most awfully touching—it's not a bad trick."

"Captain Hancock," Dore said, "saw that those poor beasts were almost starved to death, and asked me to send them down some sugarcane. As for the rest of your remark, I prefer not to have heard it. But at any rate, if Captain Hancock thinks I'm decent to my animals, he could hardly think the same of you, after seeing the state that yours are in."

The Baroness laughed. "Oh, not at all, my dear," she said. "He was absolutely horrified about the poor things. But he doesn't for a moment believe that I had anything to do with them. I told him they were yours."

Dore was shocked into silence.

"You'll have your work cut out explaining that away to him, won't you?" the Baroness asked.

Robert, too, was silent, standing at the Baroness's side.

"I think it might be just as well," the Baroness continued, "if you confined that extreme kind-heartedness of yours to animals. It's a lot safer."

Dore at last found her voice. "I don't know what you mean."

The Baroness clarified: it would be advisable, in the future, if Dore would concern herself only with animals—and not the state of Rudolph Lorenz's health. "Of course, we found your interest very touching and all that," she added, "but it's after all none of your business. Or are you perhaps in love with him?"

"If you have come to my house to insult me, Frau Wagner," Dore said, "I think perhaps you'd better go before I ask you to."

The Baroness laughed and then pivoted: "Your Captain Hancock is very generous to his protégés."

"Friedrich and I are nobody's protégés," Dore said, "but Captain Hancock has been very kind to us."

"He was simply charmed with my place," the Baroness said. "When he comes back we're going to make a film."

"Indeed?" Dore asked.

"Yes. It's to be called *The Empress of Floreana*. That's me."

"I wasn't aware of it," Dore said. "Have you bought the place by any chance?"

"No, but the aristocracy are the natural rulers of the places they come to. It's in my blood—you wouldn't understand—it's a feeling one has to be born to. . . . But please don't be afraid that I'll put on airs with you. I'm really very democratic, and have always got on excellently with the common people."

Dore had had enough. "Oh, my dear woman," she said. "We're not acting in your film. You know I don't believe you're any more a Baroness than I am!"

Robert interrupted. Turning to the Baroness, he said, "Come, little one."

*Said this young man to his mistress of forty-four,* Dore thought. At that moment Friedrich appeared. As the Baroness ranted and cursed at Dore, even calling her a vulgar epithet, Dore took immense satisfaction at Friedrich's shocked expression. "It astounded him," Dore witnessed, "and made him blush for her. He was offended and uncomfortable."

Dore told herself that she—and not the Baroness—had won that round. And, Dore would discover, she had been right to worry about the Baroness's donkeys. One developed a sore on its back, which the Baroness fatally treated with carbolic acid. Another died after she had forgotten to feed it. A third refused to come when she called it, and was shot dead for its defiance.

•     •     •

A few days later, after checking for mail at Post Office Bay, Heinz dropped by Friedo and shared his own frustrations. While making a cradle for baby Rolf, he managed to break both his toe and his only drill. Did Friedrich have one he could borrow? Friedrich did not; he only had one of his own and needed it. Also, despite Captain Hancock's wise advice, the hens were still eating every egg they hatched. Worst of all, he and Margret had been awaiting the delivery of forty tins of condensed milk for the baby; they were nearly out of their supply and growing desperate. He'd considered approaching the Baroness to ask if he might buy some milk and was even willing to pay her extortionist prices—but then remembered that her cows were starved to near death and wouldn't be able to produce one cup between them.

Friedrich mentioned the many gifts Captain Hancock had given to the Baroness. "Among other things," he said, "there was a whole crate of tinned milk for your wife, so that she should have a good reserve for herself and the baby."

Heinz was livid. It was one thing for the Baroness to steal his rice, but now she was stealing gifts meant for his newborn son. After consulting with Margret, he called upon the Baroness and asked, politely, if she had the milk that Hancock had left for them. She produced one tin.

• • •

The Baroness's transgressions disturbed Dore even when she was not the intended target. Friedrich, infuriatingly, still did not take her concerns seriously. She could not burden Heinz, who was rightfully concerned with his own family's survival. And she could not consider confiding in Margret, who, in Dore's opinion, was "an ordinary type of woman and a great gossip"—not someone she would trust with her most personal thoughts.

Dore's gravest fear, however, was that she was failing at the very task for which she'd sacrificed her life: helping Friedrich reach the highest echelons of his own humanity, achieving the status of the *Übermensch*. Like Friedrich, she chose to confide in Hancock, trusting that he was the one person who would understand the severity of her despair. Shortly after the captain's visit, she sent him a letter:

My dear Captain Hancock:

You heard the doctor often say we must live more simple, more unassuming lives. I did not help in this direction . . . and in remembering how much I swerved from the truth and the spirit we had perceived once and understood, my soul is weeping for shame and remorse. . . .

I know that I shall not live a long life. But I will use my time. I will be thankful that I could make the acquaintance of the "Baroness." Is she not like a mirror to show me the world, which lies behind me, so far away, that I could learn how impossible it is to go back to my country—not for months, not for weeks, not for days.

Is she not like a snake to hurt my soul and put bad thoughts in my mind?

She signed off by stating her new aspiration: to "overcome the material world" and rise above her own alarming—and dangerous—"animal" instincts.

Even Dore now worried about losing control of everything.

# TWENTY-FIVE
# Fanatical Jealousy

F ar from Friedo, back in civilization, the Depression deepened. Nearly 25 percent of American workers (about 12,830,000 people) were unemployed. Almost half of America's farms faced foreclosure. Hoovervilles, the shantytowns named for the former president Herbert Hoover, sprang up across the country, and many of their residents adopted the structure and rules of official neighborhoods, naming their streets and electing mayors and pooling resources. In New York City's Central Park, a group of war veterans erected a Hooverville along the reservoir, attracting groups of wealthy tourists.

The inauguration of President Franklin Delano Roosevelt brought a tentative sense of optimism. "From the moment he arrived here," wrote the *New York Times*, "Washington took on almost a visible air of hope." A prominent New York mathematician and numerologist declared that the name "Roosevelt," which contains nine letters, would prove fortuitous since the number nine "has controlled our social, political, and domestic reactions from the beginning of time."

Amid the bleak headlines, newspapers across the country printed stories about Hancock's travels, offering a glimpse into a world so fantastic and bizarre it hardly seemed real. Who wasn't mesmerized by reports of exotic cargo, including ten "Hancocki" lizards, so called because they were discovered by the captain and his crew? How could anyone resist the heartwarming story of the first baby to be born on the remote island of

Floreana? What to make of the newest settler, a sex-crazed baroness? Who didn't envy Friedrich and Dore anew for escaping the world's various ills? "Whether the world staggers or runs, they don't care," wrote the *Brooklyn Eagle* in a report on Hancock's excursion. "They are living in a garden of Eden, in a little paradise of the Pacific, where there are no worldly cares. They have a little house on the rim of an extinct volcano. It is filled with books—all well-marked by use. While the rest of the world is staggering by, this couple reads, muses, or works in their garden . . . they enjoy their escape from civilization."

By the time Hancock's adventures were publicized, several other American explorers were already en route to Floreana. The Boston businessman Amory Coolidge, owner of one of the largest textile companies in the country, organized an expedition and invited several New York City doctors and Wall Street financiers. After anchoring his cruiser, *Blue Dolphin*, at Post Office Bay, Coolidge came upon a sign etched with what one colleague called "vulgarly large red letters":

Friends, whoever you are! Two hours from here lies the Hacienda Paradiso, a lovely spot where the weary traveler can rejoice to find refreshing peace and tranquility on his way through life. Life is such a tiny fragment of eternity, shackled to a clock—let us be happy in it the short time we can. In Paradiso you only have one name: Friend. We will share with you the salt of the sea, the produce of our garden and the fruits of our trees, the cool spring water that trickles from the rocks, and all the good things friends have brought us when they passed. We would have you spend with us a few moments of this restless life, we would bestow on you the peace with which God endowed our hearts and minds when we left the turbulence of great cities for the tranquility of centuries which has thrown its cloak over the lonely, romantic, miraculous Galapagos.

Baroness Wagner-Bosquet

No sooner had Coolidge finished reading this welcome than he saw a man's feet, shoved inside a ratty pair of white sneakers that exposed several of his toes. The man seemed to have been awaiting their arrival, stationed at the beach like an attentive porter, ready to hoist their luggage and show them to their rooms. On his belt he carried a knife and a handgun. He introduced himself as Robert Philippson and shared the history of the abandoned house at Post Office Bay, once occupied by aspiring settlers who had failed to achieve their dream. "It made quite an impression on us," Coolidge later wrote. "Just to think of the poor souls who had come all the way from Norway with such high hopes. What must have been their disappointment to find no water and a desolate unyielding island, which rendered all their toil in vain."

Come up to the Hacienda Paradiso, Robert urged. It was just a few hours' journey. They started off and found the path a fairly easy walk, leading up serried hills and through a pass in the mountains. As they approached the highlands, they encountered the bodies of cattle that had dropped dead from exhaustion or dehydration. Swarms of flies buzzed around the carcasses, and wild hogs picked at the bones.

The Baroness stood at the foot of her garden, waiting. Coolidge had a ready assessment: "From Paris, where she was a blonde (and furious with the society editors if they did not quote her dress correctly at Longchamp Racecourse), she has darkened into a simple, country housewife." Her bare legs bore vivid red scratches, and her white cotton dress was stained with hog's blood.

After a tour of the Hacienda Paradiso, she led them to a table draped in a decorative cloth stitched with a German motto about good food well served. The gleaming silverware bore a baronial crest. She served a luncheon of rice and garden vegetables, dressed with olive oil and juice from her wild lemons, and a dessert she called "emperior cake," made of a diced flour pancake mixed with canned pineapple and apricots. Coffee was sweetened with sugar, which, Coolidge noted, "had an ant for nearly every grain." The Baroness, upon hearing this criticism, explained that the insects were good for rheumatism. Coolidge was skeptical but overall impressed by the Baroness's operation: "They all radiate enthusiasm and energy—even Rudolph Lorenz, who is suffering from tuberculosis, and at best can only do light work around the house and garden, seems to have caught the prevalent contagion of optimism. The Baroness is very much the boss. She seems extremely intelligent and agreeable, and as happy and cheerful as can be."

The meal finished, her guests sated, the Baroness pulled out her last bottle of schnapps and began to gossip about her neighbors. Dore was an "unusual lady," to put it diplomatically, and "very jealous of the new arrivals." When she, the Baroness, first arrived on Floreana, Dore invited her to stay at Friedo but made her sleep on the porch without covers on a very cold night. Dore refused to make a fire for the Baroness, but then made tea for a male guest simply because he was handsome. Even worse, the Baroness confided, Dore grew furious with her because she, the Baroness, made her donkey carry a light load up a hill—this, when Dore badly mistreats her own animals. Here was just one example: Dore has a small spring that she covers with an iron plate. When little birds come to drink, she pulls a string to release the cover and kills the birds instantly, feeding the little corpses to her cat.

As for Friedrich Ritter, he cultivated an excellent garden, the Baroness admitted, but has failed to become self-sufficient and embarrasses himself by begging for gifts from passing ships. He was stingy and unkind and went out of his way to make life more difficult for her. He fed large pieces of sugarcane to his donkey, but gave her only a short stem for planting. He dispensed advice on building a home and garden that turned out to be harmful and wrong—perhaps a deliberate mislead? He's fully aware of his dependence on wealthy American visitors but wants to deny her the same benefit, even though she'd generously divided her seed into three lots: one for the Wittmers, who live nearby; another for Dore and Friedrich; and the third for herself.

She should add that the Wittmers are "the most kind and neighborly people" and just welcomed a baby boy. In fact, perhaps Coolidge should leave behind any cans of milk he had brought along on his journey?

* * *

Before leaving Floreana, Coolidge and his party made an impromptu decision to visit the Wittmers' home. Baby Rolf did not look as healthy as when Hancock visited just a few weeks earlier. "All goes well," Coolidge observed, "but the baby is thin and looks badly."

On the Baroness's advice, the party did not visit Dore and Friedrich.

Coolidge was dissuaded by her tales of the couple's antisocial behavior. They were stingy and disagreeable, obsessed with the idea that their Garden of Eden was being "snatched away." Friedrich would not let his neighbors near his spring, even though it was the best source of water on the island. "Such fanatical jealousy," Coolidge wrote, "creates a situation almost beyond comprehension, but then curious trend of thought is certain to develop in individuals who have chosen so isolated an existence." As for the Baroness, he offered a prediction: "Indeed I am sure it will not be long before her fame would spread abroad, which will bring her a visit from every ship that sails to Galapagos."

•   •   •

With Coolidge's departure, Heinz and Margret found themselves in a desperate situation. The Baroness had established a habit of stealing from them, and now they suspected she had done it again with Coolidge and his party. Her antics were harming the health of their newborn. Heinz did not want to confront the Baroness. Instead, hoping for help, he wrote to Hancock:

February 26, 1933

Dear Mr. Hancock:

You will perhaps remember me when I mention that I am living on Charles Island, near the Caves, and that a baby, now 8 weeks old, belongs to my family. The actions of the pretended "Baroness" Wagner, who lives in our vicinity, are causing me to write this letter.

Recently three gentlemen from Boston visited this island. The "Baroness" begged milk from these gentlemen, giving the reason that she needed it for my baby. She also told them that formerly she had provided this milk from her cows, and as these cows had died since, had contributed condensed milk from her own provisions. This statement is not true. She has not given us a drop of milk for the baby and we have not asked her to beg anything for our child. Probably the

Baroness has used the same trick on all visiting vessels in order to obtain provisions for herself.

Would you kindly let me know whether or not the Baroness has begged from you or your companions also provisions for my baby, in order that I may call her to account, if so. I would appreciate an answer at your earliest convenience.

Yours very truly,
Wittmer

That Sunday, Heinz stopped by Friedo, bringing with him half a hog, per Friedrich's request. In exchange, Friedrich gave Heinz half a pound of sugar—a rather sparing amount, considering the generous supply Hancock had left behind. Still, the three had grown to enjoy each other's company; Dore, in fact, found Heinz "so thoroughly likeable and honorable" that she couldn't fathom his choice of partner. Margret was neither so "well-bred" nor so kind as her husband, Dore had decided. Moreover, she was "quite obviously dazzled by the proximity of the nobility, and hand-in-glove with the Baroness."

Heinz shared his latest observations of the Baroness and her entourage. It appeared that she had welcomed Rudolph back into the fold and into her home, and with his return came a tentative peace. He and Robert had called a truce, and Heinz hadn't heard any of the usual clamoring and shouting. But the Baroness's larceny remained a problem, and he had no good ideas on how to address the issue.

Heinz said goodbye but returned within the hour. He had been down at Black Beach, intending to fish, when he realized that his canoe had vanished. Obviously it hadn't untethered itself and floated away, and neither Hancock nor Coolidge would have had any reason to take it.

"Why don't you ask your neighbor?" Friedrich asked. "She could probably tell you where it is."

When Heinz asked the Baroness about his missing canoe, she said that Dore and Friedrich were behind the theft. Heinz found her so convincing that he hiked back to Friedo at once, but Dore and Friedrich quickly set him straight. "Perhaps it was because he found us so unmoved by this insinuation," Dore wrote, "that Wittmer decided to examine more closely the incidents of all thefts of which he had been the victim." He concluded, ultimately, that the Baroness had indeed stolen everything that had gone missing.

• • •

While Friedrich had striven to maintain his calm, or at least the appearance of it, he now had to concede: the Baroness was a dangerous threat to his own livelihood. It perturbed him that both the American visitors and the Ecuadorian government had fallen for the Baroness's antics; she would become the island's main attraction, buoyed by both the Americans' attention and the Ecuadorians' desire for their tourism dollars. He confided his frustrations to his diary: "She is stupid enough to tell how she manages to get something from the Americans. . . . If you order a hundred corrugated metal sheets in Chatham Island, that makes the best impression on everyone; the governor must be delighted with the growth, flowering, and prosperity of their generous enterprise. . . . If we do not support this nonsensical enterprise, then we are of course selfish, jealous people and enemies of the Ecuadorian boom."

Although the Ecuadorian authorities had never responded to Friedrich's earlier complaints about the Baroness, he agreed to help Heinz draft a letter documenting the incidents of theft. In addition, he reiterated the Baroness's disruptive presence on the island and requested that a medical expert come to Floreana to examine her mental condition. At the moment, he believed that "her infirmity was nothing more serious than acute hysteria," but a more serious diagnosis was certain to come.

• • •

About a week later, on March 8, Dore and Friedrich were sorting papayas in their garden when they spotted a yacht approaching Black Beach. Its bright yellow funnels were instantly familiar: the *Nourmahal*, owned by Vincent Astor, who had just concluded a two-week excursion to the West Indies with his close friend Kermit Roosevelt, as well as Kermit's fifth cousin, the newly elected president Franklin D. Roosevelt. As soon as the *Nourmahal* returned to American shores, where the president had plans to address Britain's war debt to the United States, Astor set out again for the Galápagos, his third trip to the archipelago. This time his guest was not a politician or dignitary but Miss Eleanor Barry, described in press reports as "tall, slim, and very pretty," chosen to accompany Astor because his wife "was not a convert to the sport of yachting." Margret, perhaps jealous of the gifts and attention Astor bestowed upon Dore and Friedrich, had her own take on the millionaire's oceanic jaunts: the *Nourmahal* was a "floating brothel."

Friedrich quickly dressed and started down the path to meet Astor and his crew, while Dore tidied Friedo and fed Burro the donkey. Within the hour the group returned, Friedrich in the lead, pushing a brand-new wheelbarrow Astor had given him. Astor gave both Dore and Burro an affectionate greeting and announced that the pet's new nickname was "Caruso of Floreana" (a reference to the great Italian tenor Enrico Caruso), in honor of the distinctive bray it used solely for announcing visitors. Astor felt comfortable enough to lead the tour of Friedo himself, showing the party the netting-enclosed bedroom, the water pump, the study where Friedrich wrote his philosophy and Dore her essays, the porch that offered an unobstructed view of the sun-stippled ocean and grainy black shore.

After the tour the party sat down to relax. Astor regaled everyone with a story of a letter he'd received—an "extremely hospitable invitation" from the Baroness, urging him to visit the Hacienda Paradiso. Astor remembered how she had tortured his friend Arthur Estampa: ordering him to leave the island, training her gun on him, sending her minions to pursue him all night long. Astor had no interest in visiting the Baroness, despite her suggestive overtures and promise to receive him "in grand style."

At this, his friends protested. If Astor didn't go, then *they* couldn't go— why would he deprive them of a good show? While the men debated, Friedrich slipped away to his study, hoping to draft a quick letter to Hancock before anyone missed him:

Floreana, March 9, 1933

Dear Captain:

Due to the great haste I have to write in German. Kindly excuse my briefness, but there is no other possibility if I want to take advantage of the opportunity of Mr. Astor's visit. . . . He is only here for a short stay and has not made the acquaintance of the Baroness. . . .

Please trust our statements regarding the Baroness. I have just heard that she tried the following maneuver on Mr. Astor. Through [Robert] Philippson she sent a written invitation on board of his yacht, saying that she would entertain him with what the Lord had given her, and that he in turn should give her whatever he considered suitable. This is the new style of her "hotel" . . . of course, Mr. Astor declined to make her acquaintance. . . .

I have much to tell you still, but the time is too short. When shall we receive mail again? There are no prospects as long as the Baroness "reigns." Why does our fate include this trial? And how shall we come out of it?

When Friedrich rejoined the group, he pulled Astor aside and confessed his concerns about the Baroness, insisting that Floreana "wasn't big enough" for all of them.

"The whole thing sounds exactly like a neighborhood quarrel in a suburb," Astor said, but he could see that Friedrich was "terribly sore."

Later, Astor would regret not taking the matter more seriously.

•  •  •

In the morning, after Astor and his party left for Isabela Island, Dore and Friedrich heard a loud shouting coming from the gate. It was Robert Philippson, who didn't bother to wait for an invitation and barged inside their home, stomping through the study, his demeanor so strange that neither Dore nor Friedrich knew how to react. After a few moments of silence, Robert unleashed an outburst so vile that, in Dore's words, "it fairly took our breath away." Clearly they had used their influence to prevent Astor from visiting the Baroness, and they alone were responsible for the insult and embarrassment she felt from such a public rejection. It was only fair that the Baroness get her fair share of whatever gifts and supplies the millionaire had given Friedrich and Dore.

"My dear man," Friedrich said, "you're talking utter nonsense. We are not interested in other people's affairs and it is certainly nothing to us whom Frau von Wagner chooses to invite or who accepts or declines her invitations. I think you'd better go."

Friedrich's calm, measured response only infuriated Robert further, and in that moment he became, to Dore, a stranger: "I should never have thought it possible that this man and the Philippson we knew could be one and the same person. His good-looking features were distorted with rage. He hardly seemed to know what he was saying." When he at last ran out of words, he spun around and faced Friedrich, his fist raised high and ready to swing.

Dore looked from Robert to Friedrich and back again, keeping both men in her sight. Friedrich was growing angrier by the second, and she worried that he would leap to his feet and lunge at the younger man. A few moments passed, and she could sense Friedrich willing himself to calm. "Now quite quietly," Dore saw, "he got up and took Philippson's upraised arm, looking at him so powerfully in the eyes that the younger man, like a cowed animal, wilted before him."

Friedrich led Robert to the gate. Dore followed, watching. The young man walked slowly, each step more reluctant than the last. It seemed as though he could think of nothing more dreadful than returning to the Baroness without any of the gifts she believed belonged to her.

•   •   •

Later that same day, Friedrich went into his workshop and emerged with a machete. Wordlessly, with grim determination, he hacked away at the brush. Dore, observing from the doorway, understood exactly what he was doing. Until that point, tourists on their way to visit the Baroness had to take a trail paralleling Friedo. Now, with a new route, the Friedo path would never have to be used by strangers.

"With such people as these," Friedrich explained to Heinz the following day, "the only thing to do is to give them as little ground as possible. It's really their path I'm making—not ours—and any visitors who are inspired to go to them may now do so without even being seen by us. Perhaps that will give us a little peace in the future."

Heinz countered, arguing that the continued presence of the Baroness on the island would only guarantee the reverse.

The next time Friedrich worked on the new path, he noticed Robert sitting on a stone just off to the side, shoulders slumped, head cradled in both hands, alone in his obvious misery. For a moment, Friedrich considered consoling Robert and speaking to him as a father might to his son. Instead he stood in silence, wondering what might become of Robert as well as Rudolph, his "companion in slavery," and decided he could do nothing for either of them.

Friedrich worked for two more hours, whacking away with his machete, following the burgeoning path. At sundown, returning to Friedo, he found that Robert still sat on the same stone with his head in his hands, and hadn't moved at all.

• • •

A few days later, Robert appeared at Heinz and Margret's home looking for one of the Baroness's new donkeys, which he believed they'd stolen. Robert's suspicions were correct: the animal had been mistreated and was sick, and they were hiding it in the hope that they could restore it to health. He demanded they return the donkey to him, growing so "insolent and abusive," in Margret's words, that Heinz, just like Friedrich, threw him out.

From then on Robert left them alone.

The same could not be said of the Baroness, who, Margret reported, once again "invited Heinz and Dr. Ritter, separately, to play the star role in her wigwam." Heinz forbade Margret to associate with the Baroness in the future, but a part of Margret longed to understand her volatile, mercurial neighbor. She wondered if the trials of island life were slowly eroding the Baroness's spirit and resolve, making her "unhappy, nervous, and moody." This, Margret told herself, was the most likely explanation for the Baroness's "mischief"—as opposed to any innate evil in her character.

# PART III
## Natural Selection

# TWENTY-SIX
# You Don't Know
# the Americans

One day in the spring of 1933, soon after Heinz tossed Robert from their property, a passing ship brought a long-awaited gift: a sack of mail and packages from friends and family in Europe. Heinz and Harry tore through the boxes, unwrapping books and seeds and razors and cigars and new clothes for the baby, calling, "It's come, it's all come! Hooray, hooray!" Reading through the letters, Margret found herself alternately smiling and weeping, happy reports of birthdays and milestones interspersed with darker news. The Gestapo raided private homes and arrested thousands of German citizens without cause. The physicist Albert Einstein, whose home was among those raided, so feared the growing persecution of Jewish people that he moved to Belgium with his wife. At Dachau, in Bavaria, a concentration camp opened for "enemies of the German people."

Heinz lit a cigar, sat down at the table, and started paging through a stack of newspaper clippings. As he read, Margret noticed his worried expression.

"What is it?" she asked.

"Listen to this," he said, and read the headlines: "'Revolution on Pacific Island' . . . 'Woman Proclaims Herself Empress' . . . 'Local Opposition Imprisoned.'"

Margret picked up another newspaper and read aloud: "An Austrian Baroness, with her private army of aristocratic freebooters, has established her rule over the small Pacific island of Floreana. Dr. Friedrich Ritter, the former Berlin dentist, who opposed her reign of terror, has been captured and put in chains."

Heinz wondered if these fanciful reports were generated by Valdivieso, the Baroness's old contractor, or if the Baroness had the idea herself and ordered Robert to leak them.

"But if it's a publicity stunt, what's the point?" Margret asked. "A reign of terror doesn't sound very like a peaceful paradise. Won't it put people off coming here?"

Heinz laughed and said, "You don't know the Americans yet."

•   •   •

On his next visit to Friedo, Heinz brought two documents he'd found pinned on the barrel at Post Office Bay. How long they'd been there was unclear, he said, and any number of American tourists could have seen them. Dore read the first notice, which was a long, formally worded complaint that she and Friedrich had "defamed" the Baroness, and that Friedrich had even refused to attend to the Baroness's toothache when she needed it; of course, Friedrich had never received any such request. The second notice contained equally formal allegations against Heinz, claiming that he'd trespassed onto her property and that he'd also falsely accused her, her "husband" Robert, and her "comrade" Rudolph of receiving goods on Heinz's behalf and failing to deliver them.

There was more, Heinz said. The Baroness claimed that Hancock had secretly given her a draft of his new book under the condition that she tell no one about it. The "biggest idea" in this book, according to the Baroness, was that Dore was "soiled"—in both body and reputation. Dore immediately registered her concern in a letter to Hancock: "Her hate turned against me . . . she believes she had the right to dirty my repute. . . . The whole affair is very painful and I [will] suffer if visitors come who speak at first with this woman and then look for dirt and the soiled Dore and the unhospitality [sic] of the Ritters."

And then there were the Baroness's nicknames for Dore and Friedrich, monikers she claimed were commonly used throughout Ecuador. Friedrich was the "toothless Adam in slippers" and "insane Buddha." Dore was known as "Humpelstiltskin with the dirty ruff"—a play on the Brothers Grimm fairy tale. But the worst infraction, in Friedrich's eyes, was a story the Baroness recounted about a visit to Friedo—a story she presumably shared with all the American tourists. On this day, the Baroness claimed, she had failed to call out the requisite warning, and Friedrich and Dore did not have time to dress before she barged through their gate. As the couple stood naked, the Baroness let her gaze wander up and down Friedrich's physique and declared, "Oh, yes, you are really small."

With each new insult, Friedrich privately thought about murdering the Baroness. These fantasies recurred with an alarming frequency until they all but consumed him.

. . .

At the same time, the Baroness worked to bolster her own reputation among American visitors, Hancock in particular. She wrote to the captain about plans for her hotel and asked if he might help her obtain the following items: gutters and roofing rails; twelve pairs of men's Keds sneakers, size 9.5; six pairs of women's Keds sneakers, size 6.5; one glass cutter, one scythe, one pickax, and three hunting knives; a variety of small fruit trees in pots; three large bottles of Bain de Champagne Caron perfume from Paris; four colonies of bees with four American queens; and eleven yards of pink silk for underwear.

This list was accompanied by a letter in which she promised to "catch a flamingo" for him and implored him to ignore any rumors he might have heard about her behavior on the island—rumors, of course, that she herself had concocted:

Trusting this finds you in good health, and hoping you do not believe all the fantastic stories in the newspapers about the "Pirate Queen," I beg to remain,

Yours very truly
Baroness Wagner

• • •

Dore noticed that the Baroness's antics were taking their toll on Friedrich. He grew increasingly sullen and angry and more consistently violent; the same man who once refused to eat potatoes because they "had to be dragged from the earth by force" now did not hesitate to beat her. He even struck her in front of Heinz.

Tortured by this struggle, Dore wrote another story featuring her alter ego Gertrud and sent it to Hancock. Titled "Revolution-Evolution," it suggested that her growing defiance was a response—perhaps the only response, at present, she could make—to Friedrich's rage. It read, in part,

> She had dreamed to elevate the man to be master of her soul, but fell instead into the hands of a tyrannical pedant; she had dreamed of being a disciple willing to sacrifice, but it was demanded of her to become an obedient and humble servant.
>
> But Gertrud would not let herself become enslaved.

Dore tried to remind herself that her purpose on Floreana, and in life, was to support Friedrich's genius and assist in disseminating his philosophy throughout the world. And yet she knew she deserved a life free from the erratic whims of a man. As Friedrich's darkest urges came to the fore, so, too, did Dore's desire to challenge him.

# TWENTY-SEVEN
# Vague and Ominous Presentiments

One afternoon, after an absence of several months, Rudolph Lorenz appeared at Friedo alone. He hadn't visited since the Baroness had welcomed him back, and Dore took this as a sign he'd again been banished. He looked ill, even more so than the last time she'd seen him. He told Dore he had come from Post Office Bay, which she saw as a lie: his backpack was empty, and his shoes did not look as though they'd marched through the lava fields.

"The Baroness has no idea I'm here," he said.

"And I expect you'd better not let her find out, either, or you'll be having trouble."

"That won't matter a damn to me anymore," he said, and began talking in detail about the Hacienda Paradiso, hinting that the garden's current productivity was lower than expected, and they were suffering a dearth of fruits and vegetables. Dore realized the Baroness had sent Rudolph hoping Dore might take pity on him and send him back with offerings from Friedo's garden. Disgusted, she offered him a meal to eat as he visited, but resolved to give him nothing for the Baroness.

When Friedrich asked Rudolph how he was doing, he insisted he had improved and in fact no longer wished to leave Floreana. This, too, Dore recognized as a lie: "It was clear to see that he was far from happy, but now his whole manner expressed a terrible resignation, as of one who knew himself caught in the toils of misery from which he could no longer even make an effort to free himself."

The Baroness implored visitors to pay no mind to rumors about Rudolph Lorenz. He was not abused and miserable, no matter what they'd heard; he was merely questioning his commitment to island life. One guest, a nineteen-year-old man from Massachusetts, defended her. "It was so satisfactory an agreement and they were so friendly about everything," he said, "that I do not believe anything could have arisen that would have led to violence."

But others sensed that the Baroness's peculiar charm could—at any moment, and with no warning—yield to a deadly fury. One visitor, arriving late at Post Office Bay, spent his first night in the Casa. In the morning he awakened to the sight of the Baroness staring at him, a revolver strapped outside her silk dress, looking "far more dangerous" than anyone else he'd encountered in his travels. This first impression did not leave him. The Baroness, he later reflected, "had a profound contempt for humanity."

•　•　•

On May 30, 1933, the governor of the Galápagos, Major Luis Paredes, arrived on Floreana with an escort of seven soldiers. After nearly eight months, the Ecuadorian government was finally responding to Friedrich's complaints about the Baroness, including the incident involving Arthur Estampa, when he showed up at Friedo, bloody and frantic, convinced that the woman would kill him.

Governor Paredes called first at Friedo. He assured Dore and Friedrich that they could live on Floreana for as long as they wished, and listened to Friedrich's litany of concerns about the Baroness. The governor then visited the Wittmers, where Heinz also detailed his problems with the Baroness. Next, at the Hacienda Paradiso, the governor learned that the Baroness had gone hunting for flamingos at one of the lagoons, as she hoped to build a zoo to lure more Americans to her hotel. When she returned, she provided her own version of recent events, telling Paredes of her grandiose plans to develop tourism in the Galápagos.

Afterward, during Heinz's weekly visit, he and Dore and Friedrich compared notes. The governor had granted 50 acres to their two households, but the Baroness received four square miles, which equaled a staggering 2,560 acres. She had also won her battle with the Wittmers over the use of their spring and was free to bathe in the source of their drinking water anytime she wished. Dore claimed that the Baroness had obtained these privileges "at the price of a more than Arabian night." The Baroness had so charmed Paredes, in fact, that he invited her to vacation with him for a few weeks on Chatham Island. To reporters, he described the Baroness as a woman "in possession of a high level of refinement and mental balance."

This alarmed Friedrich. What if the governor showed the Baroness the letter he had written after the horrifying incident with Estampa? Friedrich had called the Baroness "nothing but an imaginary Princess," "spiritually unbalanced," a "megalomaniac," and a "crazy woman" who needed to be observed in a sanatorium. He could only imagine what sort of revenge she would exact. According to Margret, he again took his anxiety out on Dore. She was, Margret wrote, "struck hard on the mouth by her doctor."

Emboldened by her victory, and eager to cultivate her burgeoning fame, the Baroness composed a letter of her own, sent it to a friend in Paris, and asked him to share it with newspapers around the world. Anyone unfamiliar with the Baroness's behavior might see her as a victim—a woman who found it necessary to restore her good name and set the record straight.

The letter read, in part,

Newspapers came with the most unbelievable reports, letters from strangers, from journalists, even offers from a union of young people who want to line up under my banners to defend me. . . . We are nothing but modern hermits. My "Empire" is forty hectares of land, twenty of which belong to Robert Philippson. My "crown" are the numerous orange blossoms that fall from the trees on my head and cover my writing paper and the table and smell so lovely that they make me forget the stupidity of the world. My "scepter" is the spade and the hoe, with which tools I try to turn this tangle of lemons into a fertile vegetable garden with European and local fruits and vegetables. My "cannons" are a hunting rifle, a long rifle No. 22 (a revolver), a Browning-Pistol, thus not that many that they could darken the sun. However, they do not miss their target. . . .

I am absolutely not a belligerent heroine and I am on the best of

terms with the Ecuadorian laws. . . . Now you ask yourself who
invented this whole saga. The inventor of this fairy tale is Dr. Friedrich
Ritter, who is considered to be completely insane in this country. The
purpose of this fairy tale, pursued by Ritter, was to lure sensational
Americans to Post Office Bay to earn a living from canned meat, rice,
etc. . . .

I would be very grateful for the refutation of Ritter's lying
sensational stories. . . . Please say my thanks to all the youthful heroes
and the numerous offers [of marriage]. Even the most tempting cannot
bewitch me.

As Margret summed up the situation, "The Baroness figured, 'What the
old tooth plumber can do, I can do ten times better.'"

• • •

On June 7, the Baroness returned from her vacation with the governor,
bringing with her two dogs, ten chickens, a healthy donkey and foals, and
Knud Arends, the handsome Danish man and friend of the ill-fated Captain Bruun. Arends had been working as the governor's interpreter but
was now employed by the Baroness, describing his position as "master of
the hunt." His first task was to visit the Wittmers and warn Heinz that one
of the Baroness's donkeys had escaped and he should be careful not to
shoot it. Margret liked him right away and called him the Baroness's "masculine assistant." He enjoyed gossip, and told Margret that people thought
Friedrich settled on the island for the sole reason of finding notoriety and
a market for his writing.

Dore was disappointed Arends did not stop by Friedo, but she guessed
the reason, which Heinz confirmed: "The Baroness had found another
slave, and for every member of that household, free or bound, Friedo was
forbidden territory."

From Rudolph, who now made regular visits to Friedo, she learned
that Arends had been accepted as the Baroness's "new lover" and that
Rudolph took on the majority of his workload. At night, the Baroness
allowed Arends a rest, and Robert resumed his role as her "husband."
Hearing this, Dore felt sorry for Robert. While Rudolph had followed

the Baroness to Floreana hoping to recoup his money, Robert was motivated purely by romance. "He had lost himself entirely to love," Dore believed.

The mere presence of Arends sent Robert into violent outbursts, for which the Baroness punished him savagely, beating him with her whip and even carving a flaming welt across his face that was visible for days. She threw a bowl of scalding soup into his eyes and left on a hunting excursion without waiting to see if he had sustained any injury. Robert retaliated against the one person who couldn't dominate him: Rudolph. He treated the weaker man as he wished he could treat Arends, beating and starving him and denying him water.

Nonetheless, the Baroness enjoyed a steady flow of visitors. No longer willing to meet tourists in her garden, she commanded one of her men to receive them first and determine if they were worthy of entrance. If deemed sufficient, they were led into her silk-lined room, where she reclined on a divan, wearing an abbreviated outfit, her riding crop in hand.

One visitor described "a woman of about forty, of a somewhat extravagant appearance and behaving like a girl in her teens. Her skipping gait and gay movements were those of a flapper, dressed in shorts." Once inside the Baroness's private room, it was as though "the Queen of Sheba granted a hearing." She put on a show, affecting a "dreamy" demeanor and ordering "Kiddy" (Robert) to serve the tea. Rudolph stood "visible in the kitchen corner, a pale and thin figure like a put-out candle, afraid of making the slightest noise." The Baroness was, in a way, embodying the persona of her literary hero, Lord Henry Wotton in *The Picture of Dorian Gray*—a skillful manipulator of the weak and a hedonist who recognized the evil that can lurk in the heart of beautiful things.

Sometimes, Rudolph shared, the Baroness would be surprised by visitors arriving at inopportune times. Dore enjoyed the image of this haughty creature caught doing laundry in an old housedress, with mud-speckled legs and messy hair. But the Baroness recovered quickly, Dore lamented, and "could afford to treat the accident with humor, for a greater transformation between the laundress and the empress could hardly be imagined." Even the sight of the Baroness's platinum hair being spoiled by dark roots (her supply of hair dye had run out) brought Dore only a fleeting joy; she had to admit that the brunette hair suited her just as well. It was interesting to Dore, all the same, to watch the Baroness's journey back to the most natural representation of herself, the gradual erasure of her own creation.

.    .    .

At the end of August, Trygve Nuggerud, the skipper of a fishing boat from Santa Cruz, brought a young journalist named Werner Boeckmann to Floreana. After anchoring at Black Beach, Boeckmann hiked to Friedo, where Dore and Friedrich gave him the customary tour and invited him to spend the night; in the morning he would go off to visit the Wittmers and the Baroness.

Late in the afternoon, walking through the garden, Dore was shocked to see Arends by the fence—how brave of him to defy the Baroness's orders to avoid Friedo. She rushed over to greet him but his response was muted, as though he were terrified at being caught in her presence. He asked, was it Trygve Nuggerud who had put in at Black Beach that afternoon? Dore said it was and then chided him for not visiting earlier; he should come inside and stay awhile.

Before Arends could respond, Dore heard a feeble cough coming from the bushes just beyond the fence. She stepped closer and there, between the leaves, she saw the Baroness, arms folded and eyes narrowed—an expression so sinister that it sent a chill down Dore's back. Arends turned away, heeding the warning, and followed her down the path.

To Dore, Floreana had always carried a sense of menace. Throughout her time on the island she had felt it everywhere: in the looming towers of Post Office Bay, in the lash of volcanic fire against the sky, in the tales of pirates and tyrants, in the arrival of new settlers with unknown intentions, in the fear that she was trapped in a failed experiment of her own. "As I turned and went back to our guests," she wrote, "I knew that dire events were on the way, violence and death—and for the first time vague and ominous presentiments which I had felt before crystallized into a feeling of murder."

# TWENTY-EIGHT
## "Accident"

The following morning, after breakfast with Dore and Friedrich, Werner Boeckmann set off to visit the Hacienda Paradiso, where he and the Baroness dined on two chickens and had a spirited chat. Afterward, hoping to visit the Wittmers, he asked the Baroness for the best route. She offered some vague directions to the caves but warned that some recent flooding would make it impossible for him to reach his destination; perhaps he shouldn't even bother to try. Undeterred, Boeckmann eventually made it to the Wittmers'. They showed off baby Rolf, who now had two teeth. Boeckmann delivered some letters that had been waiting at Post Office Bay and shared stories about his visit with the Baroness. Talking with Margret and Heinz, he realized that the Baroness had intentionally given him the wrong directions, sending him to a different set of caves.

• • •

After the journalist sailed off, Margret and Heinz noticed some mysterious activity at the Hacienda Paradiso. During the daytime, it was quiet, but at night the place exploded with the commotion of trees being chopped and wood gathered, all to the backdrop of raucous laughter and song. With daybreak the perfect silence returned, continuing the pattern. Even sixteen-year-old Harry noticed.

"I bet she's looking for buried treasure," he said. "After all, there's sup-posed to be some all over the island, isn't there?"

"That's what the inhabitants of the other islands say," Heinz said. "The stories of buried treasure have gone on for hundreds of years, and I dare say there's something at the bottom of them. But vast quantities of pirate gold—that's the sort of legend you get about any island like this."

"All the same," Harry said, "I expect Boeckmann showed the Baroness some secret map giving just where the treasure lies."

"Could be," Margret said. "Your guess is as good as mine for anything to do with the Baroness. Only if it *was* treasure, why didn't she start searching before?"

A few weeks later, on October 1, the nocturnal disturbances suddenly ceased.

•  •  •

On that same day, Dore watched a schooner coast toward Black Beach. It was Boeckmann, back for another visit, this time traveling with a friend, Joseph Linde. "I think I have never seen a handsomer young man," Dore said of Linde. "I took his age to be about the latter twenties. He was very tall and had wavy blond hair and the bluest eyes imaginable. It was clear to see what would occur when the Baroness set eyes upon him." Yet Dore was hopeful that Linde would not reciprocate the interest, as he seemed "so frank and normal" and much stronger than the "weaklings" the Baroness seemed to attract. The two men were accompanied by an Ecuadorian sol-dier, presumably for protection.

The guests stayed overnight at Friedo. In the morning, they announced their plans for a visit with the Baroness and promised to be back in time for dinner.

•  •  •

At the Hacienda Paradiso, the trio found a scene of domestic bliss, with Rudolph and Robert sewing clothing and Knud Arends working in the garden. The Baroness was at the washtub, and Boeckmann clocked her change of expression as she watched Linde approach, appraising him from head to toe. Hoping to thwart the Baroness's overtures, Boeckmann introduced Linde as his brother-in-law, making it clear that he was not romantically available.

The Baroness was undeterred.

She insisted they join her on a hunting expedition to the pampa. They would not be disappointed, she assured them, as she was an expert marksman.

Boeckmann worried about being late for dinner at Friedo, but he did not want to be rude. He, Linde, the soldier, the Baroness, Arends, and Robert set off; Rudolph, as usual, stayed behind to carry out the Baroness's orders. Arends and the soldier had rifles, while the Baroness carried a shotgun. Boeckmann and Linde, who had not expected to hunt on this trip, were armed only with revolvers.

Boeckmann, walking side by side with Arends, focused on the Baroness's maneuverings. She walked a few steps ahead, keeping pace with Linde. Boeckmann could hear her voice, amplifying and sharpening. It was clear that Linde was not engaging with her. Boeckmann sensed a shift in her mood, and it unsettled him. He cocked his ear to listen closer. She began to speak of the Ritters, insisting that Linde stay with her instead of at Friedo; she was a much more skilled hostess. But she stopped speaking when they came upon the plain.

The Baroness took charge, dictating where everyone should stand: Boeckmann, Linde, Arends, and the soldier were in one group; Robert was stationed alone some distance away; and she herself stood diagonally from Robert. The cattle clustered together in a compact herd about one hundred feet away, equally distant from all of them.

The Baroness raised an arm, signaling permission to shoot. Two shots rang out.

A body collapsed on the plain.

• • •

In preparation for dinner, Dore had been working all afternoon, gathering vegetables and slicing fruits, intent on doing her "kitchen's best" for Boeckmann, Linde, and the Ecuadorian soldier. Hours passed; the sun dipped lower. Friedrich emerged from his study, where he had been writing.

A year ago she would not have worried, as it was so easy then to get lost on the way to Friedo, but now, with Friedrich's clear network of tracks and paths, even a dull bit of moonlight made the journey an easy one. Still, the men did not come. She wondered, with some annoyance, if they had decided to stay instead with the Baroness.

Unable to wait any longer, she and Friedrich sat down for dinner. Afterward she spread three mattresses across the floor, just in case the men returned. Friedrich retreated to his study to write in his diary, obsessing, as he often did, about the Baroness. He even connected her behavior to Japan's recent withdrawal from the League of Nations. "The Baroness is going to drive us away from here, but I would defend myself," he wrote. "If the fears of the pessimistic Americans were to materialize, one day the Japanese would export us from here to turn the islands into fortresses. So nowhere is there peace, least of all at the 'end of the world.'"

Later that night, Dore was awakened by pounding footsteps. She roused Friedrich and they rushed outside without bothering to light the lantern. At the door she found Boeckmann in a panic. "It was more than the pale moonlight that made him look so ghastly," Dore saw. "He had obviously been running all the way from wherever he had been and his face wore an expression of desperate alarm."

Boeckmann gasped his words: "An accident! There's been an accident!"

Friedrich asked if the accident involved Linde.

"No," Boeckmann said. "It's Arends! He's been shot!"

"Shot?" Dore asked. "How?"

"We were out hunting." He turned to Friedrich. "Will you come, Doctor?"

Friedrich was already packing his bag with various instruments and bandages and salves. He hesitated a moment and then said, "That household doesn't usually consult me. Were you asked to come?"

"She didn't want me to," Boeckmann said. "He's been shot to blazes, so the less she says the better. For God's sake come on, Doctor, though I shouldn't wonder if it's too late already."

•   •   •

On the pampa, Friedrich rushed to Arends, still sprawled on the ground. The Baroness hovered nearby, as though awaiting a verdict. Friedrich de-

The pirate caves
on Floreana

Dore shows off
her flowerpots.

Friedrich Ritter and Dore Strauch at Friedo

Friedrich demonstrates his shower.

Dore and Friedrich
aboard the *Velero III*

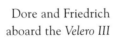

Captain Hancock with Dore, Friedrich, and Burro

Dore plays with Fleck.

Friedrich works on
his philosophy.

The Wittmer family: Margret, Rolf, Harry, and Heinz

Margret tutors Harry.

The Wittmers' home

Friedrich, Hancock, Margret, and Harry at Friedo

The Hacienda Paradiso

The Baroness
waters her garden.

Hancock and his crew visit the Hacienda Paradiso.

The Baroness with Rudolph Lorenz (*top*) and Robert Philippson (*left*)

Rudolph, exiled from
the Hacienda Paradiso

Friedrich and the Baroness

The Baroness in her boudoir

The Baroness and Robert shoot
*The Empress of Floreana.*

Dore at Friedo, December 1934

Dore is questioned by Ecuadorian officials.

Rudolph at Post Office Bay

A tragic discovery on
Marchena Island

termined that the bullet had nicked his arm and pierced through his abdomen, and he gave Arends a warning: he must stay in place and very still, as any movement could invite infection.

The Baroness began playing nurse, ordering Robert to fetch whatever Friedrich needed, and declaring she would not leave Arends's side until a boat took him to the mainland. Friedrich ignored her and asked the others what happened.

They took turns speaking, recalling where they were standing and what they had heard and seen. The Baroness interrupted, insisting that the wayward shot had been fired by either the soldier or Boeckmann, but Friedrich stopped her.

"That is impossible," he said. "Not only did this shot come from a greater distance, but the angle at which it struck does not coincide with the positions of either of these two men. Moreover, I can tell by the nature of the wounds that they were caused neither by a revolver nor by a rifle."

The Baroness did not argue. Instead, she pushed her gun at Friedrich and began to cry, begging him to take it, vowing to never shoot again. Then she knelt by the bloodied Arends and said, "Darling, forgive me."

Friedrich did not say the rest of his theory aloud, which he both recorded in his diary and shared with Dore: Based on the men's accounts of the incident, the Baroness's target had not been Arends. At the last moment Arends had switched positions, moving into the line of fire, taking a bullet that had been intended for Linde—the man who had spurned her affections. The Baroness had wished to wound him as she wounded wild animals, tending them until they transformed into domesticated pets. She'd hoped to nurse Linde back to health, convincing him he could depend on her, earning his loyalty and love.

The next morning, as Arends lay bloodied and miserable on a cot a few feet away, the Baroness wrote Captain Hancock a letter.

Floreana, The 2nd of Oct. 1933

Dear Sir:

In contrary of what I asked you in my last letter, please don't make any purchases on my account. An accident has happened, the score of my sufferings seems not yet complete. A young man, Mr. Arends, who works and lives with us, has been hurt in the stomach by a bullet, how we don't know, as the shot parted in the opposite direction from where the young man was standing. Dr. Ritter who was kind enough to attend him, says that he is out of danger, yet I prefer that Mr. Arends goes to Guayaquil in order to be roentgenized and if necessary the bullet extracted. As this will take all the rest of my resources, we cannot think of our comfort but have to do all to get Mr. Arends right again.

Hoping that this letter finds you in the best of health, with my kind regards to Mr. Swett, I remain,

Yours very respectfully,
Baroness Wagner

•  •  •

Friedrich, at the same time, synthesized his thoughts in an essay titled "A 'Hunting Accident' at Floreana":

This woman at the threshold of the "dangerous age" was desirous of possessing a young, blond man. . . . A little 6 mm. bullet shot into his thigh would be enough to detain him momentarily . . . [but] the bullet had not obeyed the command. . . . What did this woman have to do with dumb, erring bullets! She must simulate grief, a pure theatrical grief would have to bridge the tension of embarrassment. Tears and kisses of make believe despair covered the face of the wounded, a help-less youth in the claws of a beast of prey.

Friedrich gave the essay to the Ecuadorian soldier to mail from Guaya-quil, and hoped it would reach Hancock before his next visit to Floreana. The captain needed to know that the Baroness seemed more unstable and dangerous than ever.

•  •  •

Arends stayed with the Baroness as he waited for transport to Guayaquil, while Boeckmann, the soldier, and Linde stayed at Friedo. For Dore, the situation had become untenable; she feared that the Baroness might arrive at any moment to target Linde again. Every morning Robert Philippson appeared at the gate to give Friedrich an update on Arends's condition, while Dore hid inside, behind curtains, hoping to avoid him. He would insist that his "wife" had been aiming at a calf, and he couldn't understand how she missed her target.

In the afternoons, Friedrich hiked to the Hacienda Paradiso for another medical check, leaving Dore to contend with the complaints of her three guests. The Ecuadorian soldier knew that the authorities favored the Baroness, and if she wanted to place the blame on him, there was little he could do. Boeckmann berated himself for bringing Linde and setting the tragedy into motion, while Linde was bitter and vengeful. "I wish I'd seen what she was up to," he told Dore. "I'd have shot at her myself."

At the end of the week, help finally came from Guayaquil. When the officers arrived at the Hacienda Paradiso, Friedrich fashioned a stretcher for Arends by tying a mattress to a ladder. Officers informed the Baroness that one member of her household had to accompany Arends on the trip; she chose Rudolph, a decision that seemed to please him. Dressed in his best suit, he set off for Black Beach right away.

A few hours later, the others joined him: Friedrich, Boeckmann, Linde, the officers, the Baroness, and Robert, all surrounding Arends on the stretcher. As they carried Arends to the boat, an officer turned to the Baroness.

"Which of these two men was witness to the shooting?" the officer asked, motioning to Rudolph and Robert.

The Baroness admitted it was Robert.

"Then he is to come with us."

The Baroness insisted that she could not manage without Robert; she would send him to Guayaquil later if need be, but she truly could not spare him at the moment. She seemed wild and desperate, begging for Robert to stay, and Boeckmann and Linde suspected a dark reason for her behavior: after all the abuse she'd meted out to Rudolph, she was now terrified to be alone with him.

The officers denied her request.

# TWENTY-NINE
# A Wicked Plan

In November, the Child Welfare League sent a telegram to President Franklin D. Roosevelt urging him to address the growing crisis of children suffering from the Depression. By the league's estimation, more than 600,000 minors were now living in almshouses alongside "derelict old persons" and the "sick and mentally deficient." New York's citizens celebrated the landslide election of Mayor Fiorello La Guardia and the imminent repeal of Prohibition. The city's bootleggers prepared to compete with legitimate liquor dealers, filling the Hudson River with "whisky ships" bound for St. Pierre or Bimini, where they would buy booze in bulk and undersell it by 25 to 50 percent back in the city. On the West Coast, Hollywood—which the year prior had adopted the slogan "The Hell with Depression!"—was now in the throes of it; movies were perceived as an indulgence that had to be rationed or abandoned altogether, and more than eight thousand of the country's twenty-three thousand theaters were closed. Those who could still afford movie tickets flocked to see *I'm No Angel,* the latest release of Mae West, whose voluptuous figure, in this era of deprivation, became aspirational. Before filming, she admitted, she liked to "fatten up," eating creamed chicken on buttered toast, lobster Newburg, and chocolate cream cake.

Nearby, in Los Angeles, Captain Hancock, untouched by the Depression, busied himself with the reels of photographs taken during his Galápagos excursions. There were hundreds of them, depicting the Floreana settlers in various activities and moods: Dore and Friedrich lounging on Friedo's porch; the Baroness and Robert Philippson, sitting side by side on a rock; Rudolph Lorenz, alone and smiling, next to a spiky bush; a close-up of the Baroness's Minton china plates spread across her table; Heinz and Harry and Margret, with Rolf in her arms, on the steps leading to their home; Hancock himself and Charles Swett, the Baroness's favorite crew member, strolling through her garden.

Interest in Hancock's travels was so high that he embarked on a tour of forty California cities where every venue was packed. After performing a concert with the *Velero* ensemble (with Hancock playing cello), he gave a slideshow lecture titled "Strange Lands and Life of Tropic Seas," featuring all of the rare specimens he'd encountered—the birds that can't fly and fish that can't swim, the iguana with the rudimentary third eye, the vege-table "hold-overs" from prehistoric times, the settlers who came from afar with a utopian dream.

Hancock also prepared for his next expedition to the islands, sched-uled to depart December 30, 1933, with a crew of twelve scientists and a Hollywood producer named Emery Johnson. A director and celebrated silent film star of the 1920s, Johnson, his career fading, agreed to join Hancock on the trip and assist in the filming and production of *The Em-press of Floreana*, a movie that would star the Baroness. The plot, inspired by an outlandish new story circulating in the press, featured a newlywed couple stranded at sea after a violent storm. Over the course of several days, their lifeboat drifted toward Floreana. As they approached the shore, a group of men rushed toward them with weapons brandished. They bound the couple with rope and led them to a woman dressed in silk shorts and a gauzy blouse, a revolver slung around her waist.

"I am Baroness Wagner de Bosquet," the Baroness purportedly said. "I am the Queen on this island, and you are my prisoners. What are you doing here?" Without waiting for a response, she banished them back to sea without food or water or even an oar to help them row. If they weren't preoccupied with eating, drinking, or rowing, the Baroness explained, they would have more time for sex.

Even if the story weren't true—with the Baroness, one never knew—

Hancock believed it would make for a sensational short action film. He would even allow the Baroness to co-author the script.

•  •  •

As they awaited Hancock's visit (and his numerous gifts), the Floreana settlers contended with a brutal dry season. For months not one drop of rain had fallen, and the landscape was pocked with the bodies of dead animals. The Wittmers' spring had so depleted that they used it only for essentials and worried it might dry up entirely. The situation at Friedo was even bleaker, and Friedrich confessed to Heinz that he would be forced to gather and distill the ocean water if rain did not come soon.

To add to the Wittmers' troubles, Heinz developed a tooth abscess that was so agonizing he had trouble rising from bed. Margret forced herself to visit Friedo, hoping that Friedrich would be kind enough to help. Unfortunately, according to Margret, she was intercepted by Dore.

"Dr. Ritter can't do anything for that," Dore told her. "You must just see how to cope with it yourselves."

Margret retreated without a fight, but her neighbor's cruelty was not easily forgotten. "Dore did not have pity," she later said. "She was very hard."

The Baroness, meanwhile, seemed to go out of her way to encounter Margret and Heinz. He was struck by the Baroness's frazzled disposition, the way her nerves "seemed shattered." She ranted and rambled about the various ways that island life had failed her. During these encounters, Margret recorded, the Baroness wore "a most unusual garb—something too skimpy to be called even a ballet skirt. Moreover, her postures were so vulgar and her remarks so unequivocal that Heinz was glad to hurry and leave this aristocrat."

The turmoil at the Hacienda Paradiso had increased in both frequency and intensity; Margret could hear every thrash and shouted word. Rudolph resumed his habit of showing up at their home—looking, she thought, "like a small child," crying about the Baroness. "She blames me for everything that goes wrong with her," Rudolph confided, and added the Baroness had begged Captain Hancock to take her to Hollywood.

Strange, Margret thought: the Baroness continued to transport her possessions from Post Office Bay, and yet Rudolph claimed she hoped to abandon the island.

•   •   •

One morning, as Dore worked in the garden, Friedrich came to her.

"The Baroness and Lorenz are here," he said.

"What do they want?" Dore asked. "Must we see them?"

"They're standing at the gate. I haven't asked them in, and I don't want
to. They've brought us some gifts, I suppose to thank me for looking after
Arends, but I don't wish to accept the things or have anything more to do
with those people."

Without another word he walked away, leaving Dore alone to decide
what to do. This, she realized, was the first time in four years that Friedrich
had refused to engage with a visitor, a refusal that seemed, on some level,
to wound him.

Dore felt no such guilt about whom she allowed into her home, and
turned to follow Friedrich into the house. Yet she couldn't stop herself
from glancing back toward the gate: there they stood, the Baroness and
poor, beleaguered Rudolph, balancing a large pumpkin on his thin arms.
Dore turned away.

The next time she looked out to the gate she saw the pumpkin smashed
on the ground, its bright entrails spattered all around.

•   •   •

A few days later Dore's donkey, Burro, went missing. Each night she looked
out for her pet, hoping to hear his bray and his steps along the path, but
neither came.

One afternoon, walking to their orange grove, she and Friedrich heard
the Baroness's voice.

"Dr. Ritter," she called. "There's been a stray donkey at the Hacienda
lately. I wonder if it could be yours. Of course he's done a little work for us,
but you surely won't mind that, will you?"

Dore heard malice in her voice.

"Just turn him loose, then," Friedrich said. "If it's Burro, he'll come back home again. He knows the way."

When they returned to Friedo, Burro was there, but he stood alone in his pen, shabby and defeated, too exhausted even to greet Dore. Examining him closely, she saw his skin was raw and scabbed from the friction of tight ropes. She spent the next few days tending to his wounds and then let him roam free again; she could not bear to tie him up and keep him from the pampa.

He resumed his usual routine, back and forth between the pampa and Friedo, until one night he failed to appear. Dore listened for his footsteps, for the click of his corral gate, but never heard those sounds again.

•　　•　　•

Even Margret, who prided herself on her pragmatism and resilience, now felt threatened on the island, and wanted to put some distance between her family and the Baroness. Heinz and Harry set out to explore the eastern side of Floreana; if they found a suitable spring, they would move right away. After several attempts, Heinz failed to penetrate the thick mass of vegetation. He called it the "east problem," and grew desperate to solve it as soon as possible.

The Baroness continued to prove that such a move was necessary. One Sunday afternoon, while Margret and Heinz were in the lemon groves, a wild cow emerged from the trees. The animal worked itself into a rage and charged straight toward Margret. She was so gripped with terror that she felt powerless to move. When the beast was just feet away, Heinz at last shot it square in the head. Deeply shaken, she took to her bed for two full weeks.

The incident frightened Heinz, too, sharpening his vigilance. One night, he heard the clicking of an animal's nails against the steps outside their home. He opened the door, fired a shot, and then realized that the intruder was not a predator but a donkey. Walking around the grounds, he discovered that the gate that connected his property to the Baroness's had been opened; only a human hand could unlatch it. He knew, from his visits to Friedo, that Dore's donkey was missing, and realized what had happened.

The Baroness had deliberately let Burro onto his property, knowing he would kill it.

Heinz confessed his error to Margret, who was distressed by the potential repercussions; they did not need any fresh animosity with their neighbors. "It was a wicked plan," she wrote in her diary, "to stir up strife between us and the Ritters."

She and Heinz buried the animal and hoped the accident would remain their secret. On Christmas Day, still feeling guilty, Heinz lured their own pet, a turtle named Isidor, into a large sack and regifted her to Dore. She wasn't fooled. "The gift," she wrote, "convinced me that Wittmer had willingly or unwillingly been implicated in my Burro's disappearance." From then Dore's feelings toward Heinz soured, and she wondered what else he might be willing to hide.

# THIRTY
# Strange Satanic Moods

One of the first sights the *Velero* crew witnessed upon reaching the Galápagos was that of two marine iguanas in mid-coitus. The men were so transfixed they stopped to watch, with the zoologist Fred Ziesenhenne breathlessly recording the scene: "The male had the female by the nape of her neck with his mouth and held on working closer every time she moved until finally by sliding to one side he got his tail under hers and she sort of turned so the bilobed penis could be inserted. He finally made contact and after stroking for several minutes reached the climax and released his hold of her and sort of paralyzed and limp lay still and exhausted while the female crawled from beneath him he lay motionless for five minutes with his penis exposed and only moved after I had hit him several times with the net."

After all that, the iguana was easy to capture.

• • •

Three days later, on January 17, 1934, the *Velero* anchored at Black Beach. There was a brief respite from the heat, with the temperature a pleasant seventy-two degrees, and volcano peaks scratched at the sky, cloaked in hazy mist. The crew embarked on the familiar walk to Friedo, shooting small birds along the way. The trail was lined with animal dung and *Bur-*

*sera* trees, their white bark resembling peeling, pale skin. Dore and Friedrich met them at the wire gate.

The drought did not detract from the improvements at Friedo, including the new path Friedrich had carved, a substantial henhouse, and the
beginnings of a pineapple crop. Friedrich demonstrated his juice press,
which he called the "Robinson sugar swing," owing to the way his body
swiveled against the lever.

Dore introduced them to her new donkey, Fleck, whom she believed
was Burro's baby. The animal, one crew member noted, "followed Dore
around like a dog." After everyone had settled, Dore showed Hancock the
current sorry state of her teeth: many of them gone, and the ones that remained ground down to nubs and studded with painful cavities. The *Velero*'s doctor, Edwin Palmer, promised to extract them all once Friedrich
found the proper set of forceps. The conversation about Dore's teeth led
to a discussion about the merits of sugar and salt in the diet. Friedrich—
who, in their early days on Floreana, had scolded Dore for spooning sugar
into her coffee—now enjoyed it just as much as she.

While Fredrich discussed philosophy, pontificating on Nietzsche's idea
that humanity is pointless if people are mere copies of one another, Dore
pulled Hancock aside and whispered a disturbing confidence: Friedrich's
abuse had escalated. She was eager to leave the island, but he had hidden
all her clothes.

In the next breath, however, she seemed to change her mind, claiming
that she was happy.

•   •   •

Hancock invited Dore and Friedrich to stay overnight on the *Velero* and
then left to visit the Wittmers. The captain had brought a full wardrobe of
baby clothes that his granddaughter had outgrown, and Margret's effusive
joy at the gift moved the entire crew to tears. "To witness the joy of the
mother," the biologist John Garth wrote, "as she tried on one article after
another and at last put on the tiny shoes was an experience which none of
us will ever forget. Even our two young roustabouts, Ray and Al, did not
hesitate to admit that it was almost too much for them."

Margret had been studying and was able to speak in English to the crew. She confessed to Hancock that she'd had to stop breastfeeding altogether and was now forced to rely solely on tinned milk. To illustrate her point, observed one crew member, she shifted her dress and "showed how the child had sucked her down" to the extent that she had to insert padding in her dresses. The Smithsonian scientist Waldo Schmitt, still enamored with Margret, directed the crew's photographer to take pictures of her and the entire family.

Heinz had a favor to ask of Hancock: Would the captain help him explore the eastern side of Floreana? Even though Heinz had finally completed their new stone home, with a homemade sectional sofa built into a corner and a second story for Harry's bedroom, he would do anything to keep his family safe from the Baroness.

• • •

By that time the sun had dropped behind the volcanoes, and the party started back for the *Velero* to host Friedrich and Dore. She ate lavish foods with the remnants of her teeth, watched movies of herself at Friedo, and listened to the ensemble play the classical music she'd loved in her youth. In the morning, she would have a new set of teeth and a new, full smile, which might make her feel like her old self, the old self that had feared Friedrich in very different ways than she did now.

Alone with Hancock, their conversation turned to the Baroness and the movie he planned to make with her. It was, he said, to be a "pirate film." Dore told him that the story was pure invention; the Baroness had a habit of concocting and spreading wild stories about herself in the hope of luring sensation-seeking Americans to her hotel. Hancock countered, saying he'd asked the Baroness outright if the story about the newlyweds was true, and she said yes. She admitted it was a terrible thing to have treated the young couple so cruelly, Hancock added, but she was sometimes gripped by "strange satanic moods" that she was powerless to quell.

Friedrich, too, spoke to the captain about the Baroness. Hancock mused about her "neurotic state," likening it to a period in his life when he, too, acted erratically, influenced by some mysterious and malignant force. Friedrich interrupted, telling the captain that the two "neurotic states" could not be compared. Clearly Hancock's ailment was of a physical nature, the result of too much "poisoning protein stuffs" in his body; he himself had suffered a similar malady after the war, owing to an infection from a tapeworm. No, Friedrich insisted, the maladies were not similar at all. The Baroness *acted* her sickness because her "feminine instinct" told her to.

•  •  •

The following morning, with Friedrich's dental forceps and a couple of small bone saws, the *Velero*'s doctor went to work on Dore's teeth. Numbed with Novocain, Dore lay still as the doctor scraped out the septic root of an incisor and extracted three more lower ones, a lower canine, two bicuspids, and two upper wisdom teeth, all with cavities. Once her gums healed, she would be ready for the fresh set of dentures, all her own.

As Heinz had requested, Hancock took him by boat on a tour of the eastern side of Floreana, with Friedrich along for the ride. Despite what William Beebe had reported in *Galápagos: World's End*, there was no source of water on the other end of the island. "There must have been a slip of the pen in Beebe's book," Margret wrote, figuring the writer meant the west side, where they already lived. They had no choice but to stay exactly where they were, within earshot and sight of the Baroness.

And, as the Baroness had hoped, Hancock made her the star of a Hollywood film. Everyone gathered on a clear bright morning and prepared to play their roles. Hair tied back, body wrapped in a diaphanous sheath, small feet encased in grungy white Keds, the Baroness strutted and spat and peered through binoculars and smiled in a way that bared all of her teeth, the camera following her in the heat. Robert was her dashing lover, cavorting about in a loincloth, armed with a revolver. The director, Emery Johnson, and the zoologist Ray Elliott, playing the newlywed husband and wife, respectively, stood no chance.

At the end of the film, after the Baroness achieved victory and cemented her reign, she and Robert waved goodbye to the camera and returned to being themselves. He "gathered her up in his arms as one would a baby," observed Charles Swett. "She was laughing and waving to us." Glancing over at Rudolph, Swett noticed the "look of fury and hatred" that swept across his face as he watched.

After this day of make-believe, Hancock asked the Baroness for the truth: Had she aimed her gun at Joseph Linde during the hunting expedition and misfired, hitting Knud Arends instead? Had she intended to kill a human rather than an animal on that day?

She admitted her guilt, and said she had acted "in a moment of rage."

Hancock, perhaps realizing that there was no reasoning with the Baroness, approached Robert and asked him for a favor. Please, Hancock implored, "watch the Baroness, and try to be in harmony with the Wittmers and Ritters."

With that, he left the matter in Robert's hands.

•  •  •

The next day, at Black Beach, as the captain prepared to depart, he lined up the last of his gifts along the sand: groceries, petroleum, tools, milk, a lantern, an ax, guns and ammunition. Dore sat on a rock nearby, petting her new donkey and watching the action closely; the Baroness did the same, pretending to search for mussels while silently tallying the bounty. "Mr. Hancock was the very soul of tact through it all," Margret observed, "handing out the things to each person from the island himself so that there is no cause for dissension later."

Margret watched Dore and the Baroness as they watched the gift giving and each other. Finally, Dore could no longer keep quiet and, in the words of Fred Ziesenhenne, "started to accuse the Baroness of this and that." It ended, finally, with all three factions warring on the beach, fighting among themselves as the *Velero* sailed off.

Later, a Nebraska zoologist named Dr. H. W. Manter, who joined the expedition as a special guest of Hancock's, would recall his impression of the settlers. "The nine people who lived on [Floreana] may have been emotionally unstable," he said, "but I do not believe they were the kind of people who would do murder."

•  •  •

On January 27, one week after the *Velero* departed, Margret asked Harry to take care of baby Rolf so that she and Heinz could go for a swim. Approaching Black Beach, they came upon a surprise: the *Velero* in the near distance, cutting across the ocean, heading toward the shoreline. Hancock had returned to watch for the arrival of the *Stella Polaris*, the Norwegian yacht that had visited Floreana the year prior; he knew there would be many friends on board and didn't want to miss the chance to visit.

Together, the party walked up to Friedo to call on Dore and Friedrich. In the commotion, Margret noticed Dore stumbling with her cane, while Friedrich insulted her with such cruelty that she began to weep. Margret set aside her own dislike for Dore and pulled her away from him. "She began telling me about her troubles," Margret wrote. "She begged me to come to see her oftener; she had so much to put up with from Dr. Ritter, who was getting harder to deal with all the time. It was all so embarrassing."

Dore and Friedrich, once obsessed with how the public might perceive their lifestyle and relationship, now made no attempts to burnish their image at all.

•   •   •

The *Stella Polaris* had listed the Floreana settlers on its official sightseeing itinerary. At Hancock's request, they all boarded the yacht in the afternoon to mingle with the American tourists. In the salon, as waitstaff glided by offering canapés and drinks, they answered questions about life on Floreana—why they came, how they survived, what they missed, if anything, about the civilized world. Dore realized, with pleasure, that she and Friedrich were the most popular attraction, and she wished there were time enough to invite all of the tourists to visit Friedo. Friedrich was thrilled by the opportunity to talk with an American philosopher about his own ideas but found himself disappointed. "America currently doesn't know any higher intellect than Einstein," he wrote, "and I dare to say something against his greatness—not mathematically, of course, he's right, I can't judge—but epistemologically, he and all his faithful are mistaken."

During a break in the conversation, Dore spotted the Baroness in a far corner of the salon. For once, she was entirely alone, without even Robert to attend to her; Dore would later learn that he'd sneaked onto the *Velero* looking for Hancock in the hope that he might ingratiate himself with the captain. The Baroness wore green silk knee pants and an embroidered peasant blouse—"a most peculiar costume," Dore thought, "certainly de-signed to attract attention. But if it did so, one could only regret it, for those garments did not suit her."

One of the American tourists approached the Baroness, and Dore moved close enough to eavesdrop.

". . . miss the theater?" the Baroness said. "Oh no! I consider this island life my greatest role. It's like a wonderful revue . . ."

The sentence trailed off, and soon the Baroness stood alone again. Dore felt the urge to join her, but could not bring herself to move; instead, her thoughts were "riveted to the Baroness, solitary in her corner, looking so old and grotesque in that inexplicable costume."

At last the Baroness put on her brightest smile and walked toward the orchestra.

"Do play a waltz from my dear Vienna!" she said to the conductor.

The conductor glanced at her, visibly annoyed, and returned to his work.

Dore scanned the room and believed she was the only one to have wit-nessed the slight. The Baroness's cheerful confidence, an accessory she was never seen without, seemed to fall away. After a moment, unsure of what to do, she skulked back to her corner.

Even after everything the Baroness had said and done—the flirtations with Friedrich, the belittling insults, the violent abuse of Rudolph—Dore could not bear to see her so defeated and alone. She made up her mind to go talk to the Baroness, but just then another American approached with a list of questions. After their conversation, Dore checked the corner again, but this time the Baroness was gone.

Dore would never see her again.

# THIRTY-ONE
# A Woman's Natural Instinct to Play with Fire

As soon as Hancock left, Friedrich felt compelled to continue their conversation about the Baroness's neurotic state, crafting yet another letter that divulged all of his long-simmering frustrations and fears:

> She acted the spoiled, sick Baroness, because she thought I would be the naïve, good-natured, philanthropic nature-apostle I was described as in the newspapers. . . . She until now thinks of me (and Dore) as "little people," because we do not wish to gain more profit from our popularity; and because her sickness is of a psycho-criminal origin, she thought she could easily inherit that popularity from us dumb, fanciful people. . . . She is much more trained in intrigue than you all will or can see. To be sure, she came on this island to drive us away and to exploit the rich Americans; all her other motives are lies.

Outside Friedo's walls, animals rustled in the brush; donkeys brayed at the moon. Friedrich had to convince Hancock of the Baroness's true nature, which threatened all of them. Perhaps, too, he recalled her more personal insults—insults that challenged both his intellect and his physicality, insults that reduced his very manhood to a mere aspiration, a figment of an overactive and nonsensical mind.

He kept writing:

Maybe she is a "little Mata Hari" of whom it is said: "She was probably
inspired by a woman's natural instinct to play with fire." Look at her
life. It is one debauch after another, and one debauch is much the
same as another. . . . Such vampires can only be tamed if they are
constantly humbled by the surrounding milieu. If she asks for patience
with her "sickness," that only means: wait until I have found a
new trick.

He signed off "Cordially Yours, Dr. Ritter."

•  •  •

In February the drought intensified. The temperature registered 120 in the
shade, 40 degrees more than usual for the warm season. Every morning,
Margret, Heinz, and Harry filled barrels with water and lined them up
along the fence for the thirsty animals. Margret took particular notice of a
female donkey—"a real wild creature," she wrote—who strayed into the
garden and helped herself to vegetables. Hoping to minimize the damage,
Margret lassoed the donkey, bound her to a tree, and brought her "green
stuff" and water. In the morning, she found that the animal had suffered a
head injury and the wound had filled with maggots. She nursed the donkey back to health and released her, but every morning the animal returned, waiting for food and water. Margret obliged, perhaps honoring an
unspoken contract with the island and its creatures: if she tended to Floreana, then no harm would come to her family. "The solution," Margret
wrote, "is to not get tired."

Heinz and Harry made frequent runs to Friedo, and reported that Dore
and Friedrich were not faring nearly as well.

•  •  •

The sun's strength scared Dore; so ferocious was its heat that it seemed to
burn the sky around it, casting it in an eerie bronze glow. Even at night the
ground burned so hot it felt as though a volcano had erupted beneath their
feet. The spring was reduced to a weak trickle. Plants withered and leaves
blackened and animal carcasses littered the trails. Worst of all was the

wind, sweeping what Dore called "invisible fire" across the island, felling banana trees with just a single fierce gust, stirring the scent of death and decay. "We were alone again," she wrote, "yet not alone."

From Heinz, she and Friedrich learned that the Baroness's garden had stopped producing anything at all. If the drought persisted and the ships didn't come, he said, the residents of the Hacienda Paradiso would surely appear at Friedo asking for help.

Dore dreaded such a visit, expecting Robert to corner Friedrich for hours with questions about malnutrition (after all, she noted, a "prolonged drought is hard upon the health of Europeans"), but instead it was Rudolph who appeared at Friedo's gate. He looked wretched, gaunt, and wan, a young man turned suddenly old. He appeared to be on the brink of death, Dore thought, but "some strange strength, some remnant of willpower stronger than exhaustion and proof against the final hopelessness, still held him up. It was extraordinary."

He spoke of daily fights, even more violent than in the past. He regretted not leaving with Captain Hancock or Vincent Astor or the *Stella Polaris* or any of the passing ships, but his fear of the Baroness was such that he didn't dare defy her.

Now he had no choice but to leave the island as soon as possible. He had asked the Baroness for his share of their money, only to be told the money was nearly gone; a large portion of it had been sent to Knud Arends as an apology in the aftermath of the hunting incident. If she wasn't going to give him money, he asked, might she at least hand over his belongings? Yet she denied even that, locking up all his things and keeping close watch to ensure he couldn't take them. Dore felt a rush of sympathy for him; he felt as trapped by the Baroness as she did by Friedrich. Now he was determined to go, even without clothing or money or any possessions at all. Terrified that he might miss a passing boat, he decided to live in the Casa down at Post Office Bay, but that locale, too, did not have food or water. He begged for just enough to keep him alive for a day or two.

He recalled the Baroness's response: "Get out of my sight, you spawn—you dog—you low-down bastard! Go down to your damned Bay and rot there for all I care."

Robert stood next to the Baroness, Rudolph told Dore, laughing at him.

At that, Rudolph was seized with rage. No matter that he was outnumbered, and that the Baroness had her whip in the air, or that Robert had double his own strength—he grabbed a chair and swung it in the air, smashing it against the cupboard where the Baroness had hidden his things. He heard the wood splinter, saw a mocking smile on the Baroness's face, felt a heavy blow to his head—and then nothing.

When Rudolph awakened on the path outside the Hacienda, he saw fresh new welts had sprouted along his arms; he'd been beaten while unconscious. He pulled himself to his feet. He had not eaten or drunk anything that morning, and the sun inflamed his head and his stomach spun with nausea. For two days he staggered about the island. He did not stop until he reached Friedo, and now here he was—could Dore and Friedrich do him a favor and write a notice to hang at Post Office Bay, asking any calling ship to take him away? He also begged for Hancock's address; he wanted to tell the captain the "truth" of his relationship with the Baroness.

Dore and Friedrich did as he asked, although they doubted he'd have the will to defy the Baroness should she beg him to come back. Still, Dore thought, "something had changed. . . . It was like a strength but it was not strength. It was a fierce and burning desperation which, in a man less physically broken, might have blazed out in madness."

Rudolph next went to Margret and Heinz's house and begged for asylum. "Philippson's threatened to kill me if he ever sees me again," he said, and told them how he'd been knocked unconscious. Margret would later report that Dore and Friedrich, fearful of the Baroness's wrath, offered Rudolph food but denied him shelter; Dore would say that Rudolph had never asked to live with them.

Their recollections of the events on Floreana would only diverge further in the months to come.

•  •  •

Margret, too, worried about the danger of taking in Rudolph, but couldn't refuse him. He promised he would impose for only a few days. The *Manuel J. Cobos* was due to arrive; he would get to Guayaquil and from there arrange passage to Germany.

He sent desperate letters to his brother, Carl, back in Dresden, which was in the midst of plans for a "Reich Festival Week," celebrating Hitler's favorite classical works, including a "poets' congress" under the auspices of the Reich Chamber of Culture.

"Things are not going so good," Rudolph wrote. "The Baroness has hidden all the money and won't give me any. She had kicked me out and has taken in Philippson, who beats me up. I'm sick of it all and want to get back to Germany."

Then:

Please help me get off this island. Send my money care of the German Consul at Guayaquil. He will come and get me. I am still fighting with Philippson.

He even wrote to the Baroness's husband in Paris:

I left your wife two weeks ago. I find it impossible to live with her any longer, and she refuses to give me my money. If you can get me a job I should like to come back and would be glad to help you get a divorce.

Margret felt pity for the young man, but also extreme unease that he now lived beneath her roof. At any moment the Baroness and Robert could come pounding at their door, threatening Harry and the baby. "The Baroness and her 'husband' must both be insane," she worried. "There was no telling what they might do against protectors of their chief victim."

She found it difficult to sleep.

The next day, Margret watched in trepidation as the Baroness walked up their path, and was shocked to hear her calling sweetly for Rudolph. "Lori," she said, using his nickname, "do come out a moment please. Please come, dear Lori, I've got something I *must* say to you."

Off he went, against his better instincts, disappearing around the bend. Hours later he returned. At first he seemed to be in a calm and jovial mood, but then sat down at Margret's table, sobbing uncontrollably. Nothing she did or said could console him.

•   •   •

Dore, too, had trouble sleeping. The drought persevered, nothing feeding on nothing, a host and parasite in one. Hour after hour, night after night, the ceaseless wind sounded like a woman in mourning. Dore wondered when the curse might be lifted, and if the dark spirits of Floreana were waiting for a human sacrifice.

•    •    •

At this time, the Baroness might have been the most fearful of all. During a brief trip to San Cristóbal Island, she confided to a friend a premonition of her own. "No one knows what the future holds in store for us," the Baroness said, "maybe fortunes, maybe misfortunes, but what is certain is that events of which we do not even suspect will not fail to occur. It might just as well be the case that in the book of my destiny it is written that I must die in these islands."

In the event of such a tragedy, the Baroness continued, she wished to share a secret: on a certain part of Floreana Island, she had buried her family jewels, which she esteemed "more than anything else in this world."

The Baroness shared a different confidence with another friend, suggesting she might take the matter of her death into her own hands. "One day," she said, referring to herself and Robert Philippson, "we shall smoke our last cigarette and drink our last whiskey and together swim out into the big ocean."

Day after day, night after night, the island amplified its shadows and sounds. The sun grew hotter and heavier and seemed to sit lower in the sky, as if on the attack. Crops and animals continued to wither and die. Along the trail to Post Office Bay, someone had strung across the trees a macabre necklace of bleached skulls, their ghostly glare greeting anyone who happened to pass in the dark.

# THIRTY-TWO
## And Then There Were Seven

At noon on March 19, 1934—Dore later would be adamant about this date—she and Friedrich had finished their morning work and were attempting to study and write, but the heat drained their energy. The drought, now five months along, showed no sign of abating. They abandoned their books and lay down for a nap. That afternoon was unnaturally quiet, Dore remembered. The absolute stillness of everything around them—the leaves on the trees, the pages of their books, the wings of the finches—so disturbed Dore that it "weighted upon [her] soul," and in that strange quiet she could not find any rest.

A shriek rang out. "It was an outcry of such panic terror that it was hardly human," Dore wrote, "and yet it was a woman's voice. It froze the marrow in our bones, and paralyzed us for a moment."

She and Friedrich got up and walked down to the gate. If someone had been hurt in the vicinity, the logical reaction would be to call at Friedo for help. No one came, and they did not investigate. They returned to the house, telling themselves that the drought was "playing havoc" with their nerves, that the scream had merely been a cruel trick of the island's acoustics, the heat somehow throwing and distorting sound.

Or so Dore and Friedrich would later claim.

•　•　•

They expected a visit from Heinz the following day, but he did not come. Instead, on March 21, Dore claimed that Rudolph knocked at Friedo's gate. He was alone. He still looked very ill, but his demeanor had changed. Gone was the defeated minion who'd been discarded by his lover; here, in his place, was the Rudolph of old—happy, smiling, engaging. Dore would record this visit in her memoir.

"Have you made it up with the Baroness?" she asked.

"Not this time," he said.

"Oh, then you're staying at the Wittmers'?"

"Yes, I am," he said, adding that he told the Baroness "once and for all where she gets off."

"Will she remember it?" Dore asked.

"I think she will," Rudolph said. Then, in Dore's recollection, he began a strange and incoherent monologue, leaping from one subject to the next, as though he realized he'd spoken indiscriminately and hoped to bury his mistake beneath a pile of nonsense. She listened carefully, thinking that he might again make a mistake, revealing information that would be better left unsaid. Eventually, in the ambush of words, a story began to take shape.

He had been living with Margret and Heinz for three days, Rudolph said, when the Baroness appeared, standing at the gate and calling for him. Margret walked down to greet her.

"Why won't you come in?" she asked. "You needn't shout at him from here."

But the Baroness ignored the invitation. Margret returned to Rudolph and cautioned him to avoid speaking to the Baroness unless she came inside; otherwise he risked being shot. While Rudolph contemplated what to do, the Baroness changed her mind and stepped into the garden.

"I wish you'd come and help me bake some bread," she said. "You know I never can do that alone—and Robert's worse than useless as a baker!"

She delivered these words with an easy and innocent charm, as though she had never treated Rudolph with anything but kindness. He responded with a cold, even tone: "If you give me back my things I'll help you. But don't expect me to ever stay with you again. I've had enough."

She pleaded with him, to no avail, and eventually she left him alone.

At the conclusion of this story, Dore said, "At any rate you've shown her at last that you can take a stand against her."

"She'll be back again," Rudolph said. "I know her. She will never leave me in peace. She'll always find a new excuse to come around again."

Dore did not believe a word of this story. Rudolph, in her opinion, lacked the willpower to resist the Baroness, no matter the harm that might befall him.

·  ·  ·

Four days later, on March 25, Dore's thirty-third birthday, she baked a cake for herself. Heinz visited and handed her an envelope, saying, "This is for you."

Inside, Dore found an article and a letter. The article, written by a reporter neither she nor Friedrich had ever met, included several disparaging comments about them and their life at Friedo. Clearly, Dore surmised, this was more evidence of the Baroness's sending false reports to newspapers. The letter, which contained similar insults, was addressed to a stranger and signed "Antoinette, Robert, Lorenz"—Antoinette being the Baroness's real name. Dore felt disgusted; after all she'd done for Rudolph, even he participated in defaming her.

"The only thing I'd like to know," Friedrich said, "is how you came to have these compositions in your possession."

Heinz said that Rudolph had "got them off the table at the Hacienda" and brought them to him and Margret.

So Rudolph had gone back to the Baroness after all.

In the next moment, Dore claimed, Heinz behaved completely out of character, ranting about vigilante justice. "It is an outrage," he said, according to Dore. "The woman is a danger to us all. We let her get away with everything. I know you're hard to move in such matters, but what I want is for us all to get together now, and do something to put an end to all this rottenness. Now that you've got proof of the sort of story she is spreading against you, perhaps you will be more ready to join me in some action against her. It's no use appealing to Ecuador. We've tried that often enough and it leads to nothing. We've got to take our protection into our own hands now." He then turned to Friedrich and announced, "We are our own law here on Floreana!"

In Dore's telling, Friedrich then chastised Heinz: "Judge not, that ye not be judged. Everyone is responsible for his own actions. That is enough."

This calm, measured response seems incongruous with the Friedrich who abused his companion and fantasized often about murdering the Baroness. But Dore, in later recollections, adhered to this version of events, and also posed pointed questions: Why would Rudolph lie about standing up to the Baroness? How to explain Heinz's fresh rage against the Baroness, since neither he nor Margret had been mentioned in the article and letter he'd brought? She wondered if their strange behavior was somehow connected to the mysterious scream—a scream only she and Friedrich ever claimed to hear.

•   •   •

Two days later, on March 27—Margret was quite certain of the date, just as Dore knew exactly when she'd heard the scream—the Baroness came to the garden gate. She wore her riding costume: a blouse, breeches, high boots. A scarf looped neatly around her head. She called in a sweet, soft voice, "Lori!"

Rudolph wasn't there, Margret explained. He had gone with Heinz to collect wood.

The Baroness appraised Margret, looking from her head to her feet. "Then please tell him that friends of ours have come, and we're going to Tahiti with them," she said, meaning she and Robert. "I hope that'll be a better place to realize my plans." Rudolph was to look after the animals and things she left behind, until she returned or sent further word.

"Then I wish you a successful journey," Margret said, but silently had a more jubilant reaction. *I can hardly believe my ears,* she thought. *The thing that we have longed for is to become a reality.*

"Thank you," the Baroness said. "*Auf Wiedersehen* or perhaps goodbye."

Margret watched the Baroness walk away, and decided she had no reason to doubt her story; many ships called at Black Beach or Post Office

Bay without her or Heinz's knowledge. Yet Rudolph had a more sinister interpretation.

"It's a trap to lure me down there," he said, "and when I get there, they'll bump me off. I know too much about her."

Margret urged him to take some time to think it over.

After lunch, Rudolph gathered the courage to walk to the Hacienda Paradiso, even though he believed his two former companions had already dug a grave for him.

·   ·   ·

Rudolph was gone for two days, according to Margret, but she did not worry. Instead, she assumed that the Baroness had decided not to leave after all and Rudolph had stayed with her. But he returned with a strange story: He had stood outside the Hacienda Paradiso for a long time and sensed no activity within. This place, which had once been bustling with life, both good and bad—music and laughter and sex and arguments and insults and violent confrontations—now stood still.

He went inside. No one was there. The donkeys were gone, and so were the Baroness's and Robert's belongings. He next walked to the Casa at Post Office Bay and noticed some footprints in the sand. After two days of searching, those footprints were the only trace of them.

·   ·   ·

Dore and Friedrich were surprised to see Margret coming up the pathway with Rudolph; Heinz was nowhere in sight. Margret presented some belated birthday gifts—a cake and some intricately embroidered handkerchiefs—that made Dore suspect an ulterior motive for the visit. The small talk carried on for a few moments and then gave way to what Dore called a "set" story, something that seemed invented and rehearsed.

Margret related her recent encounter with the Baroness: a surprise visit from friends, setting sail for Tahiti, requesting that Rudolph take care of her possessions and the animals.

"It's rather strange she didn't wait for him to come back," Dore said to Margret. "After all, one does prefer to say such things direct."

Margret explained that she had tried to delay Rudolph as long as possible so there would be no chance for such a reconciliation. Rudolph
confirmed this and began a tirade against Robert and the Baroness.

"I hope they both get shipwrecked and eaten up by sharks," he said, and
then, just as abruptly, changed the tone of his voice, speaking with a busi-
nesslike calm. He wondered if Dore might want to buy some of the Baroness's belongings. As Dore knew, she had left him no money, and selling her
things was his only hope for leaving the island.

Dore promised to buy whatever she could and accompanied Rudolph
and Margret to the gate. Walking back to Friedo, she turned to Friedrich,
who had listened to Margret's story in silence.

"What are you thinking about?" she asked.

"You played your part extremely well," he said.

"My part?" Dore said. "What part?"

"My dear child," Friedrich said, "is it possible that you believed all that?
The whole story was nothing but lies from beginning to end. I haven't yet
made out exactly what the purpose of it was, but one thing is very clear . . ."

"Tell me what you mean," Dore said. "Hasn't the Baroness really gone?"

Friedrich took her hand. "Yes, she has gone," he said, "but no friends
came for her and there was no yacht. The Baroness has been murdered,
Dore, and so has Philippson."

He did not explain how he knew this to be true, or directly name the
person or persons involved. If Dore questioned him, she did not record
that exchange. Instead, in her written recollection of this conversation,
she seemed to soften her views toward the Baroness—a self-serving edit, it
would seem, intended to cast herself and Friedrich in the best possible
light. If it were true her old rival had been murdered, then Dore felt a
"great pity" for her. "While she lived I would have given anything to see
her leave the island," she wrote, "but now that she was dead, and dead in
so horrible a way, I would have given just as much to see her back again."

Also according to her later recollection, two events stood out for their
"unspeakable hideousness": the woman's scream on March 19, and Rudolph's behavior during his subsequent visit. She recalled his high spirits
and sense of relief, the fact that he had been jovial enough even to laugh.
She thought, too, of that long-ago luncheon after the birth of baby Rolf,
when the Baroness came to Friedo and said that Rudolph was very ill and

staying down at Post Office Bay. "I thought a murderess was sitting at our table," Dore wrote, "but all the time the fate she seemed to be preparing for another was being spun for her."

She thought, too, about the embroidered handkerchiefs Margret had brought to Friedo, gifts she claimed had been sent by her sister. But Dore now believed this to be a lie: "Somehow I knew that these had not come from Frau Wittmer's sister—they were the Baroness's. I stood and looked at them, so delicate and feminine with their fine embroidery lying shimmering on the table in the falling dusk. And suddenly I seemed to see them stained with blood."

She took them to the farthest corner of the garden, dug a hole, and buried them.

•  •  •

Margret told a different version of her and Rudolph's visit to Friedo. In her account, she did not bring a birthday cake or any embroidered handkerchiefs, and Friedrich, not Dore, met her at Friedo's gate.

"The Baroness has gone," Margret said. "Did you know?"

Friedrich shook his head.

"You don't believe it?" she asked.

"I've not seen a ship," he said. "If there'd been one here, I'd surely have seen it. Dore, come out here."

Dore came out from the house. Upon hearing the news, she danced in celebration, heedless of her bad leg, and then served hot chocolate and dessert. Margret had never seen her so welcoming and friendly, while Friedrich seemed more "strikingly silent" than usual. At least, Margret mused, she was "spared all philosophical discourse."

Friedrich turned to Rudolph and advised, "The sooner you get away from here, the better." He should sell the Baroness's belongings, make plans to get back to Germany, and never return.

Friedrich also insisted that they all draft a formal statement about the events surrounding the Baroness's sudden departure. Why the urgency, Margret wondered, when nothing was proven fact? Besides, she told Friedrich, the Baroness had said that she might return. At this, Margret later wrote, "he merely shook his head and said with conviction, almost as if he had private knowledge he was not going to give us, 'She won't come back. Take my word for it.'"

•   •   •

On this, both Margret and Dore agree: That Sunday, April 1, 1934, the remaining residents of Floreana walked to the Hacienda Paradiso to assess the Baroness's possessions. It had been another morning of eerie stillness, with not even the slightest breeze, when suddenly came a searing wind, hurling through the parched leaves of the trees. The noise sounded like cackling and whispers, Dore thought; if Friedrich had not been holding her arm, she might have fallen to her knees.

The Baroness and Robert had not taken most of their belongings, as Rudolph had claimed. Her hat rested upon the table. Against one wall her shoes lined up in a tidy row. Her trunks and suitcases were stacked as they had always been. Her cigarette tray overflowed with ashes from her favorite Russian cigarettes. Photographs of her family, and one of Robert's mother, were still on display in their frames.

Dore watched as Rudolph gathered these things and brought them forward, as though to conduct an auction. Heinz began to dismantle the Hacienda's iron roof. She pointed out two items at random, but then couldn't stand the thought of taking anything from the house. "Perhaps after all it will be better not," she said. "Suppose she were to come back?"

"Don't worry," Rudolph said. "There's no danger of that."

Dore noticed one more item that seemed to confirm Rudolph's grim word. The Baroness's copy of *The Picture of Dorian Gray*—a precious talisman she took on every trip, as she had once confided to Dore—was conspicuously sitting in its usual spot, never to bring good fortune again.

# THIRTY-THREE
# The Feeling of Tragedy

The drought stretched into April. Margret and Heinz tried to continue on as normally as possible, going hunting with Harry and tending to the baby and studying English and Spanish. Rudolph remained their guest, but in between helping with chores, he disappeared for long stretches of time. If Margret asked where he'd been, he answered, "On the heath," which she took to mean the pampa, watching the cattle graze and roam. When he returned, he spoke to her of his past, lamenting the moments that had put him in this position. "This woman wrecked my youth," he said. "What am I today? A physical and mental wreck!"

Privately, Margret agreed. Rudolph was now a thirty-three-year-old man, she wrote, "feeble and tubercular." He had "fever spots on his cheeks, coughing spells that leave him spent—in short, a deathly sick man." Unsure of how to console him, she left him alone with his thoughts. "Hours on end he sits in one spot," she observed, "crying softly to himself, saying not a word—a heart-rending picture. Outside these spells of despondency, however, he always behaved very well with us and not infrequently he has guarded the house when Heinz and I were gone."

She even trusted him with her baby.

•   •   •

Unlike Margret, Dore thought constantly about the disappearance of Robert and the Baroness. She was certain they had been "removed by violence" and believed that Rudolph was the murderer. Two persistent fears burrowed into her mind: one, if there were ever an investigation, she and Fredrich might be implicated in the deaths; and two, Rudolph, in an attempt to cover his tracks, might also try to kill them. "We said to each other," Dore wrote, "that a man who would go to such lengths to regain his freedom would not be scrupulous about securing it at the expense of anybody who he felt might be a danger to him; there-fore, the slightest slip on our part . . . would inevitably expose us to the same fate."

Dore did not search for the bodies, but wondered where they might be. The ocean seemed implausible, as Rudolph did not have the means to take them far out, and without sufficient distance the current would wash them to shore. It was more likely that they had been incinerated in a pile of acacia wood, which burned so hot that it reduced corpses to fine ash; she and Friedrich had witnessed this phenomenon with cattle bones. Or perhaps they were hidden in the caves carved into the volcanic rock all across the island. Day after day, she waited for a ship to anchor and take Rudolph off the island. She was as desperate for him to leave as he was himself.

·    ·    ·

On April 20, the day the drought finally broke, a ship anchored at Post Office Bay. The *Thalia* belonged to Thomas M. Howell, a Chicago specu-lator known as "the leader of the grain pit," an expert at predicting the price of wheat. A swarm of black clouds gathered in the sky, heavy with rain, obscuring the mountains below. The rain fell hard as Howell and his party disembarked and explored the Casa on the shore. They found no sign of life save for directions to the Hacienda Paradiso and a notice pinned to a wall:

A young man on this island is forced to leave as he has no longer anything to live on. Therefore, he asks for an opportunity to go to

Chatham or Guayaquil. I live by the track marked with red approximately 2 hours walk from here. Rudolph Lorenz

In the mail barrel they found letters addressed to Friedrich Ritter and removed them, intending to make the delivery. They started the walk up the trail, which grew fainter the higher they climbed, and came to a spot where the ground was "pawed up" by hooves—evidence, Howell realized, of a life-and-death battle between the island's creatures. They went on, passing several donkeys tied to stakes, milk goats, a garden with a stone wall around it, and a small chicken coop enclosed by a wire fence capped with bleached steers' horns.

They came to a small home constructed of large, unhewn boulders, with a gabled roof of corrugated iron. A large dog trotted out, followed by a woman carrying a naked baby in her arms, and then a man trailing behind her. They realized this was not the Hacienda Paradiso, but the Wittmers' place. Howell's German-speaking cook helped with translations, and Margret served coffee and fruit. When Howell asked about the Baroness, he was surprised to learn that she and Robert Philippson had disappeared a few weeks prior and that neither of them had been heard from since.

It grew dark. Howell would not have time to visit with Dore and Friedrich, as he had to set sail in the morning. Heinz, Harry, and Rudolph offered to escort the party back down to shore; it was too dangerous to ride donkeys, since the cattle attacked them at night. "It was one of the most weird trips I ever made," the photographer Claude Matlack later said. "The feeling of tragedy was in the air, and this was enhanced by the bright moonlight"—light that illuminated the white animal skulls lining the path down the mountain.

Howell, taking pity on Rudolph, offered passage as far as Panama, but changed his mind once he learned that Rudolph had tuberculosis. Howell then gave Heinz a packet of seeds, explaining, "Half for you—half for Dr. Ritter."

Back on the *Thalia*, Matlack could not stop thinking of Margret. She had wept almost for the entire duration of the visit, unsettled by thoughts or fears she lacked the language or will to confide.

•   •   •

In the morning, Rudolph and Heinz journeyed to Friedo, carrying the seeds and mail.

"Why didn't Howell come himself?" Friedrich asked.

Heinz explained that Howell and his party had intended to make the delivery but had run out of time. Neither Friedrich nor Dore accepted this answer.

Heinz, back home, told Margret that Dore had been so abusive that he would "have nothing to do with" her from then on. "This is the same with [Rudolph]," Margret wrote. "He and Frau Koerwin used to be good friends; now because of the latest affair, they've become enemies."

But Dore's animosity toward Rudolph went beyond the question of stolen gifts and mail. She believed he had "blood upon his hands," and that he had an accomplice in his crime; in his weakened condition, he would not have been able to dispose of two bodies on his own. Someone else on the island knew exactly what had happened to the Baroness and Robert.

Dare she confront the terrifying possibility that Friedrich was Rudolph's accomplice? What if the man she'd entrusted with her life also had blood on his hands?

•   •   •

In Los Angeles, where Captain Hancock kept busy with lectures about his Galápagos travels, he received an upsetting letter from Berlin, signed by Dore's mother.

Very honored Captain Hancock:

You will not be offended with me if I write you today. The worry about my daughter on the Galapagos Islands robs me of all my rest. Since I am in no position to do anything, due to the distance, I would like to trustfully turn to you. The last letter from her sounded so sad and discouraged, which appeared strange to me, as she has always written so happily before. I am afraid that she has great home-sickness. As I know, from my daughter, how great her trust and respect for you is, I want to beg you from my heart, that if your way should ever again take you to the Galapagos Islands, you will stand by her with advice and in deed, and place the possibility of her returning before her. You will understand my worry as a mother, when one knows one's child is in need and cannot help.

In the hope that I have not made a vain request

Signed, respectfully,
Mrs. M. Strauch

# THIRTY-FOUR
# And Then There Were Six

In May, shortly after the disappearances, Dore wrote a short story called "Why Paradise Is Lost." She could no longer confide in Rudolph or Heinz or even Friedrich—especially Friedrich—and she needed to process the disquieting thoughts roiling through her mind. The story featured her usual literary foil, Gertrud, but with a twist: this time there was another foil, named Mary; in essence, the story depicted Dore debating the dueling sides of herself.

The story begins with Mary, who is married and unhappy with her life. She lost, Dore wrote, that which "leads to the essence of life. She had stayed too long on the glittering and sparkling surface of it." Mary meets with Gertrud to debate why paradise was lost. Gertrud speaks in the way Friedrich had conditioned Dore to speak, the way she had rebelled against so many times: "If a man does what his wife wishes, then paradise is lost." She reminds Mary that Eve tempted Adam with the apple, and then repeats Nietzsche's words: "If you go to women, do not forget the whip." Mary realizes that her desires are incompatible with Gertrud's and begins to cry. Her marriage has become like most: "Every party went his own way, and nobody cared neither for his own soul nor for that of the other." The idea terrifies Mary, but she must stop looking to others for strength and guidance, and instead seek them from within.

The story marked Dore's transformation from "Gertrud" to "Mary": at last, it was clear to Dore that she must become her own master, no matter the risks or consequences.

.   .   .

Margret noticed that Rudolph's condition was worsening, but he still tried to make himself useful. When he had the energy, he began to move his belongings (all recovered from the Hacienda Paradiso) down to Post Office Bay to be prepared for the next passing ship. Occasionally he slept there overnight, afraid of missing potential rescuers, but then would grow lonely and move back in with Margret and Heinz. His shoes had worn to ragged scraps from hiking back and forth.

On one occasion, he missed a ship, and the crew members stole most of his possessions. "Tuxedo, dress suit, dress shirts—all stolen," Margret wrote. "When one looks at the sick Lorenz, one is inclined to doubt that he'll ever wear such things again though he is very hopeful and doesn't seem to realize how sick he really is."

In her diary, Margret took care to note Rudolph's gossip about Friedrich and the Baroness. They had both told stories to American reporters while accusing each other of being the sole source of scandalous news items— "building, thereby, a veritable well of envy and hate."

Friedrich, in his own writings, spoke obliquely of that hate. He had no reason now to worry about the Baroness, but he feared at least one of his remaining Floreana neighbors. "Should it ever be announced that either myself or both of us have disappeared," he warned a friend in Germany, "you can be sure that it was a bullet out of the bush that was responsible— even if there is no more Baroness."

.   .   .

On July 10, a fishing boat, the *Dinamita*, set sail from Santa Cruz Island, destined for Floreana. On board were the skipper, Trygve Nuggerud, and a Swedish journalist named Rolf Blomberg, who was exploring the Galápagos Islands in the hope of writing a book. "Nuggen," as Blomberg called Nuggerud, had a young wife on Chatham Island and was about to become a father for the first time; he "walked about," Blomberg reported, "like he was happily intoxicated and not sure what to do with himself until the big day approached." To pass the time, Nuggerud suggested a quick journey to Floreana. "I promised long ago to deliver some coffee plants to the Baroness Wagner," he'd told Blomberg. "Now is a suitable time. We should be back here in ten days at the latest."

Blomberg thrilled at the idea. He had read all about the Baroness back in Sweden, and even carried in his wallet a clipping about her reported capture of the doomed newlywed couple, titled "Den Dystra Drottningen av Galápagos" (The Grim Queen of the Galápagos) and illustrated with "what looked like a beautiful lady." Blomberg was so intrigued by the Baroness that, upon his arrival in Guayaquil, his first inquiry was to ask the authorities about this famous icon of Floreana, but they told him nothing. He then had the random luck of meeting a man who had once been a part of her entourage—Knud Arends, who, the year prior, had been shot and severely wounded by the Baroness during a hunting expedition. Despite this traumatic experience, Arends claimed he'd had a "wonderful time" with the Baroness and would see her again at any opportunity. "Oh well," he said, waving his hand. "She didn't kill me, anyhow." He wrote a letter of introduction for Blomberg to give to the Baroness, and wished him luck.

The fishing boat set off hours before dawn. For Blomberg, the trip had an eerie feeling from the start. Even the departure, he wrote, "had something unreal about it. It was pitch dark, but our wake was like a green sparkling veil of phosphorescence. And the surrounding sea was heaving deep sighs." He thought of the pirates who had haunted these waters so long ago and felt a sense of deep foreboding, but then chided himself: "How my fantasy played tricks on me in the dark!"

With each passing hour Floreana grew larger and closer, giving the impression that it was creeping in their direction, meeting them halfway. At dawn the silhouettes of the island's extinct volcanoes came into sharp focus. They could discern the shape of the famous La Corona del Diablo, the Devil's Crown—a small volcano, submerged deep into the water, with jagged tops peeking above sea level that resembled the points of a crown.

After ten hours at sea, they at last reached Post Office Bay. No one was in the Casa, but they noticed Rudolph Lorenz's handwritten letter requesting a ride from any passing ship. The men gathered the mail from the barrel and began the walk to the Hacienda Paradiso, which Blomberg called "New Eden." They passed the chain of bleached skulls, the tree trunks marked by red paint, the thickets of wild lemon and orange trees. After an hour they came to a path; the right fork led to Friedo, and the left to the homes of the Baroness and the Wittmers. They turned left.

After another hour of hiking, they arrived at a small clearing. Blomberg knew they'd found the site of the Hacienda Paradiso, but it seemed as though it hadn't been occupied in quite some time.

"Maybe she is in one of the caves," Nuggerud said, "like the first period when they were still building the house." He shouted in the direction of the caves and heard only an echo in return.

Giving up, they started for the Wittmers' home, where Heinz and Rudolph were outside. Both men grew excited. Heinz shouted, "Ah, Sie haben Post . . . kommen Sie. . . . Schnell, schnell!" *Ah, you have mail . . . come . . . quick, quick!* Blomberg made notes of their appearance: Heinz was tall, in his mid-forties, mustache, goatee, glasses; Rudolph "was emaciated and did not look well." Margret came out with Harry and Rolf, and Blomberg was especially delighted with the baby, whose birth on Floreana made him "a true Galapagonian."

"Where is the Baroness?" Blomberg asked.

"Disappeared," Rudolph said, and recounted the story: the Baroness's friends arriving on an English yacht, an impromptu decision to travel to Tahiti, his discovery of her and Robert Philippson's footprints along the shore.

Blomberg had trouble believing any of it. Who were these particular friends? Had anyone else seen the yacht? There would have been talk of an English yacht on Chatham and Santa Cruz, and yet no one on those islands had mentioned anything. If the Baroness had not left the island, where could she have gone?

Blomberg and Nuggerud stayed overnight at the Wittmers' house. In the morning, they continued on to Friedo. Rudolph accompanied them, sharing stories about the Baroness. Once, he said, she ordered twenty thousand cigarettes from an American cigarette company and signed it, "The Kaiserin of the Galapagos and Philippson, Minister." She was, Blomberg concluded, "a sensation-hungry and sadistic person, capable of mistreating animals and people alike, but who in spite of all this had a sort of winning charm."

They walked the well-trod path lined with banana trees and coconut palms. As they approached Friedo, Nuggerud warned Blomberg to call for Friedrich and Dore from a safe distance, as they "often walked about dressed in the way God had created them. [They] needed time to get dressed and get their teeth in place." Friedrich came out first, with Dore trailing behind.

Friedrich told Blomberg that in abandoning civilization, he'd had no desire to "make a sensation," although that had been the unfortunate consequence. Yet Friedrich's behavior, Blomberg observed, belied his words. "We got another impression," Blomberg wrote, "from his obvious willingness to pose in front of the cameras: Tilling the soil, pressing sugarcane while using his homemade apparatus, resting on a stone with a philosophical expression—he certainly wanted to be photographed."

Blomberg also noticed a strange dynamic between Friedrich and Dore, who appeared "trained to agree with anything he said, and if she spoke before he had finished, he either looked at her disapprovingly or gave her a scolding."

"We brought some coffee plants for the Baroness," Nuggerud said. "But now that she is no longer here, don't you want them?"

"Oh," Dore said, and clapped her hands in joy, which Friedrich quickly extinguished. "No, thank you," he said. "We do not use stimulants of any kind: no coffee, no tea, no tobacco, no alcohol."

Dore agreed with Friedrich, eager to correct her mistake. Of course coffee was "completely out of the question," she assured them—it was just a "funny thought."

•    •    •

Later, after Friedrich cooked a delicious meal of bananas and eggs ("I valued his culinary diet," Blomberg admitted, "more than his attempt of spiritual feeding"), the two men took a walk. At a pause in the conversation about Friedrich's philosophy, Blomberg changed the subject.

"What do you make of the Baroness disappearing?" he asked, and noticed that Friedrich looked "very happy" at hearing the question.

"Well," Friedrich said, "it is simply wonderful that this creator of in-trigues, this disturbance of peace, this—I simply do not know how to sum her up—has finally gone from the island."

"But how do you think she vanished?" Blomberg asked.

"I have my own theory," Friedrich said, and here he offered a different conclusion from the one he'd shared with Dore—that the Baroness and Robert Philippson had been murdered by Rudolph Lorenz.

Instead, he suggested to Blomberg that the pair had died by suicide, fol-lowing each other into the ocean. "When it became obvious to the Baron-ess that it would be impossible to realize her dream of this Paradise Hotel, when she realized that she could not continue acting the role of pirate queen repeatedly without becoming ridiculous, and when she saw the dev-astating effect the recent drought had on the island and how difficult it was to cope since Lorenz no longer worked for her, she solved it all with a desperate action, Philippson also joining her in death. That is the most natural explanation."

To this, Blomberg said nothing.

•    •    •

The next morning, Rudolph at last had the chance to leave Floreana. Nuggerud offered him a ride on the *Dinamita*, but only as far as Santa Cruz; from there he would take the first ship to Guayaquil and arrange for passage back to Germany. Blomberg would remain behind in Santa Cruz, and bid Rudolph farewell from there. All of the remaining settlers said their goodbyes. Margret and Heinz gave Rudolph a packet of letters to post from the mainland. Dore and Friedrich had lunch with Rudolph, Blomberg, and Nuggerud before accompanying them down to Black Beach.

Sitting across from Rudolph, eating Friedrich's bananas and eggs, Dore thought of her long-ago luncheon at Friedo, when the Baroness spoke of seduction and sex, Rudolph conspicuously absent. She thought about how long she'd known Rudolph—only two years in calendar time but, in the intense, claustrophobic cauldron of a remote island, it felt like so many more. She thought of the old Rudolph, optimistic and cheerful and bright with promise, and could not reconcile that memory with the image of the decrepit, bitter man sitting across from her—a man she believed to be a murderer.

She gave him the story she had just written, "Why Paradise Is Lost," and asked him to mail it to Captain Hancock from the mainland. "Don't be sad," she said. "Be happy that you can go away at last. You've plenty of years before you to make good all that you've lost, and one day you'll look back on all this and think you only dreamed it."

He spoke in low, somber tones so that no one else could hear. "I'm afraid," he said. "I don't know why, but I'm afraid of this trip."

"Why?" Dore asked.

He walked away without answering, and did not turn back.

•   •   •

For her part, Margret never remembered Rudolph's final words to her, but one observation cleaved to her mind: he took with him some cargo that seemed to be "extremely heavy."

The remains of the Baroness and Robert Philippson had still not been found.

# THIRTY-FIVE
# Scoundrelism, Rascality, and Faking

O n July 16, three days after Rudolph's departure, Friedrich finished a large section of his memoir and prepared a package for Captain Hancock. He included a letter in which he offered yet another explanation for the disappearance of the Baroness and Robert. This time they weren't murdered, as he'd told Dore, nor did they die by suicide, as he'd told Blomberg, but instead they'd simply "vanished to the South Seas." He also suggested that he had further information about the incident—information so sinister and incriminating that he would only feel safe sharing it in person. In all caps, he wrote, "WITTMERS AND WE ARE ALONE HERE NOW. WE WILL HOPE THAT YOU WILL COME ONCE MORE—THEN I MUST TELL YOU WHAT I CANNOT WRITE—BECAUSE I HAVE NO PROOF OF IT."

A few weeks later, Friedrich composed another letter to Hancock:

You would have got the manuscripts and letters more than half a year earlier if the [Wittmers] would not have prevented us from meeting American visitors who anchored in Post Office Bay. The young mother (using her baby to stir up sentimental pity in visitors) proved not to be the blameless angel she seemed to be at first; we do better to keep distance from those people. . . . They tell us that in Chatham people suppose Rudolph Lorenz would have murdered the Baroness and

Philippson. Wittmers must know what had happened. We only know
what we are told.

If Friedrich hoped to become a world-renowned philosopher, revered
for his brilliant ideas as much as for his unconventional life, then he could
not be a suspect in the disappearances.

•    •    •

After Rudolph left the island, Dore grew obsessed with the idea of her own
escape. Their carefully curated utopia was now forever ruined, and yet
they had no choice but to stay. She recognized the irony of her situation;
the Baroness, even in her absence, found a way to torment Dore. "The
woman who had been responsible for the destruction of our paradise," she
wrote, "kept us entrapped there after she was dead." The likelihood of
murder made it impossible for either she or Friedrich to leave; fleeing the
island might be seen as an admission of guilt.

So they stayed, each focusing on elements within their control. Dore
noticed that Friedrich seemed possessed by a "strange mood," one that
drove him into a morose seclusion and spurred him to write pages and
pages of his philosophy, working from morning to night in "desperate
haste," oblivious to anything else, while Dore tended to the garden and
the house and the animals alone.

This mutual solitude intensified their long-festering resentments, forcing them to the surface. They did not speak for days. He whipped her, and
any remaining love she felt for him "turned to hate." Yet, as always, she
was mindful of protecting Friedrich's public legacy, and understood how it
might be tarnished by any hint of personal strife, let alone violence. "We
had found perfect harmony and peace together," she later wrote in her
memoir. "All differences had been smoothed out, and we had reached that
infinite understanding of each other which no words can tell. Friedrich
had become considerate and tender. All storms had ceased. And amid the
debris of its outward peacefulness, the inner life of Friedo's founders had
achieved perfection."

•    •    •

In late August, three Germans arrived and settled into the caves by the Wittmers' home. They announced their intention to hunt the "thousands" of wild animals on Floreana in the hope of selling the hides, although Heinz advised them that the drought had wiped out most of the beasts and the remaining ones weren't worth anything. He and Margret called the trio "the globetrotters" owing to all the countries they'd visited; one boasted of his journalism work for American newspapers. Despite tensions between his household and the Wittmers', Friedrich invited them all to visit Friedo for dinner, requesting they bring rice and meat—"because," Heinz wrote, "he has nothing to eat." Friedrich had grown so desperate he'd finally given up all pretenses of being a vegetarian.

On September 9, a Sunday, Heinz and Margret and the globe-trotters ventured to Friedo with a roasted ham and a pound of rice, hoping it would be enough for them all. Dore was particularly interested in speaking with the journalist and began recounting her life story. Hoping to impress the guests, Friedrich distributed several essays and posed questions: Did the men understand that the earth is "not merely a small sphere in the cosmos"? Did they wish to discuss theories regarding the "point-curvature and zero curvature of the earth's surface"? To Friedrich's dismay, no one cared.

Hours into this gathering a surprise guest arrived: the Rhode Island businessman Francis Taylor, traveling on his yacht, the *Aldebaran*. He had read the journalist Rolf Blomberg's report about the disappearance of the Baroness and Robert Philippson. Titled "Deadly Revenge or American Yacht?," Blomberg's piece read, in part,

Who has not seen and remembers the blonde silhouette of the Austrian baroness as she passes through our port before embarking for Galapagos? Who does not remember the slender mermaid that made the waters of the pool shine with gold during her dives? Who does not remember her walking her body of aristocratic softness through our streets? Who has not known about her popularity in the world of snobbish adventure, distributed to the four winds by the world's largest newspapers? Today her name is wrapped in a veil of mystery, with all the contours of a sumptuous femme fatale tragedy.

Blomberg continued, describing the Baroness's dream of a luxury tourist hotel, her savage treatment of Rudolph Lorenz, her alleged departure on a yacht with Robert Philippson, the various theories of suicide and murder, the lies that seem embedded in every facet of the mystery. "Wittmer and Dr. Ritter are guests on every yacht that arrives," Blomberg wrote. "The yacht, which they have said has taken the Baroness and Philippson, has not been seen by the human eye. No one has heard of it. It is an enigma, a mystery, an invisible yacht that perhaps no human being can account for."

Other newspapers expanded upon the mystery. A German newspaper reprinted a Colombian newspaper's report claiming that visitors to the abandoned Hacienda Paradiso had discovered "numerous traces of blood" along the walls. A reporter interviewed the Baroness's brother Rudolph, a retired railway official living in Innsbruck, Austria. He had no theories about her disappearance but felt compelled to defend her honor. "It is out of the question that my sister did the kind of things that are now being said of her," he insisted. "She was always a very good-natured person, and I don't believe her able to point a revolver at another person." The *Velero* crew member Charles Swett teased revelations to come. "Find the Baroness," he told the Associated Press, "and you will find the story that will meet your deepest zest for a tale of adventure."

Taylor, the Rhode Island businessman, told the gathering at Friedo that he had come searching for answers about the Baroness. Upon docking at Post Office Bay, he and his crew had first visited the Hacienda Paradiso and found it deserted. They ventured on to the Wittmers' house, where Harry told them that everyone had gone to Friedo; so now here they were.

Friedrich attempted to strike up conversation about his philosophy, but Taylor had no interest. Instead, he began an interrogation about the disappearances. "When we broached the question of the absence of the Baroness and Philippson," reported the yacht's captain, "Ritter switched subjects, stating vaguely that the Baroness and Philippson had left the island on a yacht. Ritter would not say, or was unable to state the name of the yacht." Since they were strangers eating a meal at Friedrich's home, they decided not to question their host further. When they asked Heinz the same questions, he insisted that he, too, knew nothing about the disappearances.

After they left, Friedrich retreated into his study to write a letter to Captain Hancock. If the visitors were going to report Friedrich's evasiveness to the American press, he hoped to discredit them as quickly as possible. Taylor and his party, he wrote, "are making the situation in our garden somewhat uncomfortable. We feel strongly how much we exist outside of the diligence of these people . . . just like the Baroness, they have fallen to the depths of modern piracy. To be brought into contact with these people is distasteful."

•  •  •

In mid-October, after the globe-trotters had given up their hunting enterprise and departed Floreana, Heinz and Margret became alarmed at baby Rolf's condition. His skin was hot to the touch and he registered a fever of 105 degrees. Heinz had no choice but to ask the doctor to examine his son. Friedrich didn't hesitate to rush over, but found "nothing definite." Heinz couldn't help noticing the doctor's own poor condition; Friedrich looked "broken and old."

"The island has not given me what I hoped," he told Heinz and Margret, and seemed uncharacteristically eager to share his deepest intimacies. He confided that Dore's multiple sclerosis was "gradually getting worse." She had become "extremely difficult." She "let her tongue loose" indiscriminately and he could not "shut her mouth." At least Captain Hancock was scheduled to visit in January, he said; hopefully the *Velero* would take Dore back to the mainland and arrange for transportation to Germany. "But it's three months till then," he added, "and I don't know if I'll . . ."

He sighed, letting his sentence die, and then added one ominous line: "You never know what she might be capable of."

•  •  •

On the other side of the world, in Berlin, Germany, Robert Philippson's father was besieged with fear about what might have befallen his son. He wrote a letter to Captain Hancock asking for his help.

Dear Sir:

Referring to the tragedy which seems to have happened on one of the Galapagos Islands, known to us by recent newspaper publications, I take the liberty of addressing this letter to you, known to have a good knowledge of many things on those islands.

My son Robert Philippson, probably personally known to you as having resided on Dr. Ritter's island, seems to have left Floreana in July 34.

The last news I had from him are dated Dec. '33; since that date I have not heard the least from my son, so my wife and myself are most anxious to know what has become of him since.

You surely will understand parents [sic] helpless situation and deep sorrow about this, and therefore excuse my request to your kindness, dear Captain,—I do not know whom else I could address to—whether it is possible for you to inquire on my behalf, if anybody could inform unfortunate parents of the fate of their only son.

Whatever you will be so good to communicate to me in this matter, will be accepted with sincere thanks.

Apologizing once more for the trouble I might cause you—and for my bad English.

I remain, dear Captain

Every [sic] Yours Sincerely,
Ernst Philippson

•    •    •

In Los Angeles, Captain Hancock was in the final preparations for his next expedition to the tropics, a journey of eighty days that would begin in November. The official itinerary included stops at remote islands off the coast of Peru, Chile, and Colombia, where they hoped to capture more specimens of the rare Gorgona porpoise, a species that had caused a great deal of excitement after the *Velero*'s trip the prior year. They were noted for their sharp, attenuated jaws measuring eighteen inches long, with as many as fifty teeth in each jaw.

"The meat of some of the species is grand eating, like the breast of duck," the Smithsonian scientist Waldo Schmitt said. "Thoughts turn to the commercial food value, but these kind are too hard to catch to bring them to American tables." But that wasn't all, he added; they also had "retractable teats for suckling their young in water that would provoke the envy of a designer of retractable landing gear for airplanes."

Four days before the *Velero*'s scheduled departure, a series of fragmented wire messages came over the Mackay telegraph station in Los Angeles. The messages, transmitted by the captain of a tuna clipper in the Galápagos Islands, reported the discovery of two bodies on Marchena Island, the largest of the northern islands in the archipelago, uninhabited and lacking any source of freshwater. "Passing Marchena Island in Galapagos group today, small skiff was sighted on beach," the message read. "On investigation found bodies of man and woman. . . . One letter was addressed to Capt. Allan Hancock of Los Angeles. Man's body was found under skiff and woman's, who was dressed in lingerie, was about 50 feet away. . . . Woman appeared to have died last, as man's head had been covered with white coat and was lying on pile of clothes. There was some French money in paper near man."

This discovery came at the same time as Friedrich's cryptic letter from Floreana, in which he lamented having "no proof" for his suspicions. "I don't know what he means," Hancock told the press. "It only deepens the mystery that I want to clear up. I intend to make a first-hand investigation of this mystery." In a change of plans, he would bypass the islands near Peru, Chile, and Colombia to travel straight to Marchena, where the bodies would be left just as they'd been found.

# THIRTY-SIX
## And Then There
## Were Five

O n November 6, the American broadcaster Phillips Lord sailed into
Floreana on his four-masted schooner, the *Seth Parker*. Lord, thirty-two, a precursor to Garrison Keillor, had a weekly show on NBC radio
called *Sunday Evening at Seth Parker's*. The titular character was a preacher
and backwoods philosopher based on Lord's own grandfather, and the
sketches reimagined characters from Lord's childhood summers in rural
Maine. Since the show's debut, Lord had amassed a regular audience of
ten million listeners. For Americans, suffering from devastating droughts
and dust storms and a 22 percent unemployment rate, the show allowed
them to forget, at least for an evening, the struggles of the past week and
the week to come. "The characters were just plain folks," wrote the *New
York Times*, "the speech colloquial, friendly Down East talk, and the plots
called up a simple, old-fashioned way of life that conveyed a sense of sta-
bility in uncertain times."

Yet a backlash was building against Lord as listeners questioned whether
his "Seth Parker" persona bore any resemblance to his real-life conduct
and character. His current weekly program for NBC, *The Cruise of the* Seth
Parker, followed Lord on a world cruise, and rumors circulated that he was
far more interested in drinking and cavorting with women guests than in
dispensing homespun wisdom and singing hymns. By the time Lord
reached the Galápagos Islands, the entire enterprise was unraveling. He
had lost his lone sponsor, Frigidaire; engines quit running; bedbugs and

cockroaches had the run of the ship. He was also suffering from a lingering, low-grade illness that sometimes rendered him incapable of using his hands. He had doubted whether he'd even make it as far as the Galápagos, but now here he was, anchoring at Black Beach in the midst of an island drama far more compelling than any of his fictional scripts.

He and his crew stopped first at Friedo. Dore assessed Lord's appearance and declared him "handsome"; he was six feet tall and powerfully built, with a dimpled smile and slick black hair. She noted with pride that Lord and his crew listened to Friedrich's philosophical discourse with genuine interest. Nothing is absolute, Friedrich instructed. Time itself is an illusion, "a projection in our physical minds of a four-dimensional manifestation." Women are "vessels of pleasure." Sex is an "intellectual relaxation." Man is the pioneer, restlessly searching for new fields, but "woman has neither imagination, logic, nor desire enough to do so" and is incapable of advancement along any of the mental pathways. America is "mainly run by women" and is therefore headed for a downfall.

One of Lord's colleagues mentioned his skill at palm reading, and asked Friedrich for his hand.

Friedrich laughed and said to Dore, "Now you'll hear how long you're going to have me on your hands." Turning back to the crewman, he asked for the truth.

During this demonstration, Dore looked not at Friedrich but at the stranger, whose expression, in an instant, transformed from one of playful curiosity to one of earnestness, signaling a realization that would remain unsaid. He stared straight into Friedrich's eyes and spoke with conviction: "Oh sure I'll tell her the truth—she'll have you for another fifty years."

Everyone laughed, including Friedrich, who—perhaps forgetting his former goal of living to age 150—said he'd be ready to go by that time, anyway.

Friedrich got up to cook dinner, telling the group he had only meat to offer. He opened a jar of potted pork—leftovers from one of the invasive pigs he'd killed with poison. Lord took a sniff and said it "stank." Friedrich deemed it inedible, and Dore threw it to the chickens.

• • •

When Lord and his crew left, Dore gave voice to all of the foreboding thoughts she had collected over the years, remarking on the "strange and dark events" in Floreana's history and the similar incidents that had continued, unabated, since their arrival.

"We do not know what causes underlie the fate of men like Watkins," Friedrich said. "Nor can we really put ourselves so far into the minds of people who are alien to us—the Baroness, for instance—as to be able to interpret their destiny. But if misfortune and even tragedy should come to us two here, I shall know what it was we were punished for."

Silently, Dore decided that their time on Floreana had been worth it, no matter what had happened between them on the island—or what might happen in the time they had left.

·  ·  ·

A few days later, Lord visited Margret and Heinz and invited them on board the *Seth Parker*. The occasion was particularly momentous for Margret; it marked the first time since her arrival on Floreana two years prior that she left the island, even if it was just a short journey on a small boat, bringing her out to Lord's cruiser. She and Heinz gave Lord and his crew fruits, pumpkins, and smoked meat in exchange for a variety of groceries and six big, freshly caught fish.

In the evening, as they dined in one of the yacht's saloons, several crew members approached and said they had just returned from Friedo.

"All Dr. Ritter's chickens were found dead," one of them said. "Seems they got meat-poisoning."

"Always thought he was meant to be a vegetarian," another said.

"Well, he's not now," Lord said. He recounted his visit to Friedo and the rotten potted pork Dore had fed to the chickens. "And there you are, today they're dead."

One of the crewmen related a message from Friedrich: Could Heinz and Margret bring him a couple of hens and a cock so that he could start breeding them?

Despite the recent hostilities between the two couples, Heinz and Margret obliged, carting the animals to Friedo two days later. When they arrived, Margret was shocked by what she saw: Friedrich potting the very

chickens that had died from eating the poisoned pork—"a medically qualified man," she marveled, "and a supposed vegetarian into the bargain."

"But will they be all right to eat?" Heinz asked.

"Oh yes," Friedrich said. "It's not as bad as all that." He explained, dubi-
ously, that the poison had been "boiled out" of the chickens, and asked
Heinz if he'd like a jar to take home.

"Thanks very much," Heinz said, "but I don't think we will."

He and Margret left, and Friedrich carried on.

When Friedrich felt satisfied that the chicken was safe to eat, Dore
scooped it onto a platter and brought it to the table.

Lying in bed that night, Friedrich complained of a headache.

•   •   •

At midnight on December 2, the *Velero* approached Marchena Island—
"that strange, dead, truncated remnant of an ancient volcano," thought
Charles Swett. It had the distinction of being one of the most, if not the
most, barren of the islands. Unlike Floreana, it lacked the altitude to har-
ness enough precipitation to sustain any wildlife. No tortoises had ever
been found on its rocky paths and shores.

Swett felt a sense of dread as the crew drew closer: "An arrow of gray dry
brush which was visible for miles served as a pointer, a sign which seemed
to say to us, 'This is the spot. Thirst, tragedy, and death I have witnessed;
here you will find them.'"

Additional wire messages had come through, delivering more information about the victims. They were determined to have died of thirst. Early
speculation had been wrong: the bodies were not those of the Baroness
and Robert Philippson; nor of Margret and Heinz; nor of Arthur Estampa,
the Norwegian fisherman who had once fled to Friedo in the middle of the
night, terrified that the Baroness might kill him. The deceased were Trygve
Nuggerud, the fisherman whose wife had just given birth to a son, and
Rudolph Lorenz, who would now join the Baroness and Robert Philippson
as part of the Galápagos Islands' dark lore.

The crew anchored and took a skiff to the shore, where, noticed the
biologist John Garth, "seals lying on the beach in strange attitudes suggested the bodies we were seeking." It appeared, according to the wire

reports, that Nuggerud's boat, the *Dinamita*, likely suffered from engine trouble somewhere between Santa Cruz and Chatham Islands. The old boat had no sail and could not navigate the powerful currents that churned through the archipelago, tossing them northward toward Marchena. The crewman was swept overboard, the boat sank, and Nuggerud and Rudolph barely escaped in the skiff. Some wondered if, instead of a shipwreck, the two men had been treasure hunting and killed each other.

Rudolph's body offered no answers. He lay on his side, one arm folded beneath his body, the hand of the other clasped over his throat. He was hatless and barefoot and wore blue cutoff jeans shorts that had belonged to the Baroness; her trademark embroidery stitch encircled the hems. Baby clothes were piled on one side, a gift from Margret to her sister that Rudolph had promised to mail. His passport was found nearby, along with a clutch of letters bearing the names Hancock and Ritter and Strauch and Wittmer, and a photograph he had once held dear: a portrait of Robert and the Baroness, taken on the journey from Europe to South America, smiling and magnificently dressed, a vestige from a happier time. And, finally, there was Dore's story about paradise lost, the tale of a woman discovering that she must become her own master.

"The poor devils," Schmitt thought. "Lorenz, if murderer, got what he deserved."

The biologist John Garth had a similar conclusion: "As I gazed on the body of Lorenz, I could not help but wonder if I were looking into the face of the murderer of the Baroness and Philippson. Had conditions become worse for the poor consumptive than when we last visited them on Floreana, he might have had significant provocation. But what swift retribution to overtake him in the very act of fleeing from his crime, and what seeming injustice to involve an apparently innocent man in such a horrible death."

Garth took several photographs of the bodies, shooting from every angle. Then he filled two buckets and a colleague's shirt with sea urchins.

•     •     •

Hancock and the *Velero* crew sailed on to Charles Island—"Ritter-wards," as Schmitt called the journey, arriving on December 4 in the late afternoon. After anchoring at Black Beach and sounding three blasts of the whistle, Hancock spotted the heliographic flash of a mirror coming from on high—Friedrich's customary greeting. A boat was lowered, and they landed and hurried along the trail, waiting for the doctor to bound toward them at great speed, his hair wild with his movement, his voice calling out, "Mail! Have you any mail?"

They climbed higher and higher with still no sign of Friedrich; was he not at home? At last came a woman's shout. There was Dore, stumbling with her crude cane, crying and shaking, telling Hancock that his timely arrival was an "act of Providence." She had dashed off a letter, willing him to come, knowing full well it could sit in Post Office Bay for weeks, yet somehow the captain had heard her.

She had tragic news to share.

· · ·

Only Dore and Margret knew what had really happened in those last days of November, after Friedrich ate poisoned meat and developed a headache in bed. Once again, their versions dramatically diverged.

When Friedrich said he had a headache, Dore grew "instantly alarmed." She asked if he might be feeling some bad effects from the meat he'd eaten. But she had eaten some as well, she later wrote, and had not felt sick at all.

"It may be something else," Friedrich said, "but don't worry. I shall be all right."

She sat on a chair next to the bed, watching over him. She noted that his complexion seemed normal, neither flushed nor pale. Some time passed, and then he spoke in an odd voice, a voice that did not sound like his own: "My tongue feels heavy." She peered inside his mouth and saw that his tongue was swollen, lying slug-like across his teeth. Dore rummaged through his medical bag and made him an elixir of charcoal and calcium carbonate, which she hoped would prevent any poison from entering his bloodstream. As a chaser, she made a strong pot of coffee. Nausea set in, tormenting him for the rest of the night. A thick sheen of sweat spread across his skin—"the sweat of death," Dore said. Friedrich knew that he was dying, and Dore told herself that she could "only look on, ignorant and helpless."

She did not go to the Wittmers' and ask for their help.

Instead, she picked up a copy of Nietzsche's *Thus Spake Zarathustra* and read his favorite passages. Somehow Friedrich found a way to speak around his swollen tongue, telling her, "Mark these lines, Dore, and remember them always . . . in memory of me."

She read on. Next to her, Friedrich spasmed in pain. "Despair surged over me," she later said. She asked herself a discomfiting question: What would she do at Friedo all alone?

But she did not go for help. Instead, she claimed, she walked back over to their table and swallowed another mouthful of the poisoned chicken, with the intention of eating it all and dying with Friedrich. Just as suddenly she changed her mind, asking herself, "What if he did not die but remained ill and helpless, or even paralyzed for life? If I were dead, then I should have failed him in his hour of greatest need. I could not bear the thought, and prayed that if I had now poisoned myself, God might not punish me by killing me while Friedrich still needed my help."

She did not feel any ill effect from the meat, and still, she did not go for help.

Friedrich, she said, then roused himself from his deep sleep. She told him she was thinking about going to the Wittmers' to ask for help. He tried to answer but could not speak. She fetched a pencil and paper so that he could write his thoughts. She read his weak scribble. Don't go to the Wittmers' house, he warned. With her lame leg, she might not make it.

She defied him, and at last went for help.

•    •    •

Early in the morning Margret heard footsteps in the garden, and turned to see Dore at the gate. Margret approached her with great apprehension; Dore seldom visited the house, and Margret couldn't imagine why she'd make the trip at such an hour, considering her bad leg.

"Why didn't you come on the donkey?" she asked.

Dore avoided the question. "Something terrible's happened," she said. "Dr. Ritter had got meat poisoning. He's extremely ill, in fact I think he's dying."

Margret was stunned. She escorted Dore into the house and sat her down. Dore gathered her strength, and after a moment shared more details.

"The day before yesterday we opened some of the jars with the meat from the dead chickens," she said. "We realized at once the meat was bad, but Friedrich said I only needed to give it a good boiling, then it would be quite safe."

"And you ate some of that?" Margret asked. "You both did?"

"Yes, I had some too."

Margret went silent. Two people had eaten poisoned meat, and yet one was on his deathbed while the other had traveled a long and arduous journey to her home and still looked perfectly healthy.

"How long has he been ill?" Margret asked.

"He didn't feel well yesterday morning, and put it down to the meat. But the worst of it is that he can hardly see."

"And you didn't have any ill effects yourself?"

Here came the first discrepancy. "Oh yes," she said. "I was sick directly afterwards, and haven't felt anything since then. But Friedrich got worse and worse." She added that she had "sensed evil" in the meat and deliberately made herself vomit.

Again Margret fell silent. In that case, she thought, why hadn't Dore come for help the day before? But Dore seemed in no mood for such questions, and besides, Margret sensed that they had already wasted enough time. As she dashed off a note for Heinz, telling him to head to Friedo as soon as possible, Dore rambled on: "During this morning his tongue swelled up so badly he couldn't talk properly anymore, only a sort of mumbling it's impossible to make anything of. About the last thing he said more or less comprehensibly was that it would be very funny indeed if he as a vegetarian was going to die of meat poisoning. . . . I know I should have used a stomach pump at once, but we haven't got anything that would make one." Margret, ever resourceful, had already found a thin rubber tube that she hoped might work. The women set off for Friedo.

They traveled slowly. Dore would recall riding on Harry's donkey, while Margret said they walked the entire way, Dore's bad leg dictating the pace.

• • •

By the time they made it to Friedo, the women had the same conclusion: it was too late. Friedrich seemed to be in unendurable pain, but would not accept the needle of morphine Dore tried to inject. He gathered enough strength to scribble a note, writing that a knot of mucus had lodged into his throat, making it difficult to breathe. Dore came at him with the rubber hose and again he rebuked her; it was no use. He reached for his pencil again and wrote, "This is choking me. Give me my gun." Dore picked up the gun from his bedside table and placed it out of his reach. She then leaned in and chided him: "Die in a manner worthy of your name." Margret understood: in German, the name Ritter meant "knight."

Heinz arrived around 5:00 p.m. and asked Dore for an account of what had happened. Dore repeated the story she'd told Margret, with some variations: Their cats had also eaten the poisoned meat, and none of them died. The following morning, Friedrich had complained of impaired vision, declaring it proof that he'd been poisoned. At that pronouncement, Dore immediately stuck her finger down her throat and "vomited thoroughly." Friedrich then asked for a "stomach rinse," but she could not find the materials to oblige. Like Margret, Heinz did not ask why Dore had not come at the first sign of trouble. The three of them gathered around Friedrich's bed. Dore watched as his face "became distorted with maniacal rage, terrible to behold."

From then on, she and Margret would have different recollections of the last moments of Friedrich's life. Margret would remember a disquieting admission: Friedrich wondered if his illness was punishment for having fantasized numerous times about killing the Baroness. Margret would remember, too, that Friedrich harnessed all his energy to pick up a pencil and write, "I curse you with my dying breath." At that, he looked at Dore, his eyes "gleaming with hate." Margret was startled: "Here were two people supposed to have been living together in spiritual harmony, despising all worldly things, and now when one of them was dying his last emotion was hatred for the other."

Over the next hour Margret watched Dore, gauging her expression; she pretended not to notice Friedrich's "hate-filled eyes." If Dore came close to him, his limbs spasmed feebly, as though trying to hit or kick her.

Dore excused herself and went outside to the garden, where she lay on the ground. She thought of the five years they had spent designing and tending to their "Eden in the wilderness," a paradise that would never bloom again.

In the house, Friedrich's shaking hands pressed together and gestured toward Margret.

"You want to pray?" she asked.

He shook his head no, and again made the gesture, drifting his hands from Margret to Heinz. Margret couldn't understand what he was trying to tell them. She fluffed his pillows and dabbed at the sweat along his brow. Dore came back inside; it was now 9:00 p.m.

Dore would remember that Friedrich suddenly sat up in bed, animated by some mysterious burst of energy, and reached toward her with both arms. "All trace of pain and torment had vanished from his face," Dore claimed, "which was transfigured with a look so lucid, so triumphant, so calm, so tender, so illuminated with a knowledge that surpasses understanding, that I could only gaze upon him like one who sees a miracle."

Margret, too, watched Friedrich sit up, motivated by rage at the sound of Dore's voice. "Looking like a ghost," Margret claimed, "he tried to pounce on her."

DORE: He seemed to actually say to me, "I go, but promise you will not forget what we have lived for." I called his name in astonishment. It seemed to me as if he would draw me with him.

MARGRET: His eyes flashed with a wild feverish flame. Dore shrieked, and drew back in horror.

DORE: Then he sank back, and I began to caress his forehead tenderly. He became quite still.

MARGRET: Then he collapsed soundlessly, falling back on the pillows.

DORE: And that was death.

MARGRET: He had gone.

• • •

Heinz checked Friedrich's pulse and breath, confirming his death. Dore found a linen that she had brought from Germany and lay it over his body. Heinz and Margret decided that he should return home to be with Harry and Rolf and Margret would stay with Dore, who was distraught and murmuring incoherently. Margret tried to discern her garbled words; she managed to catch "something about a secret" that Friedrich had with Rudolph Lorenz, but Dore was unable—or unwilling—to divulge what it was.

In Margret's telling, she changed the subject, describing how Friedrich had held up his hands, as though in prayer.

"Why did he do that?" Dore asked.

Margret said she had no idea. Dore repeated her question but received the same answer; Margret did not know what Friedrich had meant by the gesture. Dore, to Margret's surprise, offered an explanation: "He was begging for your forgiveness."

"What for?" Margret asked.

"I don't know," Dore whispered. "I only know that's what he meant."

"What did he think he'd done to us?"

Dore couldn't elaborate, and said again, "I don't know."

She was up all night, mumbling fragments of thoughts, sometimes shouting. At one point, deep in delirium, she cried, "I shall be murdered here. I must get away, I must."

"Come now," Margret said, trying her best to soothe her. "There's no one on the island who would want to hurt you. Try to calm down and get some sleep."

"No, no, I must get away from here," Dore insisted, but in the next moment her voice softened to a solemn hush. "I must spread Dr. Ritter's fame through the world. They would not acknowledge him during his lifetime, but now he is gone, his writings will be ranked among the great masterpieces of philosophy. It is my task to see that they are."

It went on in this way all night long.

•   •   •

In the morning, Heinz arrived at Friedo to take Margret home. She felt relief at leaving "that bungalow of death and delirium" but felt obliged to return often and sit with Dore, listening to her fevered soliloquies about forgiveness and murder and her need to flee the island—words Margret believed were connected to the disappearance of the Baroness and Robert Philippson.

Back home, with Heinz, Margret tried to make sense of Dore's odd dialogue. There seemed little question that Rudolph Lorenz had killed the Baroness and Robert, she said—but how? He was a sick man, Margret reasoned, and could not have overpowered them by himself. With Friedrich as an ally, though, Rudolph might have been emboldened to strike.

"Perhaps," Heinz said, "he got into the chalet when they weren't there. He would know where she kept her revolver. He could have waited to trap them on their return."

"Yes," Margret said. "Or sneaked up on them somewhere." She recalled how Rudolph used to spring out from the bushes like a jack-in-the-box, scaring her out of her skin. They decided that the bodies most likely had washed out to sea, carried out by the high tide.

They lamented, as Friedrich had in one of his last letters to Hancock, that there was no proof.

• • •

For Friedrich's final resting place, Dore chose his favorite corner of the garden, one where he had toiled the most, intent on creating the perfect Friedo egg. Harry and Heinz carried the body in Friedrich's old wheelbarrow. A ribbon of congealed blood oozed from his nose and mouth. Margret picked flowers to place at the grave.

Dore, according to Margret, did not attend the funeral.

# THIRTY-SEVEN
# And Then There
# Were Four

O n the trail to Friedo, Captain Hancock was surprised to see Dore, crying and "half hysterical," with Margret just a few steps behind.

"Where are your menfolk?" Hancock asked.

"The doctor is dead," Dore said.

"My God!" Hancock said. "And he said something terrible might happen. What a series of tragedies!" They had just come from Marchena Island, he said, where they had located and identified the bodies of Rudolph Lorenz and Trygve Nuggerud. "I recognized Lorenz at once," he added. "You could still make out his features. He was lying stretched out in the hot sand, all his clothes worn to shreds. . . . Nuggerud lay quite near him. They must have died of starvation and thirst. There isn't a drop of water on the island."

In that moment, with Dore under extreme duress, Hancock did not mention the letters that had been found near Rudolph Lorenz. One letter in particular, written by a Norwegian sailor named Arthur, spoke of visiting Rudolph on Floreana in the spring of that year. Rudolph told Arthur that the Baroness and Robert had left the island on a "small English sailing boat," but also said something that could be interpreted as a confession. "He told me," Arthur wrote, "he stood it as long as he could, and finally got sick of it."

• • •

The *Velero* party decided to split up. The scientists Waldo Schmitt, Fred Ziesenhenne, John Garth, and some of the wives would escort Margret back to her home; Hancock and the rest would take care of Dore. Walking with Margret, Garth noticed that the island was greener than he'd ever seen it, with the trees heavy with fruit and the flowers in furious bloom. Great swarms of birds circled them from above—"more birds than ever," he remarked—and the pigeons and rabbits had multiplied. He could hardly believe that settlers had suffered a drought that had killed most of the cattle. Schmitt picked a dozen oranges along the way, declaring them the best he'd ever eaten, and marveled at the trees—"a hundred years old," he said, "and the very ones that Darwin saw."

The Wittmers' farm was flourishing: tobacco, avocados, squash, papaya, cucumbers, and bananas all boasted luxuriant growth. The corrugated-iron sheets that once covered the Hacienda Paradiso now served as the Wittmers' new roof. One of the women nearly fainted as Fred picked shiny black spiders from the rafters.

Margret invited the party inside and related her version of the story, beginning with the drought and ending with the disappearance of the Baroness and Robert Philippson. It was the last time she'd have to explain what she knew of the tragic events, or so she thought.

•    •    •

Even with her cane, Dore found it difficult to walk. Hancock and Charles Swett flanked her, gripping her arms, leading her back to Friedo. She seemed "out of her mind," Swett thought, calling for Friedrich in one breath and speaking of his last moments in the next. "What am I going to do?" she asked no one in particular. She did not have the strength to care for Friedo, to tend to the garden, to water the plants and fruits, and if she did not care for them, she would starve. As they climbed the trail, her donkey, Fleck, bounded down to meet her. He had grown impressively since the crew had last seen him, but now his once-handsome coat shed in large patches.

All the way she kept whispering, sometimes in German, sometimes in English, about the troubles on the island, about the abuse of Rudolph Lorenz, about the Baroness leaving her most intimate belongings behind,

about Friedrich and his manuscript, about the volatile nature of their relationship. "Yes, I loved the doctor, loved him very dearly," Swett heard her
say. "We too had strife even in our garden of Eden. . . . I too would have
left the island if I could have found a way. Now our garden will wilt and
die. Soon the drought will come again and the desert jungle will take its
own. Our garden of Eden will vanish."

They reached Friedo, already marred by neglect. The water hole Friedrich had so painstakingly dug had already collapsed. The wild pigs he
despised had broken into the garden. The insects, which he once derided
as "socialists," were descending in hordes.

Dore led the men to Friedrich's grave, shallow and half-filled, marked by
disturbed earth and a pile of flat stones. She sat down on it, crossing her
ankles, her feet encased in clean white sneakers. Her head and shoulders
seemed to wilt, and Swett leaned in to hear her next words: "The island is
an island of tragedy. It is not meant for human habitation. Thirst and
death is the lot of those who try." Swett lifted his gaze to an old papaya
tree, its branches laden with fruit, its leaves spreading a canopy over Friedrich's grave. Soon enough, he thought, those melons would ripen and
fall, the seeds would sprout, and a jumble of greenery would rise up and
cover the soil, covering the grave for good.

•    •    •

On December 7, 1934, Dore prepared to leave. At her request, Margret
stayed over the night before, helping Dore to pack, filling several boxes
and bags with seemingly everything she and Friedrich owned. A *Velero*
crewman stood nearby with a camera, filming the scene. Both women
wept; Margret hid her face with a handkerchief. For the occasion Dore
dressed in a long cotton skirt and matching top with a Peter Pan collar. A
bucket hat sat atop her head. She walked with her cane in one hand and a
handkerchief in the other, dabbing at her eyes.

She bade a final farewell to Friedrich's grave, a moment she would later
record: "I said goodbye . . . but did not feel as if I were leaving him there,
cold in the hostile Floreana earth. In some strange way that I cannot find
words for, I did not feel that he was dead, but that he had just begun to
live. . . . The gods of Floreana could have no power over Friedrich, whom

they slew; he must live on through me." When she and Hancock turned around for one last look at Friedo, the captain noticed a "merciful mist" descending from the summit of the long-extinct volcano, hiding the highlands from sight.

On the walk to Black Beach, her donkey romped around her, nearly knocking her down. She listed and stumbled all the way as though drunk. Heinz stood on the shore, waiting for them. He loaded a few of his donkeys with Dore's boxes and bags. Turning to say goodbye to Heinz and Margret, Dore began to cry again. "We and the Wittmers never had been friends," she would write, "but we had been something more than merely neighbors." She wished them well, and they promised to take care of Fleck and Friedo.

Taking Hancock's hand, Dore climbed into the dinghy that would bring her to the ship. Once on board, the captain sent a wireless message to Los Angeles: "Dore leaving Charles Island on Velero III for trans-ship for Germany at Guayaquil. Was hysterical, but improving."

•   •   •

The next day, a reporter for *El Universo,* a Guayaquil newspaper, arrived on Floreana to investigate the disappearances and interview the Wittmers. The reporter had already spoken with several people on the mainland, including a man who happened to have a letter from Margret; the letter had been intended for Rolf Blomberg, the Swedish author who had visited the island a few months earlier. The letter, written shortly after Blomberg's visit, mentioned rumors that the boat carrying Rudolph Lorenz had shipwrecked. "I am deeply sorry for the misfortune that befell Lorenz," Margret wrote, "but he has received the punishment he deserved"—a statement the reporter interpreted to mean that Margret and Heinz knew exactly what had happened to the Baroness and Robert Philippson. This suspicion was confirmed by a letter Friedrich Ritter had written to the newspaper, in which he accused Heinz Wittmer of murdering the couple. "There was no ship anywhere near Floreana on the night the Baroness is supposed to have left the island," Friedrich claimed. "But during the night I heard shots and a woman's scream. It could only have been the Baroness. And the only person who could have fired the shots is Heinz Wittmer."

Heinz and Margret recalled Friedrich's strange gestures on his deathbed—the clasping of hands as though in prayer. They had a guess as to what he'd meant to convey: an apology for defiling their good name.

• • •

Right away, Dore's presence on the *Velero* presented some difficulties for the scientists and crew. John Garth was astounded by the voluminous baggage Dore had brought with her, calling it "a great assortment of trash." Nothing had been deemed too trivial to leave behind, including old bedding, half a can of sugar, and Friedrich's shopping ledger, which listed the items he planned to request from visiting yachts. One crewman, charged with storing Dore's belongings below deck, was disgusted by the "old garments and rotted cloth." Waldo Schmitt called Dore's stash "the darndest junk" and joked that she might dump half of it once she "learned of steamer rates for impedimenta."

After departing Black Beach, the *Velero* sailed for Santa Cruz Island, where the party stopped, in Schmitt's words, to "visit acquaintances of former years and get a couple of tortoise feet." With this endeavor he was disappointed, finding only "a few punk ones" that might not be salvageable. Gossip abounded about the Floreana settlers. "Everyone is convinced Lorenz did away with the Baroness and Philippson and then tried to flee the country," Schmitt noted, "for he was in great haste to get away and to Chatham where he could catch a boat to Guayaquil; they have more frequent boat service there."

During this visit, the scientist Fred Ziesenhenne learned of other popular theories. One suggested that Rudolph Lorenz had stored the bodies of the baroness and Robert in a box at Post Office Bay and brought it on board the *Dinamita*—a rumor given credence by Margret's observation about "heavy" cargo when she'd bid Rudolph farewell. Moreover, Ziesenhenne wrote, "enough rocks were added to sink the box and bodies in very deep water." Another claimed that Dore, too, was guilty of murder: "Dr. Ritter would take his temper out on Dore when upset. During the dry season Dr. Ritter's temper really flared and poor Dore could not take any more punishment and decided to kill the Dr. and leave Charles Island."

On board the *Velero*, Dore stayed in cabin 1 of the crew quarters. Zie-senhenne found himself in the role of Dore's chaperone and assistant, run-ning back and forth to deliver messages and fetch her various comforts: fruit, cold water, writing paper, pens. She had "one crippled leg," he wrote, "and did not walk too well in a rolling sea." She spent most of her time standing at the ship's rail, gazing out at the water. When he asked if she felt lonely, she would reply that she simply loved the ocean.

At first she declined to talk about Friedrich or his death, but eventu-ally told Ziesenhenne that she had warned him not to eat the poisoned chicken—a statement she had never made before, nor would ever again. A few days later, her mood shifted. She dressed up in her nicest clothes, garments she hadn't worn in years, left her cabin, and mingled with the crew.

At 6:00 a.m. on December 14, Ziesenhenne was surprised to learn that the *Velero* was changing course, heading back to Floreana. Hancock, un-nerved by the dark rumors circling throughout the islands, wished to take depositions regarding the Baroness and Robert Philippson. Waldo Schmitt was dubbed Sherlock Holmes by his colleagues, and the student zoologist, Ray Elliott, his Watson.

Schmitt and Elliott walked to the Wittmers' house and invited them back to the *Velero*, where Hancock was waiting to talk to them. Together, Dore, Heinz, and Margret crafted a statement. It described the drought; the abuse of Rudolph Lorenz; the Baroness's claim that she and Robert were setting sail on a yacht; Margret's realization that this story was merely a subterfuge to entrap Rudolph; and, finally, Rudolph's desperation to leave Floreana and his eventual departure, funded by money he'd received by selling the Baroness's things. "We know nothing of the Baroness's whereabouts, dead or alive," the statement concluded, "and only know about her what Lorenz imparted to us before his departure."

It did not mention March 19, the day on which Dore claimed she'd heard a woman's scream. The story of the scream was likely a ruse of Dore's own—an attempt to give Friedrich an alibi, quiet any suspicion that he had been Lorenz's accomplice, and preserve, as best she could, his legacy.

After dinner and a concert by the *Velero* ensemble, Heinz, Margret, and Dore were invited to watch *The Empress of Floreana*, Hancock's movie starring the Baroness, in which she plays a pirate queen. Heinz was confused, thinking the film depicted an actual event, until one of the scientists clarified that it was fiction.

•   •   •

On December 15, Dore faced another inquiry, this time regarding the circumstances surrounding Friedrich's death. At one o'clock, after the *Velero* docked at Chatham Island, she, Waldo Schmitt, and John Garth took the launch to the shore, where the governor of the Galápagos waited for them. Together they walked to what Garth called the "Governor's Tin Palace."

Inside, Dore was escorted to a room crowded with Ecuadorian officials, among them a judge, the public prosecutor, and the chancellor of the German consulate. Dore spoke mostly in German, with Garth acting as her interpreter, translating her responses into Spanish. Dore did not mention poisoned chicken, and claimed that Friedrich had died of a stroke "due to suffocation. . . . He did not have the strength to expel his vomit due to the progressive paralysis of the muscles and nerves in his throat." Garth, aware that the governor and his associates might have heard conflicting stories of Friedrich's death, "left out a good deal in the translation." At this point, he wrote, the entire *Velero* party wanted to save Dore from an "impossible situation" and get her off their hands.

The judge ratified and signed Dore's statement, and she was free to leave the Galápagos without any further delay.

•   •   •

On the morning of December 20, the *Velero* left for the mainland. From Guayaquil, Dore would find passage back to Germany, and to the very civilization she'd once hoped to avoid for the rest of her days; Adolf Hitler was now the führer of the German Reich and its sole, absolute authority.

Hoping to spare Dore from further questioning by Ecuadorian officials, Hancock anchored the *Velero* a short distance from the quayside and told Dore to stay on board. The strategy failed: a dozen small boats and a fleet of water taxis carrying journalists and photographers ferried to the ship, eager to glimpse the "Eve" who had lost her Adam, calling for her to answer questions about the past five years—her reasons for leaving Germany, her relationship with Friedrich, the drama on Floreana, Friedrich's death, and her return to her homeland. She refused a request from a magazine editor to write articles about her life, explaining that she planned to write "several books on the subject" as soon as she reached Germany.

One reporter, however, did manage to find Dore's ex-husband, Hermann Koerwin, who lived in Berlin with his second wife and had no interest in seeing Dore ever again. He was, he said, "entirely dispassionate" toward the incidents on Floreana, and content for the Galápagos affair to remain a mystery.

• • •

On Floreana, Margret and Heinz honored their promise to Dore to take care of Friedo. Margret moved into Friedo with Rolf, leaving Harry to look after their own home, while Heinz went back and forth. Heinz was appalled by Friedo's condition. "Pots and pans lie around everywhere and there are tools of all kinds," he wrote. "Heaps of empty shells spoke eloquently of frequent hunting. The guns are of American manufacture and the many worn shoes too." The whole situation, Heinz decided, was causing the "complete upsetting" of his own family life.

On one occasion when Margret was back at her own house, which they had named Casa de la Paz (House of Peace), she saw a group of soldiers approaching with fixed bayonets, followed by the Galápagos governor and an interpreter. She was not used to seeing armed soldiers—why would they come to her home? Her heart "stood still for a moment," and she could not find her voice.

"What do you want with us?" Heinz asked. The soldiers didn't respond. They fanned out into a circle, and the interpreter asked Heinz to go inside the house. They were investigating a crime and wished to question him. Heinz did as they asked while Margret stayed outside, waiting in a quiet panic. Finally, someone appeared at the door and told her it was her turn.

"Tell me exactly what happened about the Baroness's disappearance," the interpreter said, speaking for the governor.

Margret told the story she'd already told many times, and said the governor likely knew the story himself.

He wasn't satisfied. "You're hiding something from me," he said. "You're hiding the most important thing. Let's have the truth at last."

Margret didn't know how to respond.

"Your husband killed the Baroness," he said.

"What?" she asked. "Who on earth do you get that from?"

"Dr. Ritter," he said, and then Margret understood: he was following up on the newspaper article in which Friedrich had claimed to hear a woman's scream and gunshots—gunshots that were, according to Friedrich, fired by Heinz. Margret began to laugh; she couldn't help herself. Heinz argued that this scenario would have required "superhuman hearing" on Friedrich's part, since Friedo was several miles away from the Hacienda Paradiso, with a mountain slope in between. Heinz also suggested that if the Baroness and Robert Philippson had indeed been shot, Friedrich could just as easily have been the culprit, for he and Rudolph Lorenz both had strong motives for murder.

Convinced of their innocence, the governor and his party stayed for lunch. Margret, pleased to have "no stain on our characters," made them all a plate of perfectly edible chicken.

•   •   •

At Friedo, Heinz sifted through the last of Dore and Friedrich's belongings, growing angrier with each new discovery. In the cupboards he found shelves of butter, fat, oil, sugar, canned vegetables, and the like—obviously gifts from the Americans that Friedrich had never thought to share. He recalled Friedrich's pious declarations about vegetarianism and living only on "fruits and eggs"—all of them lies, spoken in service to his own self-creation, an ideal he would never attain. "It is basically false to state that people are good," Heinz wrote in his diary. "Words and expressions sound very fine when one knows nothing of the deeds. So it was with Dr. Ritter."

In one of Friedrich's books, Heinz found a curious sentence underlined: "All thoughts of sympathy or antipathy do good or evil and when they are unable to find a fertile soil in which [to] take root, back they go to their originator and spend on him the potentialities for good or evil inherent in them."

Heinz considered the sentence for a moment, and wondered if Friedrich had predicted his own sad and sudden fate.

• • •

He and Margret decided it was not worth the effort to preserve Friedo, that it made no sense to "do good to those who meant to do us evil." He erected a plain wooden cross to mark Friedrich's grave. Over time, visitors on passing ships plundered what was left until the house itself ceased to exist, and the garden that had once been revered for its fecundity succumbed to the invasive pests Friedrich had so despised.

Friedo's demise underscored an inescapable paradox: in the settlers' desire to flee the chaos of modern civilization, they created a microcosm of it on the island. Nearly a century later, anyone drawn to explore Floreana's dark history might wonder if the legendary "Adam and Eve" had ever found Eden at all.

# THIRTY-EIGHT
# Thus Spake Floreana

During a visit to Floreana in the winter of 1935, the Galápagos governor gave Margret and Heinz a cable from a German newspaper, which asked if they were alive and, if so, interested in writing about the events on the island. The reply was prepaid, with a limit of seven words. Back on his ship, the governor signaled Margret's response—"WE ARE ALIVE RITTER DEAD WILL WRITE"—which, she later learned, was broadcast on an enormous sign outside the newspapers' offices.

She decided to take a trip to Germany, both to visit family and to "find out what the people back home know of things." She also worried about Dore, who might start "putting out stories about us which needed immediate refutation." The money they had stored away in the event that their Galápagos experiment failed would be used to fund the journey. Rolf, now two years old and known throughout the world as "Prince Charles" in homage to Floreana's English name, would accompany her, while Harry would stay behind to help Heinz. It would be a multi-legged journey—from Floreana to Chatham Island to Guayaquil to, finally, Panama, where she would board the USS *San Francisco* to Hamburg. At Panama, throngs of reporters gathered around the ship, clamoring for any comment about Floreana. Her brief interview only heightened the intrigue, as she claimed to know the secret behind the Baroness's disappearance, a secret she would be pleased to reveal—for a price.

"When was the last time you saw the Baroness?" one newsman asked.

"In March of last year," Margret answered.

"Where is your husband?"

Margret shook her head and said, "I am going to Germany now to clear up all the stories that the newspapers have published about me. I have a contract with a journalistic union there."

At the next shouted question, Margret demurred. "I prefer not to say anything else unless I am paid for the story," she said, adding that her price was for no less than "one money per word."

• • •

Margret arrived in Cologne in late April 1935, just as Wilhelm Frick, Hitler's minister of the interior, announced new requirements for full German citizenship in the Third Reich. Every German woman of childbearing age was to produce one child for the fatherland, and every German man must serve his army term before full citizenship would be granted. "Racial kinship to the German people is one of the main prerequisites for becoming a citizen," Frick said. "Enemies of the state and unworthy elements will be deprived of this right." In a related announcement, he decreed that Jewish citizens "must discontinue flying the German flag, especially the Swastika," because "much trouble has been caused by Jews who fly flags."

Margret was overjoyed to reunite with family but felt very uneasy about the political and social changes in her homeland. "When we left the country three years before," she reflected, "Hitler had not yet come to power, and it was both painful and alarming to see the Nazi regime in action, ruthlessly suppressing all possible opponents and already persecuting harmless Jewish citizens. My sister, who had many Jewish clients in her hairdressing salon, hated the Nazis and already emigrated to England the year before. . . . I did feel 'something was rotten,' and this feeling made me all the readier to leave 'civilization' again, to return to our primitive island."

After Margret's series, titled "With Wittmer at Galapagos," ran in a Cologne newspaper, the editor received a barrage of furious letters from Dore—complaints that soon "dried up," Margret noted smugly, since they adhered to facts Dore could "scarcely dispute." When Margret tried to turn the series into a short book, she encountered far more difficult resistance, this time from the Nazi regime itself. The Baroness's Nazi brother, Gustav, demanded that the work be expurgated. Years later, Gustav's daughter would write a memoir in which she addressed her aunt directly: "My father was ashamed of you. . . . He certainly never spoke of you, his sister."

Margret stayed in Germany throughout the summer and fall, giving public talks about her life in the Galápagos, supplemented with film and photographs sent by Captain Hancock. The lectures were immensely successful, she reported to Hancock; one evening, all twelve hundred seats in the hall were taken, and "there was still a crowd of men outside."

She and Rolf departed Germany in early November, arriving at Black Beach in January 1936. Her beloved dog, Lump, raced down and barked wildly at the ship. Rolf, at the sight of his father, said, "Papa, Papa, come and fetch your little boy," a command Margret had taught him during the trip. She was thrilled to see that Heinz and Harry had added a new bedroom and that Heinz had killed most of the chickens, explaining that it would have been too much work to keep them alive.

•    •    •

Dore, meanwhile, had been working on her own book, detailing her five fraught years on Floreana. Titled *Satan Came to Eden*, the book was published in London in 1935 and in New York the following year, with some tweaks in language and minor but telling additions—many seemingly intended to name Rudolph Lorenz, indisputably, as a murderer, and to cast Margret and Heinz as his accomplices. She made the most significant change in her account of Friedrich's death. In 1935, she claimed, with no equivocation, that Friedrich had suffered a stroke; in the later edition, she named meat poisoning as the likely cause of death. In both versions, she insisted that she and Friedrich heard a woman's scream on the afternoon of March 19, 1934, an event she never once mentioned at the time it allegedly occurred. Margret had no kind words for Dore's book, claiming it caused only "a minor stir" and "was not very successful."

Although Dore no longer sent Hancock stories about her alter egos, Gertrud and Mary, she wrote often with updates on her present circumstances and reflections on her past—letters that spoke of her "bodiless

Friedrich" and his persistent influence on her life, even in death. She omit-
ted any hint that she had begun to chafe under his instruction—that she
had, toward the end, reveled in the possibility of becoming her own
master—and instead reclaimed her role as his disciple, helpless without his
ghostly guidance. "I could give you a dozen of proves [*sic*] how Friedrich is
near me," she wrote, "and arranges all things to my best. My task is to be
awake and to wait till he has decided."

Privately, though, it seems her resentment toward Friedrich had only
deepened with his death. In July 1935, one month after Dore wrote to
Hancock of her enduring connection to Friedrich, the captain received a
letter from Friedrich's nephew. "I know that among the many new friends
that my uncle made in the islands, you rank highest," he wrote, "and it is
my duty to offer you in his stead unending thanks." He confessed that he
had failed to find a publisher for Friedrich's philosophy works, even after
numerous inquiries, and had to settle for publishing Friedrich's memoir
instead. He added that he had sought Dore's assistance in this endeavor,
but she had been "impossible" and refused to help, despite her oft-stated
goal of spreading Friedrich's ideas around the world.

Dore wrote to Hancock several times over the next few years, sharing
personal insights that seemed to reflect her growing loneliness. "Do you
know that there may be moments in our relations with those we love,
when we leave them to be nearer to them?" she wrote. "Absent, they are
all our own. We hold them so near, so near to us. They say only what we
wish to hear, and we say nothing to them which we wish afterwards unsaid.
We understand each other so perfectly in these solitary meetings of the
fancy, that the reality is sometimes deadly cold in comparison."

Still living in Berlin, she sent what appears to be her final letter to Hancock on May 12, 1938. "Although I never got an answer or personal note
from you," she wrote, "I am writing to you again. It should be my last step."
She told him she had been "very very sick" during the past three years,
since leaving Floreana, and lamented that she had "not one penny" of her
own. She hoped to change her fortunes by giving lectures—"I shall speak
about tropical life and so on, just about my life accidents and experiences"—
and wondered if he might send some photographs for the purpose. "The
very moment I get enough money to buy my ticket," she signed off, "I am
leaving Germany and going to Guayaquil—that means to the tropics."

Dore never made it back to Floreana. She died in Berlin's Ludwig Hoffmann Hospital on May 11, 1943, at age forty-two. The death certificate cited complications of multiple sclerosis and "menopausal bleeding." Reflecting upon the news, Margret remarked that Dore was "the last person who could have cleared up the mysteries which had surrounded our island."

Time would prove that many visitors to Floreana believed otherwise.

•   •   •

Even after the Baroness vanished, her presence loomed large over the island she once claimed to rule. One sea captain, who had traveled to the Galápagos with an American yacht in November 1934, said his "latest knowledge" of the Baroness placed her as a hostess in a Guayaquil nightclub. Another report claimed that the Baroness and Robert Philippson had gone back to Paris, where they operated a toy shop. An even wilder tale came from the former Pennsylvania governor Gifford Pinchot, who reported an encounter with the Baroness in March 1935, a year after she disappeared. After arriving at Post Office Bay, Pinchot said, he and his party followed the path that led to the Hacienda Paradiso. Walking ahead of the group, Pinchot saw a piece of white silk. At first he thought it was a handkerchief, but then the silk moved, darting behind a bush, rustling branches. He continued on the trail until a voice shouted at him from behind.

"Stop!"

Pinchot felt something on his shoulder. He swiveled his neck and saw that it was a pearl-handled revolver, held by a woman with a steady hand. He realized that this was the famous Baroness and "trembled with excitement."

She gave him a "cold look" and an order: "I don't like you. Go."

Shortly thereafter, Pinchot admitted that the reported incident was invented for the benefit of his fellow passengers on the *Stella Polaris*, which had made a recent stop in the Galápagos. "We hunted for the Baroness," he said, "but we didn't find her. We walked far inland from Post Office Bay, where the whalers left their letters for home in a barrel, but no Baroness. So with some others who went with us we put up a cock and bull story of how we found the fiery lady, and what she said, and what we said, and for about fifteen minutes we got away with it with the rest of the passengers. Then they were on to us."

Even President Franklin D. Roosevelt wasn't immune to the Baroness's mystique. In July 1938, Roosevelt took a fishing vacation on the cruiser USS *Houston*, which planned a stop at Floreana. The Smithsonian's Waldo Schmitt was on board and regaled the president with tales of the Baroness, inspiring the party to find and interview the Wittmers. "The official news report from the *Houston*," wrote *Time* magazine, "announced that the landing parties tried to pump the settlers about [the Baroness], the queer German woman who, wearing silk panties and a pearl-handled revolver, sought to rule the island several years ago until she and her retinue of young men came to mysterious ends. The settlers would not tell, and the whereabouts of the Baroness have been unknown for four years."

Hancock continued his explorations to the South Seas, including the Galápagos, overseeing research and conservation efforts that still endure today. On Baltra Island, where invasive goats were endangering the native land iguanas, his fleet of scientists moved seventy iguanas to North Seymour so they could breed and rebuild the population. Although some of the scientists' methods would be rightly considered cruel today—no modern researcher, for instance, would advocate transferring indigenous Galápagos animals to aquariums or zoos—their work contributed to and enhanced scientific knowledge, especially regarding the islands' lesser-known species, including mosses, plankton, mollusks, and lichens. In a feat that would have thrilled Darwin himself, the *Velero* crew discovered three new species of oxystomatous crabs and a new genus and species of barnacle, and conducted an intensive study of the male genitalia of noctuid moths.

During rare moments of downtime, in between collecting and filming and classifying specimens, the scientists wondered what Hancock knew about the intrigues of Floreana, now years past. "It was the general understanding among the people on the 1938 trip," wrote one scientist, "that the only one of Hancock's people who had gotten the whole story of what happened to the Baroness and Philippson was Capt. Hancock, and that he had said that what he knew would die with him."

Hancock died at the age of eighty-nine on May 31, 1965, having kept that promise to himself.

• • •

Out of all the Galápagos settlers, only Margret and Heinz achieved something close to utopia, assimilating into life on Floreana, the island sustaining them in turn. The Danish writer Hakon Mielche, during a visit to Floreana in 1932, made an eerily prescient observation, especially considering the macabre events that would come to pass. "When Ritter and the Baroness have turned to dust and 'Paradise' and 'Eden' have sunk into a smoking hell," he wrote, "Wittmer will still be sitting in his cozy little house smoking his pipe. The sun will rise and set, and he will forget to count the days."

In December 1938, Heinz and Margret held a wedding ceremony on Floreana presided over by Ecuadorian civil officials, but it wasn't until 1939 that Heinz's divorce from his first wife was finalized. By this time, Margret and Heinz had had another child together, a daughter named Ingeborg Floreanita Wittmer, the second native of Floreana. As of this writing, Ingeborg is still living on the island, running the Hotel Wittmer along with her daughter Erika (another daughter, Ingrid, runs a smaller hotel, Black Beach House, a short distance away). The ground floor of the Hotel Wittmer is a museum devoted to Margret and Heinz's life on Floreana, with many of their belongings on display: a typewriter and clothing iron; hunting rifles and a phonograph; trunks and notebooks and lanterns; a bookshelf featuring dozens of books about the Galápagos, including Friedrich Ritter's *Als Robinson auf Galapagos* (As Robinson in the Galápagos). The shelf has one notable omission: not one copy of Dore's book, *Satan Came to Eden.*

Other settlers came and went, most notably an American couple, Ainslie and Frances Conway, who lived for six months on Santiago Island before moving to Floreana. Owing to Ainslie's work for the U.S. military, rumors began to circulate that he and Frances were spies. The United States had not yet entered World War II, but some military strategists believed that Hitler's plans included invading and conquering South America, a possibility that required swift and effective intelligence work.

Both Frances and Ainslie had read Dore's book and were eager to visit the remains of Friedo. The well-worn trail leading from Black Beach to Friedo had been named El Camino de la Muerte (The Path of the Dead) by some imaginative locals, a moniker that reflected both the string of animal skulls lining the path and the suspicion that the ghosts of the former settlers—from the vicious pirate Patrick Watkins to Friedrich Ritter—haunted anyone who walked along it. "The garden was as quiet as oblivion," Frances wrote of Friedo, "except for the soft trickle of water and the rustling of the wind in palm leaves, like the swish and shush of a taffeta petticoat. . . . Perhaps it was the wind in the palm leaves, perhaps the grave in the weeds, perhaps the limbo-like atmosphere of the island itself. In any case, I felt that the eccentric Germans who had created this place were still present. You cannot build a garden on a desert island, live in it virtually alone for five years, and not come back to haunt it now and then."

During the Conways' five-year stay on Floreana, the United States continued gathering intelligence about Hitler's motives and strategic information about the Galápagos Islands, producing surveys of potential sites for submarine and air bases. In 1940, soon after the start of World War II, the U.S. Navy's first minesweeper, the USS *Lapwing,* visited the archipelago. Two months after the attack on Pearl Harbor, the Naval Office published its first *Field Monograph of Galapagos Islands,* a five-hundred-page compilation of detailed findings. Around the same time, military engineers began construction on Baltra Island for an air base and naval station.

After Germany surrendered and the war officially ended, the United States had one final mission on Floreana Island. Having heard a rumor that Heinz was a reserve officer in the German army and on good terms with Hitler—highly unlikely, considering that Heinz's old boss had been an avowed enemy of the Nazi Party—military officials sent a detachment of soldiers to Floreana in 1945. They scoured the island and knocked on the door of the Wittmers' home, but Hitler was nowhere to be found.

• • •

The curse of Floreana, which had so haunted Dore during her entire time on the island, continued long after her death. In 1951, after nearly two decades on the island, Harry Wittmer, age thirty-three, drowned when his

fishing boat capsized; his body was never recovered. "I remembered bitterly how Harry had twice lain in bed for months with rheumatic fever,"
Margret wrote, "facing death for weeks on end, how we had nursed him
back to comparative health, so that he could at last look forward to a
happy, active life; and now the sea had taken him from us."

On November 20, 1935, the front page of the *New York Times* announced that a member of the Darwin Memorial Expedition found a skeleton on Santa Cruz Island, presumed to be connected to the events on
Floreana. It was in "good condition," the report revealed, "with most of
the teeth intact, showing fillings, and with a bit of pale blond hair adhering
to the jawbone." After further examination, however, the member of the
expedition determined that the skeleton was not that of the Baroness or
Robert Philippson; rather, it belonged to one of two other men who had
come to the Galápagos several years prior and were never heard from
again.

In 1964, a seventy-year-old American tourist went on a group hike into
the Floreana highlands. She stayed behind for a moment to remove a stone
from her sandal and became separated from her group. Despite extensive
searching, her body was only found months later, under a tangle of brush.
In 1969, Ingeborg Wittmer's husband, a harbormaster named Mario Garcia, went hunting on Floreana and vanished without a trace. It was a particularly disturbing incident, as Garcia knew the islands intimately. To this
day, his body has never been found.

Ecuadorian authorities ordered an investigation, as they had after the
Baroness and Robert Philippson disappeared. "Mario, he was sick," Margret explained. "He took some bad aspirin. Then he went out hunting. He
found a steer or something that knocked him down. Then the rains came
and washed him away." Heinz had his own interpretation of the Floreana
curse. "On the Galapagos," he told one friend, "it's either okay or"—and
then he would draw his hand across his neck, indicating a gruesome death.
Heinz, at least, died of natural causes (a cerebral hemorrhage) on November 7, 1963. Doctors didn't arrive until three days later, because Floreana's
only radio was broken.

Margret published her own book about the Galápagos, *Postlagernd Floreana*, in 1959; two years later, it was translated into English, published in
the United States, and serialized in newspapers across the country. Al-

though the book offers no definitive answers about Floreana's many mysteries, tourists descended upon the island, making the pilgrimage to visit Margret, hoping she might divulge any lingering secrets. No one doubted that she knew more than what she was willing to tell; suspicions compounded, giving rise to new and enduring lore. One story went like this: A group of tourists who visited Floreana in the 1960s discovered "something" in one of the pirate caves—presumably the Baroness's remains. They asked Margret about the discovery and returned the following day to the cave, only to find it empty.

Until her death in 2000, Margret welcomed visitors to the hotel, standing at the entrance, a sign hanging above: "God helps those who help themselves." She was, in a way, the embodiment of Darwinism, a specimen that evolved to thrive in her habitat. For the right price, usually a couple hundred dollars, she would serve a glass of orange wine and sit for interviews, deigning to entertain the same questions she'd been asked for decades. What were the other settlers like? Did Dore intentionally kill Friedrich Ritter? What really happened to the Baroness and Robert Philippson? Cocking her head, eyebrows raised, she spoke a jumble of English and German, some words laced with a Spanish accent, a hint of impatience conveyed in her tone. "Everything is exaggerated by people who don't know," she said. "The farther they are away, the more mixed up the stories get." With that disclaimer out of the way, she dredged up old memories of the island she'd made her home, fragments that deepened the mystery and mystique but never quite added up to a whole:

"The Baroness put her nose into everything. The old bee—buzz buzz buzz . . . you should have seen her! The way women dress today is nothing at all, we had it all along forty years ago. She wore nothing on top or wore a bra with holes."

"She was always saying to Philippson: 'Darling, hand me my robe and light me a cigarette.'"

"Dr. Ritter and the Baroness despised each other. He couldn't stomach the old bag."

"Ritter was uncouth and rude but absolutely honest."

"The last note the doctor scribbled was to Dore: 'I curse you in this last moment.'"

"Everybody knows the Baroness was found later in Tahiti, dancing."

"It is all an inexplicable mystery."

"En boca cerrada, no entran moscas." *A closed mouth admits no flies.*

And sometimes she would abruptly reverse the conversation, looking her visitor directly in the eye and asking a question of her own:

"Do you think I did it?"

# ACKNOWLEDGMENTS

Back in 2011, while researching a different book, I came upon an old newspaper article about the "Galápagos Affair," and was immediately obsessed. I read further, learning of pioneering American scientists, mysterious deaths and disappearances, thwarted dreams, and a cast of characters unlike any I'd ever encountered. This long-forgotten incident, I realized, had a universal and timeless appeal: Who hasn't dreamt of abandoning the pressures of life for a simpler existence? Who hasn't longed to flee far from the madding crowd? I had never been so captivated by a story, and I wanted to write the book immediately. For a very long time, I was told no. My eternal gratitude to and respect for David Drake, who finally told me yes.

I could not have made this strange and fascinating journey back into the Galápagos without the wisdom and assistance of numerous people. Chief among them is my brilliant and delightful editor, Libby Burton, whose enthusiasm for this project matched mine from the start, and whose fine critical eye helped me turn my unwieldy first draft into the story I wanted it to be. Her intrepid assistant, Cierra Hinckson, has a superhuman talent for getting stuff done.

Thank you to my mighty and talented team of advocates and artists at Crown: Gillian Blake, Annsley Rosner, Maren Monitello, Lynn Buckley, Aubrey Khan, Liana Faughnan, Dustin Amick, and the dedicated sales reps who would brave a one-on-one confrontation with the Baroness to help my work find its readership. My deepest appreciation for my extraordinary publicists, Mary Moates, Chantelle Walker, Rachel Rodriguez, Nicole Dewey, and Isabel Begun, who worked tirelessly to spread the word on a very tight deadline.

I am hugely indebted to all of the booksellers and librarians who have supported me over the years and pressed my books into readers' hands. I wish I could meet every single one of you in person and buy you a stiff drink and tell you how lovely you are.

Thank you Simon Lipskar, agent and friend, for being both a softie and a shark.

In May 2022, I spent five unforgettable days on Floreana Island touring the old haunts and homesteads (or what remains of them) of the 1930s settlers. I was overwhelmed by the kindness and generosity of the people I met there, especially Juan Pablo, Junior, Santos Humberto Moreno Naula, the entire Cruz family (they *really* know how to throw a party!), and Ingeborg "Floreanita" Wittmer, Margret and Heinz's 87-year-old daughter.

In the 1970s, author and playwright Lorenzo DeStefano researched the Galápagos Affair in the hope of writing a script. He contacted surviving participants, unearthed invaluable primary source material, and donated it all to the University of Southern California in August 2020. Thanks to Lorenzo's passion and generous gift, *Eden Undone* contains a rich seam of never-been-published material. Also, he's a very cool guy.

Numerous people helped with fact-checking; translating German, Spanish, French, and Norwegian documents; and research in far-flung locales: Vanessa Prado Aibar, Roslyn Cameron, Washington "Wacho" Tapia, Manal Alyedreessy, Lorraine Caputo, Cristina Burack, Katie Ranum, Natalie Ford, Julia Wiesinger, Stein Hoff, Frances Thoms Provine, John Woram, Birgit-Cathrin Duval, Niko Hofinger, and Sebastian Ignacio Donoso Bustamante. Jane Brennan, George Allan Hancock's great-granddaughter, shared his private papers and correspondence. Fritz Hieber, Friedrich Ritter's grandnephew, gave me valuable insights into his relative's character and life.

Thank you, Erik Larson, for the title idea, and thanks to friends who read various drafts: Joshilyn Jackson, Emma Garman, Ada Calhoun, Susannah Cahalan, Maureen Callahan, Margaret Talbot, Liza Mundy, Kelly Justice, Maud Newton, Christine Gleason, Lindsey Fitzharris, Lydia Netzer, Julie Wu, Anna Schachner, Frances Langbecker, Sandy Kahler, and Katherine Abbott. And thanks to the many friends who cheered me on; I would name you all but I'm running out of room.

Thank you, person-holding-this-book. I hope you love this story as much as I do.

Thank you most of all to Chuck Kahler, my very favorite.

And a *beep* to Dexter.

# NOTES

## Prologue: Paradise Lost

xv   **The wire reports traveled:** *Los Angeles Times*, Nov. 21, 1934.

xv   **mummified the corpses:** *Los Angeles Times*, Dec. 5, 1934.

xv   **Both lay on their backs:** *Oakland Tribune*, Nov. 19, 1934.

xv   **The larger one measured:** *Los Angeles Times*, Nov. 22, 1934.

xv   **a tuft of brown hair:** *San Francisco Examiner*, Nov. 24, 1934.

xv   **punctured with wormholes:** Report of Rollan Walter Kraft, MD, box 88, folder 7, Record Unit 7312, Smithsonian Institution Archives.

xv   **presumed to be a woman:** *Los Angeles Times*, Nov. 21, 1934.

xv   **The desiccated facial skin:** Report of Kraft.

xv   **Neither wore shoes:** *San Francisco Examiner*, Nov. 19, 1934.

xv   **One of the fishermen noticed:** Ibid.

xv   **Hundreds of burnt matches:** *Kansas City Star*, Dec. 12, 1934.

xv   **The head of a seal:** Ibid.

xv   **The pair had died of thirst:** Report of Kraft.

xv   **Beneath their overturned skiff:** *Oakland Tribune*, Dec. 29, 1934.

xv   **a cache of thirty letters:** *Kansas City Star*, Dec. 12, 1934.

xv   **"a hell of horror":** *Los Angeles Times*, Dec. 11, 1934.

xv   **Another confessed they inspired nightmares:** Ibid.

xv   **A few of the letters were addressed:** *Los Angeles Evening Post-Record*, Nov. 19, 1934.

xvi   **"We will hope that you will come":** *Los Angeles Times*, Nov. 20, 1934.

## One: The Doctor and His Disciple

3   **At first the doctor terrified Dore:** Strauch, *Satan Came to Eden*, 5.

3   **It wasn't his stature:** I viewed dozens of photographs of Friedrich Ritter (and all of the Floreana settlers) in the special collections archives of the University of Southern California: the Allan Hancock Foundation Archive (0257) and the Lorenzo DeStefano collection on the Hancock Pacific Expedition (6215).

3   **his general disposition seemed:** Strauch, *Satan Came to Eden*, 5.

3   **She stopped just short of calling him brutal, and hoped:** Ibid.

3   **newly twenty-six years old:** Dore was born Dorothee Martha Mathilda Strauch on March 25, 1901, in Berlin (birth certificate on ancestry.com).

3   **which pioneered research:** "Story," the history of the Immanuel Krankenhaus Berlin's naturopathy treatments, Immanuel Krankenhaus Berlin, accessed May 20, 2020, naturheilkunde.immanuel.de/einrichtung/ueber-uns/geschicht.

3 **She had been diagnosed:** Strauch, *Satan Came to Eden,* 4.

3 **included a hysterectomy:** Ibid.

3 **this relapse brought an odd benefit:** Ibid., 5.

3 **"He is fanatic" to "the base of your illness" (including Dore's statement that she "blushed"):** Strauch to George Allan Hancock, January 1932, box 6, folder 13, Collection no. 0257, Special Collections, USC Libraries (hereafter referred to as "Hancock Foundation Archive"). Dore Strauch, "The Great Moment for Manfred Kyber," box 1, "Ritter Writings" folder, Lorenzo DeStefano collection on the Hancock Pacific Expeditions, Collection no. 6215, Special Collections, USC Libraries, University of Southern California (hereafter referred to as "Lorenzo DeStefano collection").

4 **"need not submit to illness":** Strauch, *Satan Came to Eden,* 6.

4 **He did not like sick people:** Ibid., 13.

4 **"will to mend":** Ibid., 13.

4 **"to say a thing must be":** Mulford, *Thoughts Are Things,* 9.

4 **"instinctive understanding":** Strauch, *Satan Came to Eden,* 1.

4 **"There was some task":** Ibid., 2.

5 **"the poor and poorest":** Ibid.

5 **"low instincts and passions":** Strauch, "Great Moment for Manfred Kyber."

5 **"If each one first would fulfill":** Ibid.

5 **"I might have stood the strain":** Strauch, *Satan Came to Eden,* 3.

5 **railed against the destruction:** Schopenhauer, 231.

5 **"My soul was starving":** Strauch, "Great Moment for Manfred Kyber."

5 **a family friend and high school principal:** Ibid.

5 **"thaw him out with sunshine":** Strauch, *Satan Came to Eden,* 3.

5 **Hermann was excessively frugal:** Ibid., 4.

5 **she found it offensive and repellent:** Ibid.

6 **an opportunity to reevaluate:** Ibid., 5.

6 **After ten days under Friedrich's care:** Ibid., 6.

6 **she walked him to work:** Ibid., 9.

6 **Der Stahlhelm, or "Steel Helmet":** "The Political Parties in the Weimar Republic," Administration of the German Bundestag, Research Section WD 1, March 2006, www.bundestag.de/resource/blob/189776/01b7ea57531a60126da86e2d5c5dbb78 /parties_weimar_republic-data.pdf.

6 **They protested against the Weimar Republic:** *Western Mail* (Cardiff), April 30, 1929.

6 **Motor Transport and Motorcycle Unions:** Ibid.

6 **attacked communist citizens:** Sven Reichardt, "Violence and Community: A Micro-study on Nazi Storm Troopers," *Central European History* 46, no. 2 (June 2013).

6 **a popular "transvestite venue":** Gordon, *Voluptuous Panic,* 25.

6 **openly gay man:** Marhoefer, *Sex and the Weimar Republic, Ernst Röhm,* 151.

6 **"business relationship":** Eleanor Hancock, 89.

6 **"I'm not his client":** Ibid.

6 **a fervent believer in excessive mastication:** Strauch, *Satan Came to Eden,* 21.

6 **"horny" enough to substitute:** *Los Angeles Times,* May 27, 1934.

6 **map the human brain:** Mielche, *Let's See,* 117.

6 **"fantastic crank":** *Pittsburgh Post-Gazette,* Feb. 3, 1930.

6   "someone who takes his own path": *B.Z. am Mittag,* 1934, No. 292.

7   He intended to live: Finsen, "Debunking," n.p.

7   hasten the end of European culture: *Reclams Universum,* Feb. 27, 1930.

7   He lived in a cheap: *Pittsburgh Post-Gazette,* Feb. 3, 1930.

7   sowed his own oats: Ibid.

7   He never wore clothes at home: Ibid.

7   He did not trust manufactured clothing: Ibid.

7   "civilized shoe": Strauch, *Satan Came to Eden,* 14.

7   Born in May 1886: Friedrich Adolf Ritter was born May 24, 1886, in Wollbach, Baden, Germany (birth certificate on ancestry.com).

7   both the town's mayor and a wealthy shopkeeper: Fritz Hieber, interview by author, Sept. 2021.

7   "firm believer in the virtues": Ritter, "Adam and Eve in the Galapagos," *The Atlantic,* Oct. 1931.

7   "peculiar nature boy": *B.Z.,* Jan. 10, 2009.

7   *Leatherstocking Tales* and *Robinson Crusoe:* Ritter, "Adam and Eve in the Galapagos."

7   the German philosophy of *Lebensreform:* Lyra Kilston, "The Remarkable Nature Boys of Los Angeles," March 5, 2015, lyrakilston.com.

7   William Pester: Ibid.

7   the father of the detox bath: Ibid.

7   "cook-less" book: Ibid.

8   "soups for the toothless": Ibid.

8   "What a great prophet": Ritter, "Settlers and Real Monkeys," *Als Robinson auf Galapagos,* 164.

8   "A man is more of an ape": Ibid.

8   "painless state of eternal being": Sur, *Tod am Äquator: Die Galapagos Affäre.*

8   He recalled a specific incident: Ritter, "Adam and Eve in the Galapagos."

8   A relative told a different story: Fritz Hieber, interview by author, Sept. 2021.

8   "It was a somewhat dangerous": Sur, *Tod am Äquator.*

8   studying chemistry, physics: Ritter, "Adam and Eve in the Galapagos."

8   aspiring singer named Mila Clark: Sur, *Tod am Äquator.*

9   the roles of Carmen, Mignon, and Amneris: Strauch, *Satan Came to Eden,* 14.

9   Mila's destiny: Ibid., 15.

9   They had long, intense arguments: Sur, *Tod am Äquator.*

9   Once he hurled a vase: Ibid.

9   Sometimes he struck her: Ibid.

9   that was itself tinged with violence: Ibid.

9   She escaped to his mother's house: Ibid.

9   "psychic experience": Strauch, "Great Moment for Manfred Kyber."

9   compelled him to volunteer: Elke Hundt (local historian), interview by Cristina Burack, published in 2002 in the local Wollbach Protestant Parish: "His thinking was crucially influenced by his experience in the Great War, in which he served voluntarily."

9   "Great mustard-coloured suppurative blisters": Brittain, *Testament of Youth,* 395.

9   he was treated for liver damage: Fritz Hieber, interview by author, Sept. 2021.

9   The experience changed him: Ibid.

9   he argued with Mila and slapped her: Sur, *Tod am Äquator.*

9    chopped his sister's piano: Ibid.

9    shot both of the dogs dead: Ibid.

10   gave lectures about chemistry: Ibid.

10   the effect of sunlight on human skin: *Oakland Tribune*, Jan. 31, 1930.

10   a short walk away: Hoffmann, *Einstein's Berlin*, 10.

10   a casual acquaintance: Fritz Hieber, interview by author, Sept. 2021.

10   he was convinced that there would one day exist: Sur, *Tod am Äquator.*

10   "a huge, impersonal monster": Ritter, "Adam and Eve in the Galapagos."

10   "I cannot have a love-sick woman": Strauch, *Satan Came to Eden*, 12.

10   "fellow pilgrim on the way": Ibid., 8.

10   She suspected she was the only: Ibid., 10.

10   "There were no scenes": Ibid., 9.

10   "triumph of the masculine": Ibid., 11.

11   "the evil inventions of modern costume": Ibid., 14.

11   State Library in Berlin: Ibid., 19.

11   "a little world within itself": Darwin, *Voyage of the* Beagle, 454.

11   "sterile and incapable of supporting life": Ibid., 458.

11   "When I enter a tropical jungle": Beebe, *World's End*, 61.

11   "If his Satanic Majesty": *New York Times*, April 25, 1930.

11   "one unbroken holiday": *Chicago Tribune*, Sept. 30, 1923.

12   A successful retreat from the world: Ritter, "Adam and Eve in the Galapagos."

## Two: Dying in One World

13   she would persuade Friedrich's wife: Strauch, *Satan Came to Eden*, 15.

13   Friedrich urged Dore to disguise herself: Ibid., 16.

13   a striking Italianate mansion: Author visit to Wollbach, Sept. 2022.

13   Mila even became enthusiastic: Strauch, *Satan Came to Eden*, 16.

13   "Mrs. Ritter, very opposite" and "She is a shining example": Strauch, "Great Moment for Manfred Kyber."

13   they embraced each other: Ibid.

14   Dore must write a letter: Strauch, *Satan Came to Eden*, 16.

14   Two large wooden boxes: Ibid., 21.

14   Mosquito netting would be vital: Ibid., 22.

14   Dore bought a full set: Ibid., 21.

14   Friedrich packed carpenter's tools: Ritter, "Adam and Eve in the Galapagos."

14   She gave her finest clothes: Strauch, *Satan Came to Eden*, 22.

14   Dore urged him to include: Ibid.

14   When he suggested taking a gun: Ibid.

14   "A great melancholy": Ibid., 24.

14   "I shall see you again": Ibid.

14   One of the most popular tunes: An operetta with that title played in various German cities in 1929 and 1930. American newspapers tied the production to Friedrich and Dore's adventure: *Tampa Times*, July 11, 1930.

15   made his final public appearance: B.Z. am Mittag, 1934, No. 292.

15   "He looked pale and outwardly wretched": *Reclams Universum*, Feb. 27, 1930.

15   The few colleagues aware: Ibid.

15 "I feel as if I am dying in one world": Ritter, "Final Letter from Germany," *Als Robinson auf Galapagos.*

15 he had all his teeth extracted: Ritter, "Adam and Eve in the Galapagos."

15 the teeth would not stay in: *New York Daily News*, Jan. 7, 1934.

15 On July 3, 1929: Strauch, *Satan Came to Eden*, 25. Friedrich recalled the day being July 4. See Ritter, "Adam and Eve in the Galapagos."

16 A smoker sometimes spoiled the air: Ritter, "Journey Across the Atlantic," *Als Robinson auf Galapagos.*

16 "Of course, overfed, alcohol-addled brains": Ibid.

16 "portly farmwife": Ibid.

16 At least, Friedrich noted, no one snored: Ibid.

16 He and Dore were mesmerized: Ibid.

16 "colorful, geometric corpuscles": Ibid.

16 a monkey climbed Friedrich and perched: Ibid.

16 "the stronger of the two": Ibid.

16 "rippled glass": Ibid.

16 "I was gripped by a pantheistic longing": Ibid.

17 At last, on July 31: Ibid.

17 a reception they both found encouraging: Ibid.

17 a term that is now considered derogatory: Roslyn Cameron (the former public support and outreach coordinator at the Charles Darwin Research Station on the Galápagos Islands), email message to author, March 7, 2022.

17 civilization would eventually spoil them: Ritter, "South American Harbors," *Als Robinson auf Galapagos.*

17 A plane could take them: Ibid.

17 They couldn't purchase land: Ibid.; Strauch, *Satan Came to Eden*, 26.

17 In case of a future emergency: Strauch, *Satan Came to Eden*, 61.

17 a packed, pungent, second-class car: Ritter, "The Journey to Quito," *Als Robinson auf Galapagos.*

17 "There are a striking number": Ibid.

18 "completely intolerable cult": Ibid.

18 "an attack of feminine vanity": Strauch, *Satan Came to Eden*, 27.

18 his grave disappointment: Ibid.

18 "One should not eat even fruit": Ritter, "The Journey to Quito," *Als Robinson auf Galapagos.*

18 "not blind" to "to any other": Strauch, *Satan Came to Eden*, 10.

18 But she believed that she alone: Ibid., 7.

18 "very human": Ibid., 12.

18 "We felt a oneness": Ibid., 31.

## Three: The Enchanted Isles

19 several hundred thousand to millions of years: Moore, *Galápagos: An Encyclopedia*, 3.

19 The archipelago numbers eighteen main islands: Q&A with the Galápagos specialists Roslyn Cameron and Washington "Wacho" Tapia, general director of Conservando Galápagos/Galápagos Conservancy.

19  other rocky promontories: Ibid.

19  a few square meters: Ibid.

19  rarely visited by humans: Kricher and Loughlin, *Galápagos: A Natural History*, 17.

19  "It seems as though some time": Moore, *Galápagos: An Encyclopedia*, 364.

20  "Take five-and-twenty heaps": Melville, *Encantadas*, 21.

20  sixty-seven square miles: Moore, *Galápagos: An Encyclopedia*, 382.

20  a freshwater spring: All of the Floreana settlers used an artisan spring at the base of Cerro Olympus. Water from this area is still piped to the town today. Email message from Rosyln Cameron to author, April 24, 2024.

20  produced the first map of the Galápagos: Gibbs, Cayot, and Tapia Aguilera, *Galápagos Giant Tortoises*, 3.

20  an homage to Juan José Flores: Moore, *Galápagos: An Encyclopedia*, 382.

20  first penal colony: Ibid., 296.

20  Patrick Watkins, was likely the first true: Jackson, *Galápagos: A Natural History*, 3.

21  He built a ramshackle hut: Stewart, *Galápagos: The Islands*, 50.

21  "The appearance of this man": Porter, *Memoir*, 129.

21  "rolling among the rocks": Ibid.

21  "lunatic and murderer": Strauch, *Satan Came to Eden*, 42, 43.

21  could not dispel his crimes: Ibid., 43.

21  The *Manuel J. Cobos* had once belonged: Treherne, *The Galapagos Affair*, 20.

21  minted his own currency: Baarslag, *Islands*, 198.

21  revolted and murdered him: Moore, *Galápagos: An Encyclopedia*, 131.

21  In 1925, a group of twenty-two Norwegians: *Los Angeles Times*, Aug. 11, 1926.

21  "venture to a more beautiful": *AZ am Morgen Munich*, April 10, 1926.

21  the nation's strict immigration laws: *Los Angeles Times*, Aug. 11, 1926.

21  launched an ambitious settlement plan: Woram, *Charles Darwin*, 231–32.

22  "the problem of water": Ibid., 232.

22  a number of modern conveniences: *Los Angeles Times*, Aug. 11, 1926.

22  the *Floreana,* named after: Woram, *Charles Darwin*, 233.

22  working with the National Museum: *Pittsburgh Press*, Feb. 21, 1929.

22  "for a dozen eyes": Beebe, *World's End*, 59.

22  transparent eels, living coral: *New York Times*, July 30, 1930.

22  a fish with spiky horns: *Cincinnati Post*, Jan. 18, 1930.

22  *galápago* is an old Spanish word: Roslyn Cameron, email message to author, April 26, 2022.

22  An examination of the logbooks: *New York Times*, Sept. 6, 1925.

22  Pinchot heard of one tortoise: Pinchot, *To the South Seas*, 197.

22  it was possible to cross an island: *Tampa Tribune*, June 15, 1958.

23  Pinchot marveled at the guileless animals: *Philadelphia Inquirer*, Sept. 16, 1929.

23  "lap dragon": Pinchot, *To the South Seas*, 198.

23  "mailbox" erected long ago: Tour and interview with Santos Humberto Moreno Naula, representative with the Centro Comunitario Floreana. Author visit to Floreana, May 2022.

23  "friendly and home-like": Pinchot, *To the South Seas*, 219.

23  the place was undeniably eerie: Ibid.

23  After knocking on the doors: For descriptions of the abandoned Casa, see Ibid., 219–223.

23   The final entry: Ibid., 220.

24   clearly, Pinchot mused: Ibid., 222.

24   Captain Paul Edvard Bruun: Woram, *Charles Darwin*, 257.

24   only two Norwegians and one Ecuadorian: Treherne, *The Galapagos Affair*, 24.

24   this time their stay was brief: Ibid.

24   Dore watched the island: Strauch, *Satan Came to Eden*, 32.

24   a fourteen-year-old Ecuadorian boy: Ibid.

25   "I should never dare to risk": Ibid., 35.

25   He assured her: Ibid.

25   rumored to have spied: Treherne, *The Galapagos Affair*, 2.

25   Casa Matriz: Strauch, *Satan Came to Eden*, 34; Ritter, "Dangerous Bull Hunting," *Als Robinson auf Galapagos*.

25   They slept on its floor that first night: Treherne, *The Galapagos Affair*, 26.

## Four: Friedo

26   "like weird sentinels": Strauch, *Satan Came to Eden*, 35.

26   "our Indian Victor Hugo": Ritter, "Dangerous Bull Hunting," *Als Robinson auf Galapagos*.

26   deepened by donkeys and cattle: Gibbs, Cayot, and Tapia Aguilera, *Galapagos Giant Tortoises*, 53.

26   Dore's feet burning with each step: Strauch, *Satan Came to Eden*, 38.

27   "We have come here": Ibid.

27   the first Dore had ever seen: Ibid.

27   From a distance Dore spotted: Ibid., 39.

27   Friedrich grew silent and sullen: Ibid.

27   if Hugo must continue: Ibid.

27   With great reluctance: Ibid.

28   "Friedrich was jealous": Ibid., 40–41.

28   dark gray pockets resembling: Author visit to Floreana, May 2022.

28   A rat scuttled out: Strauch, *Satan Came to Eden*, 43.

28   "a train of specters": Ibid., 45.

28   Friedrich estimated that the spot: Ritter, "Floreana," *Als Robinson auf Galapagos*.

28   Quickly they made their way down: Ritter, "Adam and Eve in the Galapagos."

28   "The spring": Strauch, *Satan Came to Eden*, 48.

29   "This is our place, Dore": Ibid., 49.

29   Dore immediately understood: Ibid.

29   She began to cry: Ibid.

29   Friedrich reached for her hand: Ibid.

29   "We'll christen the valley": Ritter, "Adam and Eve in the Galapagos."

29   She spun in circles, dancing as she once danced: Ibid.

29   "In the name of the Ritters I take possession of thee": Ibid.

29   He pointed his finger: Strauch, *Satan Came to Eden*, 49.

29   Watkins had murdered someone: Ibid.

29   "I see you haven't yet put": Ibid., 51.

30   "cast out the foe": Ibid., 52.

30   "almost terrifying hideousness": Ibid.

30  Friedrich declared that they should discard: Ritter, "Adam and Eve in the Galapagos."

30  "a toiling Adam and Eve": Ibid.

30  El Viejo, "The Old": Strauch, *Satan Came to Eden*, 55.

30  At night, they slept in hammocks: Ibid., 57.

30  She vowed to herself: Ibid., 55.

31  "In spite of all our differences": Ibid., 139.

31  "We had fled from the society" to "by their preserve": Ritter, "Adam and Eve in the Galapagos."

31  "perverted creatures": Ibid.

31  "devilish attempts": Ibid.

31  "Cut by the Equator": Melville, *Encantadas*, 34.

31  Little rain fell from July to December: Cassidy, *Biological Evolution*, 12.

31  "feverish fertility": Strauch, *Satan Came to Eden*, 58.

32  "as a baby's head": Quoted in Treherne, *The Galapagos Affair*, 37.

32  a primitive pressing machine: Strauch, *Satan Came to Eden* (1935 ed.), 151.

32  her body and spirit both inched: Ibid., 55.

32  "He did not even see" to "follow him into this world": Ibid., 60.

32  with great concentration: Ibid., 62.

32  Hugo caught up with them: Ibid.

32  "defense psychology": Ibid., 63.

33  Friedrich insisted that they suspend: Ibid., 64.

33  "If vegetarianism is to mean" to "every meal of meat": Ritter, "My Vegetarianism," *Als Robinson auf Galapagos*.

33  Friedrich complained of becoming: Ibid., "Floreana."

33  "stained with murder": Dore, *Satan Came to Eden*, 66.

34  "¡El toro me mata!": Ritter, "Dangerous Bull Hunting," *Als Robinson auf Galapagos*.

34  the horn had slashed: Ibid.

34  Hugo whispered: Strauch, *Satan Came to Eden*, 69.

## Five: A Moment Lived in Paradise

35  "Thank God we are rid" to "painful for us": Ritter, "Floreana," *Als Robinson auf Galapagos*.

35  peered through the thickets: Strauch, *Satan Came to Eden*, 71.

35  she had barely made an impression: Ibid., 75.

35  "We have gained the better world" to "the animal in yourself": Ibid., 78, 79.

36  "breathe the rarefied air": Ibid., 79.

36  "tropical eternal dwelling": Ritter, "Our Settling," *Als Robinson auf Galapagos*.

36  a very "light" building: Ibid.

37  Nirosta: Ibid.

37  mosquito-proof wire mesh: Ibid.

37  "like the skeleton": Ritter, "Adam and Eve in the Galapagos."

37  corrugated iron: Ibid.

37  "Friedo egg": "Friedo Egg," box 1, "Ritter Writings" folder, DeStefano collection.

37  "garden symphony": Ibid.

37  "A moment lived in paradise": Ritter, "Friedo," *Als Robinson auf Galapagos*, April 1932.

37  "Something on Floreana had changed": Strauch, *Satan Came to Eden*, 84.

38  "sinister, emaciated creatures" to "own bad conscience": Ibid., 73.

38  She pictured him strangling to death: Ibid., 82.

38  He whispered something: Ibid.

38  "strong defense psychology": Ibid., 63.

38  it would be two weeks: Ibid., 82.

38  They still had not transported: Ibid.

38  The second planting of the garden: Ritter, "Satan Walks in the Garden."

38  almonds and hazelnuts refused: Ibid.

38  the radishes were riddled: Ibid.

39  all their belongings were gone: Strauch, *Satan Came to Eden*, 83.

39  Dore did not trust the man: Ibid.

39  How foolish they'd been, she thought: Ibid.

39  They walked back to Friedo: Ibid.

## Six: The First of the Dollar Kings

40  held a press conference in Miami: *Palm Beach Post*, Jan. 6, 1930.

40  the loss of $14 billion: Stock Market Crash of October 1929, Social Welfare History Project, VCU Libraries, socialwelfare.library.vcu.edu/eras/great-depression /beginning-of-great-depression-stock-market-crash-of-october-1929.

40  the Dow Jones had lost: Gary Richardson et al., "Stock Market Crash of 1929," Federal Reserve History, Nov. 22, 2013, federalreservehistory.org.

40  a Chicago investor died: Christopher Klein, "1929 Stock Market Crash: Did Panicked Investors Really Jump from Windows?," History, Feb. 25, 2019, history.com.

40  a civil engineer from Pennsylvania: Ibid.

40  a stockbroker in St. Louis: Ibid.

40  Even bootleggers who had accrued: *Nottingham Evening Post*, Dec. 21, 1929.

40  "returning to the not less exciting": Ibid.

40  "I do not know what has happened": Ibid.

40  selected a diverse team: *Miami Herald*, Jan. 4, 1930.

41  "After the stop at the Virgin Islands" to "beforehand": Ibid.

41  at a cost of $1.3 million: *Camden (N.J.) Morning Post*, April 20, 1942.

41  the *Mizpah* measured 185 feet long: *Lincoln Star*, Oct. 20, 1929.

41  cruising range of seven thousand miles: *Camden (N.J.) Morning Post*, April 20, 1942.

41  a specially constructed cabinet: *Miami Herald*, Jan. 4, 1930.

41  "The Mizpah should return" to "of the expedition": Ibid.

41  It was rumored: *Escanaba Daily Press*, Jan. 24, 1930.

41  he dropped out of high school: *Chicago Tribune*, May 16, 1958.

41  he drove a car up the steps: Ibid.

41  he operated a telegraphone: Bryant and Cones, 13.

42  made history: Sterling and O'Dell, 894.

42  Phonevision: *Life*, Feb. 5, 1951.

42 "could drink a lot" to "he was doing": *Chicago Tribune*, February 5, 1960.

42 He ended each day: Ibid.

42 On the weekends he amplified: Ibid.

42 Once he fired shots: Ibid.

42 On another occasion, while the *Mizpah:* Ibid., Feb. 5, 1960.

42 "Land," he often said: *Miami News*, April 2, 1950.

42 sold $1 million worth of stock: Sterling and O'Dell, 894.

42 The actor John Barrymore: *Los Angeles Times*, March 18, 1929.

42 no "lost world," Barrymore reported: Ibid.

42 Vanderbilt, like Pinchot: *Miami Herald*, March 29, 1926.

43 "entirely new to science": *New York Times*, April 1, 1926.

43 "We gave them sliced beef meat" to "our fault": *Louisville Courier-Journal*, May 27, 1928.

43 Next came Charles Kettering: *Boston Globe*, April 12, 1930.

43 "Noah's Ark": *Cincinnati Enquirer*, March 26, 1930.

43 Charles Townsend: *Los Angeles Times*, June 3, 1928.

43 One tortoise, likely captured: Author Q&A with Tapia, Oct. 2021.

43 Huntington R. "Tack" Hardwick: *Miami Herald*, April 30, 1929.

43 Inspired by Melville's *Moby-Dick:* *Hartford Courant*, May 7, 1929.

43 it was harpooned at 9:30 in the morning: Ibid.

43 For six hours: Ibid.

43 only to be harpooned a second time: Ibid.

43 spouting blood instead of water: Ibid.

44 removed 120 pounds: Ibid.

44 he'd thought that the island: Eugene McDonald, foreword to *Satan Came to Eden*, by Strauch, xvii.

44 "rather shaky": *St. Louis Post-Dispatch*, March 16, 1930.

44 close to the highlands: Tour and interview with Santos Humberto Moreno Naula.

44 Their supplies had been stolen: *St. Louis Post-Dispatch*, March 16, 1930.

44 The best they could do was fire guns: McDonald, foreword to *Satan Came to Eden*, by Strauch, xvii.

44 split into four search parties: Ibid.

45 "Gott sei dank": *San Francisco Examiner*, April 6, 1930.

45 white duck trousers: *St. Louis Post-Dispatch*, March 16, 1930.

45 His left arm hanging limply: *San Francisco Examiner*, April 6, 1930.

45 gleamed in the sun: *San Francisco Examiner*, Jan. 10, 1932.

45 McDonald couldn't help but notice: *San Francisco Examiner*, April 6, 1930.

45 Friedrich would take her hands: Ibid.

45 "understood everything" and "released": *Pittsburgh Post-Gazette*, Feb. 3, 1930.

45 "Why don't you use": *St. Louis Post-Dispatch*, March 16, 1930.

45 "I do not think that is right": Ibid.

46 Dore spoke to the men's wives: Strauch, *Satan Came to Eden*, 88.

46 "We in Europe" to "as German women": Ibid., 90.

46 Dore was surprised: Ibid.

46 "extreme attempt to solve": Ibid.

46 "terribly efficient": Ibid., 88.

46 he eagerly accepted the Commander's gifts: *San Francisco Examiner*, April 6, 1930.

46   from "picks and shovel" to "fifteen hundred rounds of ammunition": Ibid.

46   Friedrich also asked for a supply of dynamite: Ritter, "Satan Walks in the Garden."

46   Friedrich assured him: Ibid.

46   "How long do you intend": *St. Louis Post-Dispatch*, March 16, 1930.

46   "We shall stay here always" to "natural things": Ibid.

47   "Yes," Brownell replied: Strauch, *Satan Came to Eden*, 91.

47   "almost mystical light": Ibid.

47   "That may be true" to "to die": Ibid., 91–92.

47   "Oh, Friedrich": Ibid., 92.

47   Everyone laughed: Ibid.

## Seven: Catalyst

48   he sent a message via radiogram: McDonald, foreword to *Satan Came to Eden*, by Strauch, xviii.

48   "German Robinson Crusoe": *Pittsburgh Post-Gazette*, Feb. 3, 1930.

48   One journalist noted that they bore: *Pittsburgh Press*, Dec. 19, 1934.

48   this time at Union Station: *Camden (N.J.) Morning Post*, Feb. 13, 1930.

48   "white vest and West Point bearing": *Camden (N.J.) Courier-Post*, Feb. 13, 1930.

48   "With tears in their eyes": *San Francisco Examiner*, April 6, 1930.

49   "unless," McDonald joked, "he expects": Ibid.

49   "avalanche of publicity": McDonald, foreword to *Satan Came to Eden*, by Strauch, xviii.

49   "Modern Adam and Eve": *Fort Lauderdale News*, Feb. 22, 1930.

49   "Garden of Eden": *San Francisco Examiner*, Jan. 10, 1932.

49   arrived after a monthlong cruise: *Oakland Tribune*, June 23, 1930.

49   "imps of darkness": *Life*, Sept. 8, 1958.

49   re-homed at the Steinhart Aquarium: *Chico (Calif.) Enterprise*, June 23, 1930.

49   "The doctor and frau were rather scantily clad": *Los Angeles Times*, June 17, 1930.

49   "Why go so far to be a nut": *Richmond Times-Dispatch*, July 6, 1930.

49   an $87 million fortune: Madsen, *John Jacob Astor*, 286.

49   "a game of stalking sharks" to "racing from view": *San Francisco Examiner*, June 22, 1930.

49   "a natural laboratory full of mysteries": Ibid.

49   "The Galapagos stands practically unchanged": Ibid.

50   "floating hotel": *New York Daily News*, Feb. 5, 1933.

50   bold patterns and chintzes: Ibid.

50   Astor's guests enjoyed: Ibid.

50   His scientific party included Kermit Roosevelt: *Atlanta Journal*, May 4, 1930.

50   "pleasure trips": Joern Olshausen, "Galapagos Lure and Lore," box 1, "Joern Olshausen" folder, DeStefano collection. Olshausen traveled to Floreana in the 1970s and conducted a series of interviews with Margret Wittmer.

50   invited a woman companion: Ibid.

50   "testudo porteri": *Chicago Tribune*, May 3, 1930.

50   "puppy-like affection": *San Francisco Examiner*, June 22, 1930.

50   small in stature and solemn: *Philadelphia Inquirer*, May 3, 1930.

50   named Paddlewing: *New York Daily News*, Nov. 16, 1931.

50   "he calmly surveyed his surroundings" to "went to sleep": *Philadelphia Inquirer,* May 3, 1930.

50   his friends died one by one: *New York Daily News,* Nov. 16, 1931.

51   The press claimed "heartbreak": *Washington Post,* Nov. 17, 1931.

51   "had to be dragged": Vincent Astor article in the *New York American,* Dec. 4, 1934.

51   Dore was missing a few teeth: *Pittsburgh Press,* Dec. 19, 1934.

51   textile slump: *New York Times,* May 4, 1930.

51   cotton slump: *New York Times,* July 2, 1930.

51   auto slump: *New York Times,* Oct. 5, 1930.

51   marriage slump: *New York Times,* May 4, 1930.

51   canal traffic slump: *New York Times,* Dec. 3, 1930.

51   potato sale slump: *New York Times,* March 15, 1930.

51   Latin America slump: *New York Times,* May 10, 1930.

51   orchid slump: *New York Times,* March 16, 1930.

51   Three million American citizens: Worster, *Dust Bowl,* 10.

51   Rainfall was perilously low: Hurt, *The Dust Bowl,* 20.

51   measures that stirred social and political unrest: Straumann, 75.

51   "One can't help believing" to "how much a ticket costs": *Austin Statesman,* Sept. 9, 1932.

52   "great force which draws" to "people on two continents": *New York Herald Tribune,* April 13, 1930.

53   Such a deal would foster: *Chicago Tribune,* Oct. 12, 1930.

53   "Yankee Menace": *New York Times,* Oct. 23, 1930.

53   would lead to a takeover: *Sunday Province* (Vancouver, B.C.), Nov. 2, 1930.

53   with "seagoing launches" to patrol: *Honolulu Advertiser,* Nov. 11, 1930.

53   from "foreign intrigue": Ibid.

53   It was on May 5: Strauch, *Satan Came to Eden,* 99.

53   the letters were all from strangers: Ibid.

53   the "South American Society": *New York Times,* April 16, 1930.

53   3,000 marks ($720): Ibid.

53   solitude being "in vogue": *B.Z. am Mittag,* 1934, No. 292.

53   "like-minded souls": Ritter, "Eve Calls It a Day," *The Atlantic,* December 1931.

54   "a flabby and hysterical sentimentality": Ibid.

54   her divorce had been finalized: Dore's divorce from Hermann Koerwin was finalized July 6, 1930. Official document from the registrar office in Berlin Lichterfelde, available on ancestry.com.

54   "A radio telegram" to "off from their world": Strauch, *Satan Came to Eden,* 99.

54   "What has happened?": Ibid.

54   "Why are you crying?": Ibid.

54   She pressed the paper into his hands: Ibid.

54   "This is the end of everything": Ibid.

## *Eight: The First Intruders*

55   "Nothing was further from us" to "two people": Ritter, "Other Questions and Reasons," *Als Robinson auf Galapagos.*

55   "call or yodel": *New York Herald Tribune,* April 10, 1932.

55  "Knock strongly": Eichler, *Snow Peaks*, 184.

55  It would be much grander: Strauch, *Satan Came to Eden*, 129.

55  "of how near we were": Ibid., 131.

55  The roof would extend beyond: Photographs of Friedo, Hancock Foundation Archive.

55  furnish with a large table and five chairs: Strauch, *Satan Came to Eden*, 130.

56  screens of wire netting: Ibid.

56  a dedicated study area: Ibid.

56  furniture they fashioned from curved sticks: Ibid.

56  set on pillars: Ritter, "Eve Calls It a Day."

56  The sharp lava rocks prevented them: Ritter, "Satan Walks in the Garden."

56  To protect their chickens: Ibid.

56  "It is a romantic error" to "all its freshness": Strauch, *Satan Came to Eden*, 135.

56  "eternal dissatisfaction": Ibid.

56  "high ambition": Ibid.

56  the pounding of the drops: Ibid., 95.

56  both of them wondering: Ibid.

56  Dore dragging the tar paper: Ibid., 96.

56  doubling over in laughter: Ibid.

57  "The socialism of the ants": Ritter, "Garden Art," *Als Robinson auf Galapagos*.

57  Bruun himself had dispatched: Strauch, *Satan Came to Eden*, 103.

57  "It's all very well": Ibid.

57  He let this statement linger: Ibid., 104.

57  "I have decided" to "here to live": Ibid., 104–5.

57  "What?" to "this island soon": Ibid.

58  "Until he comes, Floreana will" to "to be short": Ibid., 105.

58  "of more than usual good looks": Ibid., 109.

58  Five young German men: Ibid., 106.

58  A woman from Berlin brought her husband: Ibid., 107.

58  "little paradise": Ibid., 108.

58  "It sounds discourteous" to "we never did": Ibid., 121.

59  "They came expecting" to "do with them": Ritter, "Eve Calls It a Day."

59  The five young men deserted: Ibid.

59  Captain Bruun died in a drowning accident: Strauch, *Satan Came to Eden*, 118.

59  She confessed to Dore: Ibid., 108.

## Nine: Appearances

60  "two absolutely naked figures": *American Weekly* article reprinted in the *San Francisco Examiner*, Jan. 10, 1932.

60  eager for news of the outside world: John Thomas Howell, extracts from his 1932 Templeton Crocker expedition journal, box 2, "Correspondence and Notes," DeStefano collection.

60  "Am I not Faust?": Margret Wittmer, "Death over Galapagos," *Liberty Magazine*, Dec. 4, 1937, box 88, folder 3, Record Unit 7231, Schmitt Papers.

60  "glittering, stainless steel": *American Weekly* article reprinted in the *San Francisco Examiner*, Jan. 10, 1932.

61  "With these he could": Ibid.

61  placed a notice in European newspapers: *Daily Telegraph* (London), April 4, 1930.

61  outright lied: Photographs of Friedo taken by American explorers around this time show a simple, one-floor structure with open walls. Various photographs of Friedo, Hancock Foundation Archive and Lorenzo DeStefano collection.

61  "Perhaps in America" to "for anything more": Ritter, "Eve Calls It a Day."

61  Visitors to Friedo were treated: Various photographs of Friedrich Ritter, Hancock Foundation Archive and Lorenzo DeStefano collection.

62  he continued to give the impression: Ritter, "The Last Letter from Dr. Knight," *Als Robinson auf Galapagos.*

62  "The doctor taught me": Charles Swett's journal of 1931–1932 expedition, box 249, Hancock Foundation Archive.

62  her misgivings about their relationship: Strauch, *Satan Came to Eden*, 135.

62  At times their relationship seemed to be: Ibid.

62  she felt a slight shift within: Ibid., 137.

62  "by many queer discrepancies": Ibid., 136.

62  exhibiting a strange envy: Ibid.

62  "My friendship": Ibid., 138.

63  he pulled them again: Ibid., 137.

63  this time he left it alone: Ibid.

63  asking her to come to Floreana: Ibid., 139.

63  "not be unhappy": Ibid., 139.

## Ten: Our So-Called Paradise

64  stood in front of a haberdashery: Wittmer, *Floreana*, 16.

64  Although both were still married: Divorce file for Heinrich Wittmer and Anna Ebel. Their divorce was finalized in 1939. Heinrich Wittmer and Anna Ebel divorce trial proceedings and decision, housed in Landesarchiv Nordrhein-Westfalen, Abteilung Rheinland, Schifferstraße 30, 47059 Duisburg. Margret Waldbröl's marriage to Josef Decker was finalized on Jan. 31, 1933. Margret Waldbröl and Johann Decker marriage certificate, housed in Landesarchiv Nordrhein-Westfalen, Abteilung Rheinland, Schifferstr. 30, 47059 Duisburg. The marriage certificate also contained a margin note on their divorce.

64  claimed that, on this occasion: Ibid.

64  Heinz's twelve-year-old son: *Los Angeles Times*, Feb. 27, 1938.

64  "Yes or a rifle" to "I can't decide which": Wittmer, *Floreana*, 16.

64  "A rifle?" and "What on earth?": Ibid.

64  "In case we go" to "Harry's sanatorium": Ibid.

64  "Just think": Margret Wittmer, "What Happened on Galapagos?," MS, box 6, folder 10, Hancock Foundation Archive.

64  "People are writing all sorts" to "pleasant delusion": *Ottawa Journal*, March 21, 1931.

65  "My companion and I" to "so-called paradise": Ibid.

65  "My husband could use him": Anna Wittmer to George Allan Hancock, July 5, 1935, box 6, folder 13, Hancock Foundation Archive.

65  a native of Warburg: Birth certificate of Heinrich Albert Wittmer, Personenstandsregister Warburg Stadt 1891/67, Stadtarchiv Warburg.

65  **He wore thin-framed glasses:** Various photographs of Heinz Wittmer, Hancock Foundation Archive and Lorenzo DeStefano collection.

65  **"quite an ordinary person":** Mielche, *Let's See*, 118.

65  **Heinz was a veteran of the Great War:** Heinrich Wittmer's military records (Abteilung Personenbezogene Auskünfte zum Ersten und Zweiten Weltkrieg, Referat PA 2 Auskünfte, Bundesarchiv, Berlin).

65  **He suffered a minor wound:** Ibid.

66  **this time for syphilis:** Ibid.

66  **secretary to Konrad Adenauer:** Heinrich Wittmer was an *Oberstadtsekretär*, a high-ranking official, and likely in the then mayor Konrad Adenauer's inner circle of advisers. Personal file for Heinrich Wittmer, Stadt Köln—Die Oberbürgermeisterin, Historisches Archiv.

66  **his voice and hands still shook:** Mielche, *Let's See*, 119.

66  **for the future of his homeland:** Lange, "The Wittmers of Floreana," Sacramento, Calif. Heinz and Margret told Lange, a U.S. soldier, that they had left Germany to escape Hitler.

66  **"[Hitler] began to talk" to "a classical thundergod":** *Atlanta Constitution*, June 14, 1931.

66  **tools and an abundance of provisions:** Wittmer, *Floreana*, 16.

66  **"I know they are good hands" to "a bit pathetic":** Margret Wittmer, "The End of the World?", "What Happened on Galapagos?"

66  **Margret's mother had died:** Wittmer, *Floreana*, notes from the editor (n.p.: Beaufort Books, 2014).

67  **"Good night, see you tomorrow":** Ibid., 17.

67  **"good night" in response:** Ibid.

67  **aware that she would miss:** Ibid.

## Eleven: Mr. Hancock of Los Angeles

68  **On January 3, 1932:** Swett's journal of 1931–1932 expedition.

68  **On the shore Hancock and his crew found:** Ibid.

68  **Hancock and his colleagues trudged through:** Ibid.

68  **They passed:** Ibid.

68  **They climbed:** Ibid.

69  **"He looked over at us appraisingly":** Ibid.

69  **called Allan by friends and family:** Hadley Meares, "How Velero III, a Fantastic Watercraft, Enriched Early Ocean Research," PBS SoCal, April 14, 2020, pbssocal .org.

69  **a flamboyant Hungarian count:** Laura Meyers, "A Comedy of Manors," *Los Angeles Magazine*, Jan. 2020.

69  **the first Hungarian immigrants:** Hadley Meares, "The Lady of La Brea: Madame Ida Hancock Ross, Los Angeles' Forgotten Matriarch," PBS SoCal, Feb. 23, 2016, pbssocal.org.

69  **along with a twin brother:** Ibid.

69  **the ranch was deep in debt:** Ibid.

69  **a problem Ida confronted:** *Santa Maria Times*, Oct. 1, 2017.

69  **a one-room schoolhouse:** *Santa Maria Times*, Feb. 16, 1977.

69  Hancock resolved to never leave: Clover, A *Pioneer*, 66.

70  more than 3.8 million barrels: Ibid.

70  they brought to the surface: Ibid.

70  dire wolf, a saber-toothed cat, and a giant ground sloth: Ibid.

70  "the most extraordinary storehouse": DeWitt, *Voyages*, 29.

70  "They belong to Los Angeles": *Los Angeles Times*, April 8, 2004.

70  "would be away for days": *Los Angeles Times*, April 8, 1945.

70  "very indifferent": Ibid.

70  He had an intense fear: "The Makers of Los Angeles," *Out West*, Jan. 1909, 358.

70  "Jumping from one thing": *Boston Globe*, June 3, 1965.

70  cost nearly $1 million to build: Hadley Meares, "How Velero III, a Fantastic Watercraft, Enriched Early Ocean Research," PBS SoCal, April 14, 2020, pbssocal .org.

70  "floating laboratory": *Santa Maria Times*, Feb. 21, 1940.

70  thousands of glass vials: *Salt Lake Tribune*, April 11, 1937.

70  electrically heated and irrigated: Palmer, *Third Galapagos Trip*, 1.

71  underwater electric lights: *Los Angeles Times*, Dec. 1, 1931.

71  A thick cork insulation: Clover, *A Pioneer*, 177.

71  Two systems of freshwater: Ibid.

71  "doctor's room": Palmer, *Third Galapagos Trip*, 2.

71  one grand flourish: G. Bruce Newby, "A New Type Business and Research Cruiser," *Pacific Marine Review*, Sept. 1931.

71  "The ship rides like a swan": Palmer, *Third Galapagos Trip*, 2.

71  distinguished scientists from various institutions: Clover, *A Pioneer*, 182.

71  gifted musicians: *San Pedro News Pilot*, Dec. 29, 1932.

71  collecting twenty-seven iguanas: *Santa Maria Times*, Feb. 29, 1932.

71  unidentifiable lizard-like creatures: Ibid.

71  a white seal: Ibid.

71  hermit crabs and five-hundred-pound tortoises: *Californian*, April 10, 1937.

71  sea elephants and booby birds: *Santa Maria Times*, Sept. 2, 1932.

71  boa constrictors and ringtail monkeys: *Californian*, April 10, 1937.

71  "A little energetic man": Swett's journal of 1931–1932 expedition.

72  dirtying their shoes: Ibid.

72  "direct manners" and "friendly like a boy": Ibid.

72  her smile was marred: Ibid.

72  Nothing about her seemed capable: Ibid.

72  "almost fluent": Ibid.

72  the best, Friedrich had decided: Ritter, "Dangerous Bull Hunting," *Als Robinson auf Galapagos*.

72  "No one who came cruising" to "a psychological zoo": Strauch, *Satan Came to Eden*, 138–39.

72  "Music is the alcohol": Strauch, "Dollar Kings Visit Us," box 6, folder 11, Hancock Foundation Archive,

73  ridiculing him so pointedly: Swett's journal of 1931–1932 expedition.

73  "mutuality and happiness": Ibid.

73  a "Reform Warehouse" for "healthy and harmonious living": Ritter to Hancock, Feb. 1932, box 6, folder 13, Hancock Foundation Archive.

73 **"Beauty is fitness and nothing else":** Ibid.

73 **"The best form for a desk":** Ibid.

73 **exhibit it at the upcoming World's Fair in Chicago:** Ibid.

73 **"very, very interesting view":** letter from Dore Strauch and Friedrich Ritter to George Allan Hancock, Oct. 14, 1932, box 6, folder 13, Hancock Foundation Archive.

73 **how miraculous the treats tasted:** Strauch, "Dollar Kings Visit Us."

73 **"It seemed to me" to "how rich we are":** Ibid.

74 **copies of *Vogue*:** Swett's journal of the 1931–1932 expedition.

74 **"It is too much" and "You must let me":** Ibid.

74 **"When I first heard of you":** Strauch, "Dollar Kings Visit Us."

74 **He urged them to write:** Ibid.

74 **"Life grows drab" to "critically analyzed":** Swett's journal of the 1931–1932 expedition.

## Twelve: And Then There Were Five

75 **Harry ran along the shore:** Wittmer, *Floreana*, 10.

75 **"Tell me—are you people crazy?" to "taken in by him":** Wittmer, "What Happened on Galapagos?"

75 **She had endured seasickness:** Ibid.; Wittmer, *Floreana*, 12.

75 **"go no further":** Wittmer, *Floreana*, 12.

75 **But now, she told herself:** Ibid.

76 **"excitable Rhinelander":** Ibid.

76 **"How about getting us something":** Ibid., 15.

76 **"Social call?" and "Oh yes":** Ibid.

76 **they had learned a bit more:** Ibid., 17.

76 **did not much concern Margret:** Ibid.

76 **only out of politeness:** Ibid.

76 **"Gray and brown" to "dry as powder" :** Margret Wittmer, "Within Reach of Floreana," in "What Happened on Galapagos?"

76 **A pelican, resting in its nest:** Ibid.

76 **She served rice pudding:** Wittmer, *Floreana*, 17.

76 **they took a swim in the ocean:** Ibid.

76 **Heinz went to greet:** Strauch, *Satan Came to Eden*, 156. Margret says she accompanied Heinz on this trip to Friedo; Dore claims that Heinz first came alone and then returned with Margret. Wittmer, *Floreana*, 17; Strauch, *Satan Came to Eden*, 156.

76 **Dore and Friedrich noticed:** Strauch, *Satan Came to Eden*, 156.

76 **potential new woman friend:** Ibid.

77 **"odd to the point":** Ibid.

77 **At once she gave up hope:** Ibid., 157.

77 **"Do you have any mail?":** Margret Wittmer, "Arrival and Visit to Dr. Ritter," "What Happened on Galapagos?"

77 **pressed a packet of letters:** Ibid.

77 **Did Heinz have some connection:** Ibid.

77 **Did he intend to do:** Ibid.

77 Heinz answered no: Ibid.

77 Heinz soon understood: Strauch, *Satan Came to Eden*, 157.

77 Dore assumed that was the end: Ibid.

77 Heinz reappeared: Ibid.

77 "changed his absurd costume": Ibid.

77 Heinz explained that he had chosen: Ibid.

77 "threw a certain light": Ibid.

77 "whole jaw and head sag": Olshausen, "Galapagos Lure and Lore."

77 "shifted uneasily": Wittmer, *Floreana*, 18.

77 "had a gleam in them": Ibid.

77 Dore, however, took Margret's hand: Ibid.

78 "Aren't you a bit too well-dressed": Ibid.

78 "Oh well" to "wear an overall": Ibid.

78 She found it all wonderful: Ibid.

78 "one can live on nothing but figs": Ibid., 19.

78 "How do things look" to "in Berlin": Ibid.

78 His voice carried a note: Ibid.

78 the discovery of a large cache: *Guardian*, Aug. 10, 1932.

78 Dore wandered over: Wittmer, *Floreana*, 19.

78 Privately, she was intrigued: Strauch, *Satan Came to Eden*, 157.

78 "very touching": Ibid.

78 She wondered what would motivate: Ibid.

78 "a heroine, a victim, or an idiot": Ibid., 158.

78 Nor did she understand: Ibid.

79 "What do you think of Nietzsche?": Margret Wittmer, "Arrival and Visit to Dr. Ritter," in "What Happened on Galapagos?"

79 Margret silently scoffed: Ibid.

79 "Our equipment": Ibid.

79 Dore once again felt: Strauch, *Satan Came to Eden*, 159.

79 she and Heinz never intended: Wittmer, *Floreana*, 17; Wittmer, "Arrival and Visit to Dr. Ritter."

79 "Friedrich was anything but pleased": Strauch, *Satan Came to Eden*, 159.

79 Dore believed that the Wittmers: Ibid.

79 She worried that these people: Ibid.

## Thirteen: A Direct Order from God

80 In the 12th arrondissement of Paris: The Baroness lived at 9 Rue Cannebière in the 12th arrondissement. *Paris-Midi*, Feb. 19, 1933.

80 had a dream in which: *Paris-Soir*, Feb. 9, 1935.

80 belonging to God: Ibid.

80 He would speak to and provide: Baroness to a friend, June 19, 1933, printed in *L'Intransigeant*, Nov. 23, 1934.

80 At first Paris seemed relatively immune: Pierre-Cyrille Hautcoeur, "The Great Depression in France (1929–1938)," in *Business Cycles and Depressions: An Encyclopedia*, ed. David Glasner (New York: Garland, 1997), 39–42.

80 Exports suffered: Ibid.

80    tourism had dipped: *New York Times*, Aug. 31, 1931.

80    "Champagne bottles are going begging": *Arizona Daily Star*, March 6, 1931.

81    "Hitler is not yet master": Quoted in *New York Times*, April 25, 1932.

81    "Those who lived it still dream of it" to "madness in the air": *Paris-Soir*, Feb. 6, 1935.

81    "by the same orgy culture": Ibid.

81    spoke all languages and sold rare-edition books: Ibid.

81    climbed through each other's windows: Ibid.

81    "fantasy countess": Ibid.

81    a proud demimondaine: Ibid.

81    a wealthy English gentleman: Ibid.

81    called Antoinette or Toni: *Paris-Soir*, Jan. 8, 1935.

81    ran a lingerie and trinket shop: *Paris-Midi*, Feb. 19, 1933.

81    claimed to be an intimate of Hitler's: Ritter and Strauch to Hancock, Oct. 1, 1933, box 6, folder 13, Hancock Foundation Archives.

81    Antonia Henrika Jole Wagner-Wehrborn: Baptism book for the town of Zell am See: data.matricula-online.eu/de/oesterreich/salzburg/zell-am-see-st-hippolyt /TFBXII/?pg=105.

81    Her mother was an actress: *Illustrierte Kronen Zeitung*, Feb. 22, 1935.

81    a supervisor with the Baghdad Railway: Ibid.

81    a skilled actor who became a Nazi loyalist: Bregenzer/Vorarlberger Tagblatt, Oct. 6, 1931; *Arbeiter Zeitung*, July 17, 1933.

81    serving as a financier: Bregenzer/Vorarlberger Tagblatt, Oct. 6, 1931.

82    leader of the Nazi Motor Corps: Ibid.

82    well-to-do family but not obscenely wealthy: addresses for the Baroness's family can be found in an old Viennese address book: "Adolph Lehmann's allgemeiner Wohnungs-Anzeiger: nebst Handels- u. Gewerbe-Adressbuch für d. k.k. Reichshaupt- u. Residenzstadt" by Wien Bibliothek.

82    high-ranking military and political officials: Géza Csergheö and Iván Nagy, *Der Adel von Ungarn samt den Nebenländern der St. Stephanskrone* (Nuremberg: Bauer und Raspe, 1893).

82    German princes of the house of Glücksburg: The Baroness's grandmother was Aloysia Balog de Manko-Bück. German princes of both the House of Glücksburg and the House of Lippe-Weissenfeld are direct descendants of the marriage between the Baroness's grandparents. Wikipedia entry for Balog de Manko Bük: en.wikipedia .org/wiki/Balog_de_Manko_Bu%CC%88k.

82    a grandmother who belonged: Ibid.

82    who received the nobility: *Salzburger Volksblatt*, Nov. 30, 1934, 4.

82    "grant a higher general education": Original decree of Dec. 11, 1900.

82    she did become a polyglot: *Paris-Soir*, Jan. 8, 1935.

82    reportedly required her young charges: Ibid.

82    "The girl was very gifted" to "gossip about her": *Wiener Sonn-und Montags-Zeitung*, Nov. 26, 1934.

82    told people she'd "escaped": *Paris-Midi*, Feb. 19, 1933.

82    friends who told her she was beautiful: *Paris-Soir*, Jan. 8, 1935.

82    "male-murdering Austrian": Guadalupi and Shugaar, *Latitude Zero*, 134.

82    "who ate her way": Ibid.

82    Her entire family had been massacred: *Paris-Soir*, Jan. 8, 1935.

83    Possibly true: Guadalupi and Shugaar, *Latitude Zero*, 134.

83    Two Russian aristocrats: Ibid.

83    A third Russian aristocrat: Ibid.

83    Toni took a job as a waitress: Ibid.

83    In 1920, she met a French war hero: Military records of Roger Pierre Armand Bosquet, service recruitment number 1482. Archives municipals de Toulouse.

83    Roger Pierre Armand Bosquet: Bosquet was born July 30, 1894, in Toulouse, Ibid.

83    he suffered a gunshot wound to the stomach: Ibid.

83    "kept a cold-blooded": Ibid.

83    Before the war he'd been: *Paris-Soir*, Jan. 8, 1935.

83    "belong to any man": Ibid.

83    by the city's mayor: *Paris-Midi*, Feb. 19, 1933.

83    Toni soon bored of being a housewife: *Paris-Soir*, Jan. 8, 1935.

83    seducing men and women alike: Ibid.

83    forever on the verge of neurasthenia: Ibid.

83    "The Baroness is small" to "call a canter": Mielche, *Let's See*, 111.

84    turning to violence in moments of anger: *Paris-Soir*, Jan. 8, 1935.

84    She developed a habit: Strauch and Ritter to Hancock, Oct. 1, 1933, box 6, folder 13, Hancock Foundation Archives.

84    Robert Philippson: Birth certificate in Standesamt Charlottenburg.

84    "as though he might have been a gigolo": Mielche, *Let's See*, 112.

84    Rudolph Lorenz: *La Phare de la Loire 20*, Nov. 1934.

84    Rudolph joined the Baroness's household: Ibid.

84    the Baroness's husband traveled frequently: *Paris-Midi*, Feb. 19, 1933.

84    Robert was content to do nothing: *La Liberté*, Nov. 21, 1934.

84    which she named Antoinette: *Paris-Midi*, Feb. 19, 1933.

85    "These islands," she confessed to a friend: *St. Louis Post-Dispatch*, Nov. 23, 1934.

85    "Nothing can keep me": *Der Morgen: Wiener Montagblatt*, Nov. 26, 1934.

85    tired of her antics: Strauch, *Satan Came to Eden*, 184.

85    she had murdered someone: Anderson, *Zigzagging the South Seas*, 68.

85    falsifying the books: Ibid.; Strauch, *Satan Came to Eden*, 185.

85    her "engineers" and recruited a third: *El Telégrafo*, Sept. 18, 1932.

85    would serve as her contractor: Ibid.

85    "Real travelers are those" to "'Forward!'": *Illustrierte Kronen Zeitung*, Nov. 28, 1934.

85    the steamship *Bodegraven*: *Der Morgen: Wiener Montagblatt*, Nov. 26, 1934.

85    Over the years her particular copy: Diary of Amory Coolidge, box 1, DeStefano collection.

## Fourteen: A Pity That They Should Be So Unpleasant

87    "You must have a look at it" to "temporary residence": For Margret's first trip to the caves, see Wittmer, *Floreana*, 20–27.

87    The following morning, Margret made coffee: Ibid.

87    She found herself disoriented: Ibid., 20.

87    cactus branches stabbing: Ibid., 22.

88 "I must have a rest": Ibid.

88 "We've been going three hours": Ibid.

88 "Oh dear": Ibid.

88 Heinz replied: Ibid.

88 "Our house": Ibid., 23.

88 Margret did not like: Ibid.

88 "You forgot": Ibid.

88 a fireplace and chimney: Ibid., 24.

88 She took solace: Ibid.

88 "This really" to "up here?": Ibid., 25.

88 "Say no more" to "house-warming": Ibid.

89 white tablecloth: Ibid.

89 "Happy?": Ibid., 26.

89 half-hopeful, half-anxious: Ibid.

89 "Yes," she reassured him: Ibid.

89 from Cologne, no less: Ibid., 27.

89 "I felt," she wrote: Ibid.

89 saved the head of the boar: Margret Wittmer, "The March into the Interior," in "What Happened on Galapagos?"

89 "meat for my chickens": Ibid.

89 discovered Dore picking through: Wittmer, *Floreana*, 28.

89 "Live and let live": Ibid.

89 "All right" to "so unpleasant": Ibid.

89 "He was met by Dore" to "couple easy neighbors": Ibid., 27.

90 "seemed to appreciate" to "an eloquent tale": Strauch, *Satan Came to Eden*, 158–59.

90 He was cordial, even kind: Margret Wittmer, "Death over Galapagos," *Liberty Magazine*, Nov. 13, 1937, box 88, folder 3, Record Unit 7231, Schmitt Papers.

90 aroused her suspicions: Ibid.

90 they began to settle: Margret Wittmer, "Breaking Ground," in "What Happened on Galapagos?"

90 They were alarmed: Wittmer, "Death over Galapagos," Nov. 13, 1937.

90 their fatal mistake: Ibid.

## Fifteen: Before the Storm

91 On the last day of August: *L'Intransigeant*, Nov. 24, 1934.

91 The Baroness had expected: Ibid.

91 the Depression had stirred political upheaval: Sebastián Ignacio Donoso Bustamante (Ecuadorian historian), email message to author, Oct. 19, 2020.

91 leading to the resignation: Ibid.

91 opponents challenged his legitimacy: Ibid.

91 By a narrow majority: Ibid.

91 "I defended mysef like a tigress": *L'Intransigeant*, Nov. 24, 1934.

91 her antics worked: Ibid.

91 "I pull out my most gracious": Ibid.

92 nevertheless asked the official: Ibid.

92    The governor of the Galápagos: *San Francisco Examiner*, Oct. 7, 1932; *El Universo*, Dec. 8, 1934.

92    "with full Castilian gallantry": *L'Intransigeant*, Nov. 24, 1934.

92    "All this," she boasted: Ibid.

92    The temperature was lovely: Ibid.

92    the mice so tame: Ibid.

92    "The idea came to me" to "heart has hardened": Ibid.

92    "The purpose of your trip": For the baroness's exchange with the editor, see *El Telégrafo*, Sept. 18, 1932.

92    "Nothing can compare with them" to "Europe and North America": Ibid.

93    the talents of her partners: Ibid.

93    "pure crystals": Ibid.

93    "sensitive, sweet in expression": Ibid.

93    "Have you thought, madam": Ibid.

93    "I have thought" to "especially in Hollywood": Ibid.

93    "The woman is capable" to "than the male": Ibid.

93    "got to know": *L'Intransigeant*, Nov. 24, 1934.

93    "I have a conviction": Ibid.

## Sixteen: Dead Sun

94    she regretted leaving: Wittmer, *Floreana*, 31.

94    Why not, she thought, write a letter: Ibid.

94    he started to laugh: Ibid.

94    "But I've read about": Ibid.

94    Friedrich laughed again: Ibid.

94    "My dear Frau Wittmer": Ibid.

94    "I suppose mail isn't": Ibid.

94    Without her machine: Ibid., 35.

95    teaching Harry about the history: Ibid., 32–35.

95    a dull, persistent fear: Ibid., 35.

95    "We've at least got a qualified doctor" to "go wrong": Ibid.

95    "I'm afraid not" to "as a doctor": Ibid.

95    "You mustn't" to "go off smoothly": Ibid.

95    only sharpened: Ibid.

95    The husband, she argued, should never assist: Wittmer, "Death over Galapagos," Nov. 13, 1937.

95    eating only papayas: Ibid.

96    the wood of lechosa trees: Wittmer, *Floreana*, 38.

96    his favorite island meal: Margret Wittmer, "Herta Dies," in "What Happened on Galapagos?"

96    "One would have to watch": Ibid.

96    "Our day, the short tropical" to "brooding": Ibid.

96    All three of them held: Ibid.

96    Dore sensed the eruption: Strauch, *Satan Came to Eden*, 160.

96    "If fate willed that we go": Ibid., 161.

96    "The asses were undisturbed": Friedrich Ritter, "Eruption of the Volcano on

Marborough [*sic*]," box 6, folder 11, Collection no. 0257, Special Collections, USC Libraries. Ritter surely meant Albemarle Island, although the only volcanoes visible from Floreana are located on Isabela (Roslyn Cameron, email message to author, Dec. 2, 2022). It turns out this incident wasn't a volcanic explosion at all, but, in Dore's words, "the combustion of a field of sulphur deep in one of the volcano's craters." Cameron further explains, "There are 'sulfur fields' on the west side of the Sierra Negra Volcano. Exposed sulfur is only mildly flammable under normal atmospheric conditions. However, sulfur deposits deep inside the volcano would catch fire from the heat generated from volcanic activity causing sulfur dioxide gas to be released from a volcano when magma is relatively near the surface. So in theory Dore is describing pre-eruption activity."

96    a "dead sun": Strauch, *Satan Came to Eden*, 162.

## Seventeen: And Then There Were Nine

99    **Margret heard her surviving dog:** Wittmer, *Floreana*, 40.
99    **Behind him came a woman:** Ibid.
99    **Aged about forty years old:** Strauch, *Satan Came to Eden*, 164.
99    **she wore men's overalls:** Ibid.
99    **a beret perched askew:** Ibid.
99    **a wide mouth:** Ibid.
99    **by dark glasses:** Ibid.
99    **"Herr Lorenz" and "Baroness Bosquet":** Margret Wittmer, "Notes in My Diary," in "What Happened on Galapagos?"
99    **"Where's the spring?":** Wittmer, *Floreana*, 40.
99    **"Just over there":** Ibid.
99    **Margret was appalled:** Ibid.
99    **"Perhaps you would care":** Ibid.
100   **With a mumble:** Ibid.
100   **"What an extraordinary couple":** Ibid.
100   **"Well, I don't suppose":** Ibid., 41.
100   **"I'm afraid they might be" to "if I were you":** Ibid.
100   **"Oh dear"; "That doesn't sound":** Ibid.
100   **a serious construction error:** Ibid.
100   **"You won't mind, will you?":** Ibid.
100   **they minded very much:** Ibid.
100   **"In return for your kind hospitality" to "Post Office Bay":** Ibid., 41–42.
101   **a journey of three hours:** Heinz Hell, *Kölnische Illustrierte Zeitung*, April 1, 1932.
101   **a "certain artificial charm":** Strauch, *Satan Came to Eden*, 164.
101   **expecting it to be kissed:** Ibid.
101   **"If this was a mere Baroness":** Ibid.
101   **the flicker of annoyance:** Ibid.
101   **She believed that Floreana:** Ibid., 165.
101   **Dore did not believe the legitimacy:** Ibid., 184.
101   **"At least she was no little bourgeois" to "one's steel":** Ibid., 165.
101   **"a distinguished visitor":** Ibid.
101   **"cunning contraptions" and "marvelous" grounds:** Ibid.

102   "Rudi! Take off my glasses"; "Oh, Rudi darling"; "Oh, Rudi, come": Ibid., 166.

102   Dore managed to exchange: Ibid.

102   both candor and naïveté: Ibid.

102   "must have caught him early": Ibid.

102   "menacing inquiry": Ibid., 167.

102   Dore offered blankets: Ibid.

102   Friedrich strung up a hammock: Ibid.

102   "It was no cough": Ibid., 168.

102   "It is now 1 o'clock" to "no longer than the first": Ritter, "Floreana," Als Robinson
        auf Galapagos, Oct. 1932.

103   The Baroness tossed and turned: Ibid.

103   "You could perhaps" to "the rooster is already crowing": Ibid.

103   which the Baroness did not touch: Strauch, Satan Came to Eden, 169.

103   "To come to Floreana": Ibid.

103   "so little trace was there": Ibid.

103   "Oh," he said, "none of us believe": Ibid.

104   "I know that lot already" to "slaughter against us": Wittmer, Floreana, 42.

104   "Well anyhow," Heinz said: Ibid.

104   "That's funny" to "They've been opened" : Ibid., 43.

104   "Not by me": Ibid.

104   "No, of course": Ibid.

104   he saw one from Captain Hancock: Ritter and Strauch to Hancock, Oct. 1, 1932,
        box 6, folder 13, Hancock Foundation Archive. They mention receiving Hancock's
        recent letter.

104   "She's even taken photos": Wittmer, Floreana, 43.

104   "I see" to "the better": Ibid.

104   "Goes for me too" to "as I think you know": Ibid.

104   "It could be so beautiful": Ritter, Als Robinson auf Galapagos, July 1934. The
        quotation is in a letter to a friend that Friedrich reprinted in his memoir.

## Eighteen: Dentist and Doctor Indeed

105   Rudolph Lorenz appeared in Dore's garden: Strauch, Satan Came to Eden, 171.

105   He looked exhausted and red-faced: Ibid.

105   He said that he was transporting: Ibid.

105   He was so sorry: Ibid.

105   A few days later, on October 24: Margret Wittmer, "Death over Galapagos,"
        Nov. 13, 1937.

105   "dressed to kill": Ibid.

105   ignoring Harry entirely: Wittmer, Floreana, 43.

105   "very much engaged": Wittmer, "Death over Galapagos."

105   They both wore rings on their fingers: El Universo, Dec. 8, 1934.

105   Heinz appraised Robert: For Heinz's visit to the Casa, see Wittmer, Floreana, 44, 45.

106   "So sorry" to "off at once": Ibid.

106   Heinz suppressed a laugh: Ibid.

106   "You know my plans": Ibid.

106   Heinz shook his head: Ibid.

106   "Oh, but haven't I": Ibid.

106   She smiled and handed him: Ibid.

106   "Dentist and doctor indeed": Ibid.

106   "Dental mechanic at most": Ibid.

106   "Oh yes, of course": Ibid.

106   "That will be": Ibid.

106   He argued that: Ibid.

106   "It costs" to "that is": Ibid.

106   "I should be obliged": Ibid.

106   "I wouldn't dream" to "any chance?": Ibid., 45.

106   "We have three men": Ibid.

106   With that, she settled a hand: Ibid.

106   Heinz and Harry left: Ibid.

107   He was "in a fury": Strauch, *Satan Came to Eden*, 172.

107   Even so, Heinz stressed: Ibid.

107   Dore did not share: Ibid., 173.

107   Heinz wanted to know: Ibid.

107   "neighborly sentiments": Ibid.

107   "Dear Captain Mr. Hancock": Friedrich Ritter to George Allan Hancock, undated n.d. (fall 1932), box 6, folder 13, Hancock Foundation Archive.

108   He concluded by requesting: Ibid.

108   Friedrich sent the same list of items: Eugene McDonald telegram to George Allan Hancock, telegram, courtesy of Hancock's great-granddaughter Jane Brennan.

109   crouched down, beckoning: Wittmer, *Floreana*, 45.

109   He glanced behind his shoulders: Ibid.

109   "Nobody can hear us?": Ibid.

109   "I don't think so" to "is it?": Ibid.

109   "They're not really married" to "rid of her": Ibid.

109   "Really?" to "Dr. Ritter's letters?": Ibid.

109   "Yes" to "yours too": Ibid.

109   "There was a spy": Ibid., 46.

## Nineteen: Ready for All Crimes

110   On the evening of November 9: Margret Wittmer, "Pleasant Guests, New Friendships," in "What Happened on Galapagos?"

110   Arthur Estampa: *St. Louis Post-Dispatch*, Nov. 24, 1934.

110   a good friend of Vincent Astor's: Ibid.

110   a German scientist and writer named Paul Franke: *The Sacramento Bee*, Feb. 10, 1933.

110   He was Ecuadorian, Estampa assumed: *St. Louis Post-Dispatch*, Nov. 24, 1934.

110   and stood about six foot three: Ibid.

110   Estampa himself was: Ibid.

110   The woman had a revolver: The *Fremont (Ohio) News Messenger*, Feb. 10, 1933.

110   she called out a warning: Ibid.

111   She asked Estampa his nationality: *Sacramento Bee*, Feb. 10, 1933.

111   he intended to hunt: Ibid.

111   At this the woman ordered: Strauch, *Satan Came to Eden*, 175.

111 **He laughed:** Ibid.

111 **The island was now hers:** Ibid.

111 **A chorus of frantic shouts:** Ibid.

111 **did not visit willingly:** Ibid.

111 **"a person whose love of sensation":** Ibid., 176.

111 **with trepidation:** Ibid.

112 **"far-gone case of hysteria":** Ibid.

112 **"single proper man":** Dore, 179.

112 **a rifle slung over her shoulder:** *Fremont (Ohio) News Messenger,* Feb. 10, 1933.

112 **"I am the sole master of this island" to "my permission":** *La Liberté,* Feb. 19, 1933.

112 **Estampa told her:** Strauch, *Satan Came to Eden,* 178.

112 **told her that he would do as she requested:** *St. Louis Post-Dispatch,* Nov. 24, 1934.

112 **one of her guards lifting his gun:** Strauch, *Satan Came to Eden,* 178.

112 **woken again by shouts:** Ibid., 177.

112 **his clothes tattered:** Ibid.

112 **"Why did you not wait?":** Ibid., 178.

113 **"Highly esteemed Mr. Governor" to "in a sanitarium":** Reprinted in *El Universo,* Dec. 8, 1934.

## Twenty: And Then There Were Ten

114 **nevertheless felt her presence:** Strauch, *Satan Came to Eden,* 181.

114 **who began visiting Friedo:** Ibid.

114 **"If you hear any sort of eccentricities" to "in a few months":** Ritter to Hancock, n.d. (late 1932), box 6, folder 13, Hancock Foundation Archive.

114 **It seemed Rudolph Lorenz:** Strauch, *Satan Came to Eden,* 182.

115 **any perceived slacking was met:** Ibid.

115 **Sometimes Dore wondered:** Ibid.

115 **root vegetable called *otoy*:** Ibid. *Otoy* (*Xanthosoma sagittifolium*) is a non-native plant, meaning that it does not occur naturally in the islands and was likely gifted to Dore. It produces an edible, starchy tuber that is used much like a potato, where it can be boiled in stews, baked, or fried. Roslyn Cameron, email message to author, Dec. 2, 2022.

115 **"You don't know" to "brain him":** Ibid., 183.

115 **Kiddy; Mein Bubi:** Eicher, 185; Margret Wittmer, "Death over Galapagos," Nov. 13, 1937.

115 **Mousie:** Ibid.

115 **"I want to go" to "elsewhere":** Strauch, *Satan Came to Eden,* 183.

115 **She could tell his hands:** Ibid.

116 **practicing her "roles":** Ibid., 184.

116 **"which the Baroness herself":** Ibid., 186.

116 **"creeping through the bush":** Wittmer, *Floreana,* 90.

116 **had already tired of island life:** Wittmer, "Pleasant Guests, New Friendships."

116 **"I was up at Friedo" to "to eat":** Wittmer, *Floreana,* 55.

116 **"It is very moving":** Wittmer, "Pleasant Guests, New Friendships."

116 **She was hugely pregnant:** Margret Wittmer, "Childbirth in the Wilderness," in "What Happened on Galapagos?"

116    seventy-five in one day: Ibid.

116    take turns guarding the crops: Wittmer, *Floreana*, 50, 53.

116    "strange, nocturnal concert": Ibid.

117    killed it with one shot: Ibid.

117    a true log cabin: Ibid., 53.

117    could now easily lift: Margret Wittmer, "Grand Hotel Floreana," in "What Happened on Galapagos?"

117    reminded her of the thatched cottages: Wittmer, "Death over Galapagos," Nov. 13, 1937.

117    She passed the time by monitoring: Wittmer, "Grand Hotel Floreana."

117    about sixteen hundred feet: Ibid.

117    the Baroness would be willing: Ibid.

117    "Don't call me" to "at your house": Wittmer, "Death over Galapagos," Nov. 13, 1937.

117    She had stocked up: Wittmer, *Floreana*, 56.

117    "Would it be enough?" to "that now": Ibid.

118    "Dear God," she prayed, "let it all go": Ibid.

118    prepare meals for the days ahead: Wittmer, "Death over Galapagos," Nov. 13, 1937.

118    She was desperate: Wittmer, *Floreana*, 57.

118    "more than flesh and blood": Ibid.

118    She couldn't breathe: Ibid.

118    "Heinz!": Ibid.

118    She couldn't hear: Ibid.

118    All around her everything looked: Ibid.

118    remembered that she had a real bed: Ibid.

118    She called for Heinz again: Ibid.

118    Her vision darkened: Ibid.

118    She heard the hooting: Ibid.

118    and the bellowing: Ibid., 58.

118    She was too weak: Ibid.

118    "I heard a cry" to "seeing and hearing": Ibid.

119    "It's a boy": Ibid.

119    didn't know whose voice: Ibid.

119    "It was over for the little creature": Ibid., 58.

119    "Dr. Ritter. Get Dr. Ritter": Ibid.

119    three miles: *El Universo*, Nov. 28, 1934.

119    "For the first time" to "quite in order": Wittmer, *Floreana*, 59.

119    "Have you still got pains?": Ibid.

119    "Yes. Very bad ones": Ibid.

119    "I must operate" to "cold compresses": Ibid.

119    he had to go off and speak: Ibid.

119    with neither gloves nor an anesthetic: Ibid.

119    "You've been very brave" to "on that, too": Ibid.

119    regretting that she had once: Ibid.

120    "A fine strapping boy" to "worthwhile characters": Ibid., 60.

120    "special philosophy": Ibid.

120    "We do appreciate" to "we owe you?": Ibid.

120    "Money" to "every fortnight": Ibid.

120    **Margret turned her face:** Ibid.

120    **He suggested Rolf:** Wittmer, "Childbirth in the Wilderness."

120    **Prince Charles:** Diary of Coolidge.

120    **"I have seldom seen" to "Friedrich's child":** For Dore's reaction to Margret's giving birth, see Strauch, *Satan Came to Eden*, 186.

120    **She wasn't bitter:** Ibid.

120    **she felt calm enough to inquire:** Ibid.

121    **a convivial mood settled:** Ibid., 187.

121    **"long and pleasant" chat:** Ibid.

121    **One image in particular:** Box 8, DeStefano collection.

## Twenty-One: The Man Isn't Born Who Can Resist Me

122    **inspired Dore to reconsider:** Strauch, *Satan Came to Eden*, 187.

122    **the Baroness had even given:** Ibid.

122    **She had the urge:** Ibid.

122    **so "soft and gentle":** Ibid.

122    **It would be the perfect opportunity:** Ibid.

122    **"pleased and attracted":** Ibid.

122    **she had done the Baroness an injustice:** Ibid.

123    **"this lazy lying around":** Wittmer, "Death over Galapagos," Nov. 13, 1937.

123    **strange footsteps, she realized:** Wittmer, *Floreana*, 61.

123    **Lump barked:** Ibid.

123    **in an exceptionally pleasant mood:** Margret Wittmer, "The Baroness Comes to See Rolf," in "What Happened on Galapagos?"

123    **"Congratulations on your son":** Wittmer, *Floreana*, 61.

123    **gripped both of Margret's hands:** Ibid.

123    **she claimed were from her shop:** Ibid.

123    **Dore and Friedrich arrived:** Strauch, *Satan Came to Eden*, 187, 188.

123    **"had the talent":** Ibid., 188.

123    **where "you can talk":** Ibid.

123    **"a very promising specimen":** Ibid.

123    **"I am afraid" to "This on Floreana!":** Ibid.

123    **"too weak":** Margret Wittmer, "A Short Legal Procedure," in "What Happened on Galapagos?"

123    **"I was surprised to see":** Strauch, *Satan Came to Eden*, 188–89.

124    **they planted the date palm:** Ibid., 190.

124    **"When they left" to "every man she met":** Wittmer, "Death over Galapagos," Nov. 13, 1937.

124    **Friedrich explained that he:** Ibid.

124    **Dore had to admit:** Strauch, *Satan Came to Eden*, 190.

124    **Often in the dark of night:** Diary of John Garth, Jan. 28, 1933, box 25, folder 13, Collection no. 0257, Special Collections, USC Libraries.

124    **nothing short of astonishing:** Strauch, *Satan Came to Eden*, 190.

124    **"told a great deal":** Ibid., 191.

125    **"She had a most attractive" to "phenomenon":** Ibid.

125    **Among her many talents:** Ibid.

125   "For the first time" to "full of charm": Ibid.

125   "It did not take me long" to "with my own man": Ibid.

125   "The man isn't born" to "probably turn up": Ibid.

125   "I suppose you think" to "keeps them": Ibid.

126   Dore sensed a challenge: Ibid.

## Twenty-Two: A Hunter Since His Kitten Days

127   at the behest of the Ecuadorian government: *Los Angeles Times*, Dec. 28, 1932.

127   assist in the establishment: Author Q&A with Tapia, Oct. 2021.

127   He also told the press of his plans: *Santa Maria Times*, Dec. 28, 1932.

127   his thoughts about *The Journal of a Recluse*: Ritter to Hancock, Winter 1933, box 6, "Letters 1933/34/35/Depositions" folder, Collection no. 0257, Special Collections, USC Libraries.

127   Little did Friedrich—and likely Hancock himself: *St. Louis Post-Dispatch*, Nov. 17, 1912.

128   "I have had in my life" to "generally": Ritter to Hancock, Winter 1933, box 6, "Letters 1933/34/35/Depositions," folder, Collection no. 0257, Special Collections, USC Libraries.

128   "Peter Charles is a huge tomcat" to "of the brush": Dore Strauch, "The Cat," box 6, folder 11, Collection no. 0257, Special Collections, USC Libraries.

129   Despite the Baroness's crude behavior: For the Baroness's visit to Friedo, see Strauch, *Satan Came to Eden*, 194–99.

129   "grew like weeds": Ibid.

129   She told herself: Ibid.

129   With great disappointment she noticed: Ibid., 195.

129   The poor boy was sick: Ibid.

129   "It was all terribly" to "find him dead": Ibid.

129   Wasn't it strange, Dore thought: Ibid.

129   Dore waited for Friedrich: Ibid.

129   almost imperceptible smile: Ibid.

129   "mask-like absence": Ibid., 197.

129   "I knew that" to "between them": Ibid.

130   Moreover, Dore wondered: Ibid.

130   "violent quarreling": Ibid., 196.

130   "You know," she explained to Dore: Ibid., 198.

130   saved again by Burro's call: Ibid.

130   "If you treat your husband": Ibid.

130   She hoped to capture: Ibid.

130   "Men and dogs" to "their master": Ibid., 199.

130   She took them home: Ibid.

131   "as Eve must have felt": Ibid.

131   "Dr. Ritter" to "arsenic poisoning?": Ibid.

131   "Such a waste of time": Ibid., 200.

131   "You must" to "a criminal?": Ibid.

131   "My dear child" to "theatrical too": Ibid.

131   a sudden sharp fear: Ibid.

131   **"Listen, my dear" to "shrewd enough":** Ibid., 200–201.

131   **"There would be inquiries" to "you suspect":** Ibid., 201.

132   **the *Stella Polaris*, carrying wealthy:** *Miami News*, Jan. 15, 1933.

132   **seized by German forces:** Henrik Reimertz, "Stella Polaris," Great Ocean Liners, Feb. 12, 2024, thegreatoceanliners.com.

132   **130 crew members to attend:** "The History Behind the M/Y *Stella Polaris* Ship and Their Fancy Dress Ball & Au Revoir Event Menus," Digital Humanities Studio, Loyola University, Dec. 16, 2021, docstudio.org/2021/12/16/the-history-behind-the -my-stella-polaris-ship-and-their-fancy-dress-ball-au-revoir-event-menus.

132   **Smoking Room, Music Salon, Social Hall, Reading and Writing Room:** ssmaritime. com/Stella-Polaris.htm.

132   **a state-of-the-art gymnasium:** thegreatoceanliners.com/articles/stella-polaris.

132   **deck for outdoor exercising:** Ibid.

132   **exotic menus:** Menu for the M/Y *Stella Polaris*, July 10, 1938, New York Public Library, menus.nypl.org/menus/30970.

132   **clear turtle soup:** Ibid.

132   **the latter now illegal:** David A. Steen, "Why Don't People Eat Turtle Soup Anymore?," *Slate*, Jan. 4, 2016, slate.com.

132   **allowed only 198 passengers:** *Birmingham Gazette*, June 27, 1930.

132   **in exchange for a free trip:** Jeffrey Manley, "The Saga of the Stella Polaris," Evelyn Waugh Society, March 27, 2020, evelynwaughsociety.org/2020/the-saga-of-the -stella-polaris.

132   **commenced in New York:** *Shreveport Journal,* Jan. 18, 1933.

132   **Carl Block of Peoria:** *Decatur (Ill.) Herald and Review,* Dec. 15, 1934.

132   **Friedrich gave him a tour:** Ibid.

132   **"A cook-pot had mysteriously disappeared":** Ibid.

133   **had tried to escape:** Ibid.

133   **"The next time that rascal":** Ibid.


## Twenty-Three: What a Girl

134   **"the gaping jaws":** Waldo L. Schmitt, "The Hancock Expedition of 1933," box 86, folder 1, Record Unit 7231, Schmitt Papers.

134   **They launched harpoons:** Diary of Fred C. Ziesenhenne, 1933–1934, box 87, Record Unit 7231, Schmitt Papers.

134   **"more pets every day":** Ibid., Jan. 25, 1933.

134   **A female sea lion:** Ibid., Feb. 21, 1933.

134   **After she died:** Ibid.

134   **They slaughtered more seals:** Ibid.

134   **They took an albatross:** Ibid., Jan. 24, 1933.

134   **They shot finches and mockingbirds and hawks:** Ibid., Jan. 28, 1933. "The Galapagos hawks are very tame and become a nuisance," Ziesenhenne wrote in Feb. 3, 1933. "I saw fourteen of them rotting just where they fell after being shot."

134   **They filched four eggs:** Ibid., Feb. 1, 1933.

134   **with the butt of a gun:** Ibid.

134   **the *Stella Polaris* was already there:** *Decatur Herald and Review,* Dec. 15, 1934.

134   **noticed a heliograph message:** Diary of Ziesenhenne, Jan. 26, 1933.

134   **He at once understood:** Schmitt, 1934.

135   **"It was a wild tale":** Schmitt, "Hancock Expedition of 1933," 12.

135   **"his clothes half torn":** Ibid.

135   **blaming her fondness:** Strauch to Hancock, June 1933, box 6, "Letters 1933/34/35 /Depositions" folder, Collection no. 0257, Special Collections, USC Libraries.

135   **traded them back and forth:** Wittmer, "Death over Galapagos," Nov. 13, 1937.

135   **Dore refused to speak at all:** *New York World Telegram,* n.d. (date cut off), box 8, DeStefano collection.

135   **"I am happy" to "the taste sensation":** Ritter, *Als Robinson auf Galapagos,* "Friedo," Oct. 5, 1931.

135   **home movies of the couple:** Diary of Ziesenhenne, Jan. 27, 1933.

135   **a stockpile of presents:** Ibid.

135   **"Dore got quite an outlay":** Ibid.

135   **"It would not be bad":** Ibid.

136   **The next bit of business:** John S. Garth, "Personal Recollections of John Garth, PhD," box 4, folder 81, Collection no. 0257, Special Collections, USC Libraries.

136   **Immediately Friedrich agreed:** Ibid.

136   **"Dore felt no pain" to "a Spartaness":** Ibid.

136   **At Schmitt's request:** Schmitt, "Hancock Expedition of 1933," 13.

136   **At 8:30 in the morning:** Ibid.

136   **riding a donkey and wearing:** Ibid.

136   **shooting olive and vermillion flycatchers, yellow warblers, and finches:** Ibid.

136   **They followed a path:** Diary of Ziesenhenne, Jan. 28, 1933.

136   **The crew was impressed:** Schmitt, "Hancock Expedition of 1933," 14.

136   **Friedrich gave an enthusiastic demonstration:** Diary of Ziesenhenne, Jan. 28, 1933.

136   **He took a shower and smiled:** Various photographs of Ritter, Hancock Foundation Archive and DeStefano collection.

136   **The overall effect:** Schmitt, "Hancock Expedition of 1933," 14.

136   **Even Friedrich's machetes:** Ibid.

136   **one zoologist in the party:** Diary of Ziesenhenne, Jan. 28, 1933.

137   **catching butterflies:** Schmitt, "Hancock Expedition of 1933," 14.

137   **"A pitiful figure" to "glad to see you":** Charles Swett, "Floreana," MS, box 5, DeStefano collection.

137   **Some tree trunks were splashed:** Diary of Ziesenhenne, Jan. 28, 1933.

137   **"the mansion":** Ibid.

137   **"convinced us that some royalty":** Ibid.

137   **Lingerie of various colors:** Garth, "Personal Recollections."

138   **thick clouds of flies:** Ibid.

138   **In the garden they met:** Diary of Ziesenhenne, Jan. 28, 1933.

138   **who spoke perfect English:** Garth, "Personal Recollections."

138   **full of questions:** Treherne, *The Galapagos Affair,* 107.

138   **clad only in underwear:** Garth, "Personal Recollections."

138   **Crazy Panties:** *San Francisco Examiner,* Dec. 21, 1941.

138   **She even had a few kind words:** Treherne, 108.

138   **crisp white linens:** Diary of Ziesenhenne, Jan. 28, 1933.

138   **Stacks of clothing and supplies:** Ibid.

138   **"no good ideas of housekeeping":** Garth, "Personal Recollections."

138    She spoke eight languages: Ibid.

138    had lived in: Ibid.

138    excellent connections in Hollywood: Ibid.

138    Had they heard that she was: Diary of Ziesenhenne, Jan. 28, 1933.

138    And that another ancestor: Ibid.

138    "It happened during the war": Swett, "Floreana."

139    "very jolly and witty": Diary of Ziesenhenne, Jan. 28, 1933.

139    "Haven't I seen you somewhere before?": Barnacle, Jan. 29, 1933, box 5, DeStefano
       collection.

139    "I heard that gag before": Ibid.

139    her menagerie of pets: Diary of Ziesenhenne, Jan. 28, 1933.

139    warmed the liquid: Ibid.

139    regurgitated it directly: Ibid.

139    an impressive structure: Garth, "Personal Recollections."

139    "Besides having the prestige" to "big day for us": Wittmer, "Baroness Comes to See
       Rolf."

139    "She was the most beautiful": For the visit of Hancock and crew to the Wittmers',
       see Diary of Ziesenhenne, Jan. 28, 1933.

139    Heinz gave a tour: Ibid.

139    it had taken him four short months: Ibid.

140    a phalanx of dried jerk meat: Ibid.

140    "And you had that baby here?": For Hancock's exchange with Margret, see Wittmer,
       Floreana, 65.

140    "Oh, so you keep chickens?": Ibid.

140    "Do you?": Ibid.

140    "Well I've got" to "a day": Ibid.

140    "Twenty thousand" to "small way": Ibid.

140    "cannibal hens": Ibid.

140    "old friends": Wittmer, "Death over Galapagos," Nov. 13, 1937.

140    "Naturally" to "treat for us": Wittmer, "Baroness Comes to See Rolf."

140    "Waldo's interest in the Galapagos": Blackwelder, 120.

140    The group, including: Diary of Ziesenhenne, Jan. 28, 1933.

140    "felt equally bound to refuse": Garth, "Personal Recollections."

140    "sharp gleam of resentment": Strauch, Satan Came to Eden, 202.

140    he flinched: Ibid.

141    "the unhallowed mutual understanding": Ibid.

141    "We are glad" to "you'd been ill": Ibid., 203.

141    "Herr Lorenz" to "Dr. Ritter": Ibid.

141    "Another doctor?": Ibid.

141    "Oh, yes" to "Didn't I?": Ibid.

141    assessed him carefully: Ibid.

141    Yet he agreed with the Baroness: Ibid.

141    also related to: Garth, "Personal Recollections."

141    "Oh, that's just the way": Ibid.

141    she and Garth discussed Sanskrit: Ibid.

142    would he mind bringing her a textbook: Treherne, 209.

142    **some cans of milk:** Heinz Wittmer to Hancock, Feb. 26, 1933, courtesy of Jane
       Brennan.

142    **She invited both men:** Diary of Fred C. Ziesenhenne, January 29, 1933.

142    **"What a girl!":** Diary of Ziesenhenne, Jan. 29, 1933.

142    **"festering sex complex":** Robinson, 206.

142    **They shouted, circling each other:** *Los Angeles Evening Post-Record,* Nov. 21, 1934.

142    **"But the Baroness"** to **"in the bush":** Ibid.

142    **"I have to get away":** Quoted in Lundh, "Floreana."

142    **"Notwithstanding"** to **"at all times":** *El Universo,* Dec. 10, 1934.


## Twenty-Four: The Empress of Floreana

143    **"women's bickerings":** Strauch, *Satan Came to Eden,* 204.

143    **"She is not harmless"** to **"self-control to you?":** Ibid.

143    **"How can you ask?":** Ibid.

143    **"Very well then"** to **"afford to wait":** Ibid.

144    **"My dear Captain Hancock":** Ritter to Hancock, Feb. 1, 1933, box 6, folder 13,
       Hancock Foundation Archive.

144    **After a Nietzschean:** Ibid.

144    **"I hope you know"** to **"all people":** Ibid.

145    **"Too kind of you"** to **"bad trick":** Strauch, *Satan Came to Eden,* 204.

145    **"Captain Hancock"** to **"yours are in":** Ibid.

145    **The Baroness laughed:** Ibid., 205.

145    **"Oh, not at all"** to **"they were yours":** Ibid.

145    **Dore was shocked:** Ibid.

145    **"You'll have your work cut out":** Ibid.

145    **"I think it might be"** to **"safer":** Ibid.

145    **"I don't know what":** Ibid.

145    **"Of course"** to **"with him?":** Ibid.

145    **"If you have come to my house":** Ibid.

145    **"Your Captain Hancock is very":** Ibid.

145    **"Friedrich and I":** Ibid.

145    **"He was simply charmed":** Ibid.

145    **"Yes. It's to be called":** Ibid.

146    **"No"** to **"common people":** Ibid.

146    **"Oh, my dear"** to **"than I am!":** Ibid.

146    **"Come, little one":** Ibid., 207.

146    *Said this young man:* Ibid.

146    **"It astounded him"** to **"uncomfortable":** Ibid.

146    **Dore told herself that she:** Ibid., 208.

146    **And, Dore would discover, she had been right to worry:** *San Bernardino County
       Sun,* Jan. 1, 1934.

146    **While making a cradle:** Margret Wittmer, "War on Floreana," in "What Happened
       on Galapagos?"

146    **despite Captain Hancock's wise advice:** Ibid.

146    **Worst of all, he and Margret:** Strauch, *Satan Came to Eden,* 209.

146 **He'd considered approaching:** Ibid.

147 **"Among other things":** Wittmer, *Floreana*, 66.

147 **She produced one tin:** Ibid.

147 **"an ordinary type of woman":** Strauch, *Satan Came to Eden*, 210.

147 **"My dear Captain Hancock":** Strauch to Hancock, Feb. 27, 1933, box 6, folder 13, Hancock Foundation Archive.

## Twenty-Five: Fanatical Jealousy

149 **Nearly 25 percent:** Great Depression Facts, Franklin D. Roosevelt Library, www .fdrlibrary.org/great-depression-facts.

149 **Almost half of America's:** Carey Moncaster, "This Land Is Your Land: The Great Depression, Migrant Farm Workers, and the Legacy of the New Deal," Stanford Program on International and Cross-Cultural Education, Sept. 22, 2022, spice.fsi .stanford.edu/news/land-your-land-great-depression-migrant-farm-workers-and -legacy-new-deal.

149 **many of their residents adopted:** Andrew T. Carswell, ed., "Hoovervilles," 302.

149 **In New York City's Central Park:** *New York Daily News*, Jan. 3, 1933.

149 **"From the moment":** *New York Times*, March 3, 1933.

149 **A prominent New York mathematician:** *New York Daily News*, March 5, 1933.

149 **"has controlled our":** Ibid.

149 **"Hancocki" lizards:** *Santa Maria Times*, March 21, 1938. The "Hancocki" lizard was likely an invention of Hancock's crew. In the Charles Darwin Foundation species database, there are seventeen results for "hancocki," but none are lizards. Only one species (a fish) is cited as having been named specifically for George Allan Hancock: *Acanthemblemaria hancocki*. Roslyn Cameron, email message to author, April 24, 2024.

150 **"Whether the world" to "from civilization":** *Brooklyn Daily Eagle*, April 13, 1933.

150 **Boston businessman Amory Coolidge:** *Boston Globe*, April 4, 1933.

150 **"vulgarly large red letters":** Mielche, 111.

150 **"Friends, whoever you are!" to "Baroness Wagner-Bosquet":** Wittmer, *Floreana*, 67.

150 **exposed several of his toes:** Coolidge, 79.

151 **On his belt he carried:** Ibid., 80.

151 **"It made quite an impression" to "in vain":** Ibid., 80.

151 **Swarms of flies buzzed:** Ibid., 81.

151 **"From Paris, where she was":** Ibid., 83.

151 **Her bare legs:** Ibid.

151 **stitched with a German motto:** *St. Louis Post-Dispatch*, Nov. 22, 1934.

151 **The gleaming silverware bore:** Ibid.

151 **She served a luncheon:** Coolidge, 83.

151 **"emperior cake":** Ibid.

151 **"had an ant for nearly every grain":** Ibid.

151 **The Baroness, upon hearing:** Ibid., 85.

151 **"They all radiate" to "as can be":** Ibid., 87.

152 **pulled out her last bottle of schnapps:** Ibid., 83.

152 **Dore was an "unusual lady":** Ibid., 85.

152   Dore invited her to stay at Friedo but: Ibid.

152   Dore refused to make a fire: Ibid.

152   Dore grew furious: Ibid.

152   When little birds come to drink: Ibid.

152   but gave her only a short stem: Ibid.

152   He dispensed advice on building a home: Ibid.

152   wants to deny her the same benefit: Ibid.

152   "the most kind and neighborly": Ibid., 85.

152   In fact, perhaps: Heinz Wittmer to Hancock, Feb. 26, 1933, courtesy of Jane
      Brennan.

152   Baby Rolf: Coolidge, 79.

152   "All goes well": Ibid.

153   "snatched away": Ibid.

153   "Such fanatical jealousy": Ibid., 89.

153   "Indeed I am sure": Ibid., 89–90.

153   "Dear Mr. Hancock": Wittmer to Hancock, Feb. 26, 1933, courtesy of Jane
      Brennan.

154   bringing with him half a hog: Wittmer, "Death over Galapagos," *Liberty Magazine*,
      Nov. 27, 1937.

154   In exchange, Friedrich gave: Ibid.

154   "so thoroughly likeable": Strauch, *Satan Came to Eden*, 210.

154   was neither so "well-bred": Ibid.

154   It appeared that she had welcomed: Ibid., 211.

154   "Why don't you ask" to "where it is": Ibid.

154   "Perhaps it was because" to "the victim": Ibid., 218.

155   "She is stupid enough" to "Ecuadorian boom": Ritter, "'Modern Piracy' in
      Galapagos," *Als Robinson auf Galapagos*, Feb. 1933.

155   he agreed to help Heinz: Treherne, *The Galapagos Affair*, 115.

155   "her infirmity was nothing more serious": Quoted in Treherne, *The Galapagos
      Affair*, 115.

155   About a week later: Wittmer, "Death over Galapagos," Nov. 27, 1937.

155   on March 8: Strauch and Ritter to Hancock, March 8, 1933, box 6, folder 13,
      Hancock Foundation Archive.

155   Dore and Friedrich were sorting papayas: Strauch, *Satan Came to Eden*, 212.

155   with his close friend Kermit Roosevelt: *New York Daily News*, Feb. 12, 1933.

156   had plans to address Britain's war debt: *Chattanooga Times*, Feb. 5, 1933.

156   "tall, slim, and very pretty": *New York Daily News*, Jan. 18, 1933.

156   "was not a convert to the sport": *New York Daily News*, Feb. 12, 1933.

156   "floating brothel": Olshausen, "Galapagos Lure and Lore."

156   "Caruso of Floreana": For Astor's visit to Friedo, see Strauch, *Satan Came to Eden*,
      213.

156   Astor felt comfortable: Ibid.

156   an "extremely hospitable invitation": Ibid.

156   "in grand style": Ibid.

156   At this, his friends protested: Ibid.

156   "Dear Captain" to "come out of it": Friedrich Ritter to Hancock, March 9, 1933,
      box 6, folder 13, Hancock Foundation Archive.

157  **"wasn't big enough":** *New York Herald Tribune,* Dec. 11, 1934.

157  **"The whole thing sounds exactly like":** Ibid.

157  **"terribly sore":** Ibid.

157  **"it fairly took":** Strauch, *Satan Came to Eden,* 215.

157  **"My dear man"** to **"better go":** Ibid.

158  **"I should never have thought"** to **"he was saying":** Ibid.

158  **she worried that he would leap:** Ibid.

158  **"Now quite quietly"** to **"before him":** Ibid.

158  **The young man walked:** Ibid.

158  **Wordlessly, with grim determination:** Ibid., 216.

158  **Dore, observing from the doorway:** Ibid.

158  **"With such people as these"** to **"in the future":** Ibid., 216–17.

159  **The next time Friedrich worked:** Ibid., 217.

159  **"companion in slavery":** Ibid.

159  **hadn't moved at all:** Ibid.

159  **A few days later, Robert appeared:** Margret Wittmer, "A Beautiful Row," in "What Happened on Galapagos?"

159  **"insolent and abusive":** Ibid.

159  **"invited Heinz and Dr. Ritter":** Wittmer, "Death over Galapagos," Nov. 27, 1937.

159  **"unhappy, nervous, and moody":** Margret Wittmer, "The Sensation," in "What Happened on Galapagos?"

159  **"mischief":** Ibid.

## Twenty-Six: You Don't Know the Americans

163  **"It's come, it's all come! Hooray, hooray!":** Wittmer, *Floreana,* 68.

163  **The Gestapo raided private homes:** *Daily Telegraph,* March 23, 1933.

163  **The physicist Albert Einstein, whose home:** Ibid.

163  **"enemies of the German people":** Ibid.

163  **Heinz lit a cigar:** Wittmer, *Floreana,* 69.

163  **As he read, Margret noticed his worried expression:** Ibid.

163  **"What is it?":** Ibid.

163  **"Listen to this"** to **"'Imprisoned'":** Ibid.

163  **"An Austrian Baroness"** to **"in chains":** Ibid.

164  **Heinz wondered if:** Ibid.

164  **"But if"** to **"coming here?":** Ibid.

164  **Heinz laughed:** Ibid.

164  **"You don't know":** Ibid.

164  **Heinz brought two documents:** Strauch, *Satan Came to Eden,* 218.

164  **"defamed":** Ritter, "Again This Dame With Her Wiliness," *Als Robinson auf Galapagos,* Aug. 1933.

164  **refused to attend to the Baroness's toothache:** Ibid.

164  **claiming that he'd trespassed:** Strauch, *Satan Came to Eden,* 219.

164  **he'd also falsely accused her, her "husband" Robert, and her "comrade" Rudolph:** Ibid.

164  **The "biggest idea" in this book:** Strauch to Hancock, June 1933, box 6, folder 13, Hancock Foundation Archive.

164 Dore was "soiled": Ibid.

164 "Her hate turned" to "of the Ritters": Ibid.

165 "toothless Adam in slippers": *Illustrierte Kronen Zeitung*, Nov. 28, 1934.

165 "insane Buddha": Eichler, *Snow Peaks*, 155.

165 "Humpelstiltskin with the dirty ruff": *Illustrierte Kronen Zeitung*, Nov. 28, 1934.

165 "Oh, yes, you are really small": Fritz Hieber, interview by author, Sept. 2021.

165 With each new insult: Waldo Schmitt, Hancock-Galapagos Expedition, 1934–1935: Diary, Record Unit 7231, Schmitt Papers.

165 These fantasies recurred: Ibid.

165 She wrote to the captain: Baroness to Hancock, Aug. 31, 1933, box 1, "Baroness" folder, DeStefano collection.

165 "catch a flamingo": Ibid.

165 "Trusting this finds" to "Baroness Wagner": Ibid.

166 now did not hesitate to beat her: Wittmer, "Death over Galapagos," Nov. 27, 1937.

166 "Revolution-Evolution": Dore Strauch, "Revolution-Evolution," July 1933, box 6, folder 4, Hancock Foundation Archive.

## *Twenty-Seven: Vague and Ominous Presentiments*

167 which she saw as a lie: Strauch, *Satan Came to Eden*, 221.

167 "The Baroness has no idea": Ibid.

167 "And I expect": Ibid.

167 "That won't matter": Ibid.

167 Dore realized the Baroness had sent: Ibid.

167 "It was clear to see": Ibid.

168 The Baroness implored visitors: *Cincinnati Enquirer*, May 14, 1935.

168 "It was so satisfactory" to "led to violence": Ibid.

168 "far more dangerous" to "had a profound contempt": Finsen, *Debunking*, n.p.

168 He assured Dore and Friedrich: Strauch, *Satan Came to Eden*, 222.

168 had gone hunting for flamingos: Ibid.

168 The governor had granted: Treherne, *The Galapagos Affair*, 126.

169 but the Baroness received: Ibid.

169 She had also won her battle: Strauch, *Satan Came to Eden*, 222.

169 "at the price of a more than Arabian night": Treherne, 126.

169 The Baroness had so charmed: Strauch, *Satan Came to Eden*, 222.

169 "in possession of a high level": *El Universo*, Dec. 8, 1934.

169 This alarmed Friedrich: Wittmer, "Death over Galapagos."

169 "struck hard on the mouth": Ibid.

169 "Newspapers came" to "cannot bewitch me": Baroness to a friend, June 29, 1933, reprinted in *Illustrierte Kronen Zeitung*, Nov. 28, 1934.

170 "The Baroness figured": Olshausen, "Galapagos Lure and Lore."

170 "master of the hunt": Wittmer, "Death over Galapagos."

170 "masculine assistant": Ibid.

170 told Margret that people thought: Ibid.

170 "The Baroness had found another slave": Strauch, *Satan Came to Eden*, 223.

170 accepted as the Baroness's "new lover": Ibid.

170 At night, the Baroness allowed: Ibid., 224.

171 "He had lost himself": Ibid., 224.

171 beating him with her whip and even carving a flaming welt: Ibid.

171 No longer willing to meet tourists: Ibid., 226.

171 One visitor described "a woman of about forty" to "in shorts": Eichler, *Snow Peaks*, 184.

171 "the Queen of Sheba": Ibid.

171 "dreamy": Ibid.

171 "Kiddy": Ibid.

171 "visible in the kitchen": Ibid.

171 "could afford to treat the accident": Ibid.

171 she had to admit: Ibid.

172 Dore was shocked to see Arends: Ibid., 228.

172 his response was muted: Ibid.

172 Dore heard a feeble cough: Ibid.

172 sent a chill down Dore's back: Ibid., 229.

172 "As I turned" to "feeling of murder": Ibid., 229.

## Twenty-Eight: "Accident"

173 dined on two chickens: Wittmer, "Death over Galapagos."

173 warned that some recent flooding: Ibid.

173 who now had two teeth: Wittmer, *Floreana*, 71.

173 Talking with Margret and Heinz: Wittmer, "Death over Galapagos."

173 Margret and Heinz noticed: Wittmer, *Floreana*, 73.

174 "I bet she's looking" to "isn't there?": Ibid.

174 "That's what the inhabitants" to "like this": Ibid.

174 "All the same" to "treasure lies": Ibid., 73–74.

174 "Could be" to "searching before": Ibid., 74.

174 A few weeks later, on October 1: Ibid.

174 "I think I have never" to "upon him": Strauch, *Satan Came to Eden*, 230.

174 "so frank and normal": Ibid.

174 "weaklings": Ibid.

174 The two men were accompanied by: Wittmer, *Floreana*, 74.

174 promised to be back: Strauch, *Satan Came to Eden*, 231.

174 At the Hacienda Paradiso, the trio found: Ibid., 234.

174 Boeckmann clocked her change of expression: Ibid.

175 Boeckmann introduced Linde as his brother-in-law: Ibid.

175 join her on a hunting expedition: Ibid., 235.

175 Boeckmann worried about being late: Ibid.

175 Boeckmann sensed a shift in her mood: Ibid.

175 The Baroness took charge: Ibid.

175 "kitchen's best": Ibid., 231.

176 She wondered, with some annoyance: Ibid., 232.

176 "The Baroness is going to drive" to "end of the world": Ritter, "Four Years on Friedo," *Als Robinson auf Galapagos*, Sept. 1933.

176 "It was more than the pale" to "desperate alarm": Strauch, *Satan Came to Eden*, 232.

176 **"An accident! There's been an accident!":** Ibid.

176 **"No," Boeckmann said. "It's Arends! He's been shot!":** Ibid.

176 **"Shot?" Dore asked. "How?":** Ibid.

176 **"We were out hunting" to "Will you come, Doctor?":** Ibid.

176 **"That household" to "to come?":** Ibid.

176 **"She didn't want" to "too late already":** Ibid.

176 **Friedrich rushed to Arends:** Ibid., 237.

177 **The Baroness interrupted, insisting:** Ibid.

177 **"That is impossible" to "by a rifle":** Ibid.

177 **"Darling, forgive me":** Ibid.

177 **the rest of his theory:** Friedrich Ritter, "A 'Hunting Accident' at Floreana," box 6, folder 11, Hancock Foundation Archives.

177 **"Dear Sir" to "Baroness Wagner":** Baroness to Hancock, Oct. 2, 1933, box 6, "Letters 1933/34/35/Depositions" folder, Hancock Foundation Archive.

178 **"This woman at the threshold" to "beast of prey":** Ritter, "'Hunting Accident' at Floreana."

178 **For Dore, the situation:** Strauch, *Satan Came to Eden*, 238.

179 **behind curtains:** Ibid.

179 **insist that his "wife":** Ibid., 239.

179 **"I wish I'd seen" to "myself":** Ibid.

179 **"Which of these two men":** Ibid., 240.

179 **The Baroness admitted:** Ibid.

179 **"Then he is to come":** Ibid.

## Twenty-Nine: A Wicked Plan

180 **In November, the Child Welfare League:** *New York Herald Tribune*, Nov. 1, 1933.

180 **"derelict old persons":** Ibid.

180 **"sick and mentally deficient":** Ibid.

180 **celebrated the landslide election:** *New York Herald Tribune*, Nov. 8, 1933.

180 **"whisky ships" bound for St. Pierre or Bimini:** *New York Daily News*, Nov. 1, 1933.

180 **"The Hell with Depression!":** *Hollywood Reporter*, March 19, 2022.

180 **"fatten up," eating creamed chicken:** *Cincinnati Post*, Sept. 12, 1933.

181 **a tour of forty California cities:** *Arroyo Grande Valley Herald Recorder*, Nov. 10, 1933.

181 **"Strange Lands and Life of Tropic Seas":** Ibid.

181 **featuring all of the rare specimens:** *San Bernardino County Sun*, Nov. 21, 1933.

181 **the vegetable "hold-overs":** Ibid.

181 **prepared for his next expedition:** *Santa Maria Times*, Dec. 29, 1933.

181 **and a Hollywood producer named Emery Johnson:** Ibid.

181 **a newlywed couple:** *San Francisco Examiner*, Nov. 25, 1933.

181 **a woman dressed in silk shorts:** *Buffalo News*, Nov. 21, 1934.

181 **"I am Baroness Wagner" to "doing here?":** Blomberg, *Underliga Människor.*

181 **If they weren't preoccupied:** Ibid.

182 **For months not one drop of rain:** Wittmer, *Floreana*, 77.

182 **The Wittmers' spring:** Ibid.

182 **The situation at Friedo:** Ibid.

182    "Dr. Ritter can't do anything" to "yourselves": Ibid.

182    "Dore did not have pity" to "hard": Olshausen, "Galapagos Lure and Lore."

182    "seemed shattered": Wittmer, "Death over Galapagos."

182    "a most unusual" to "aristocrat": Ibid.

182    Margret could hear every thrash: Wittmer, Floreana, 77.

182    "like a small child": Ibid.

183    Strange, Margret thought: Margret Wittmer, "The Galapagos Treasure," in "What
       Happened on Galapagos?"

183    "The Baroness and Lorenz" to "those people": Strauch, Satan Came to Eden, 243.

183    This, she realized: Ibid.

183    couldn't stop herself: Ibid., 244.

183    The next time she looked: Ibid.

183    A few days later Dore's donkey: Ibid.

183    "Dr. Ritter" to "will you?": Ibid.

184    Dore heard malice: Ibid.

184    "Just turn him loose" to "the way": Ibid.

184    Dore listened for his footsteps: Ibid., 245.

184    Even Margret: Margret Wittmer, "Christmas on Floreana," in "What Happened on
       Galapagos?"

184    "east problem": Ibid.

184    Deeply shaken, she took to her bed: Margret Wittmer, "Philippson Returns," in
       "What Happened on Galapagos?"

185    The Baroness had deliberately let Burro: Margret Wittmer, "Burro Is Fired At," in
       "What Happened on Galapagos?"

185    "It was a wicked plan": Wittmer, "Death over Galapagos."

185    Heinz lured their own pet: Ibid.

185    "The gift," she wrote: Strauch, Satan Came to Eden, 247.

185    From there Dore's feelings: Ibid.

## Thirty: Strange Satanic Moods

186    "The male had the female" to "with the net": Diary of Ziesenhenne, Jan. 14,
       1934.

186    After all that: Ibid.

186    Three days later, on January 17: Garth, "Personal Recollections."

186    There was a brief respite: Ibid.

186    volcano peaks scratched: Ibid.

186    shooting small birds: Ibid.

187    improvements at Friedo: Edwin Palmer, "Third Galapagos Trip of the Velero III in
       the Winter of 1933–1934: From the Log Book of the 'Medicine Man' of the
       Trip," 15, box 25, folder 2, Hancock Foundation Archive.

187    "Robinson sugar swing": Ritter, "Sugar Manufacturing," Als Robinson auf Galapagos,
       Dec. 1930.

187    "followed Dore around": Palmer, "Third Galapagos Trip," 15.

187    promised to extract them: Ibid.

187    a discussion about the merits: Ibid.

187     now enjoyed it just as much: Ibid.

187     **Dore pulled Hancock aside:** Diary of Ziesenhenne, Jan. 17, 1934.

187     **She was eager to leave:** Ibid.

187     **In the next breath, however:** Ibid.

187     **"To witness the joy" to "too much for them":** Garth, "Personal Recollections," Jan. 18, 1934.

188     **"showed how the child had sucked":** Diary of Ziesenhenne, Jan. 17, 1934.

188     **Would the captain help him:** Wittmer, "Christmas on Floreana."

188     **a homemade sectional sofa:** Wittmer, "Galapagos Treasure."

188     **he would do anything:** Diary of Ziesenhenne, Jan. 17, 1934.

188     **watched movies of herself:** Ibid.

188     **listened to the ensemble:** Ibid.

188     **a "pirate film":** Strauch, *Satan Came to Eden*, 249.

188     **he'd asked the Baroness outright:** Ibid.

188     **"strange satanic moods":** Ibid.

188     **Hancock mused about her "neurotic state":** Ritter to Hancock (in which he recalled their conversation), Jan. 25, 1934, box 6, folder 13, Hancock Foundation Archives.

188     **the two "neurotic states":** Ibid.

189     **"poisoning protein stuffs":** Ibid.

189     **her "feminine instinct":** Ibid.

189     **Numbed with Novocain:** Palmer, "Third Galapagos Trip," 21.

189     **"There must have been":** Wittmer, "Death over Galapagos."

189     **And, as the Baroness had hoped:** Footage of *The Empress of Floreana*, Hancock Foundation Archive.

189     **"gathered her up" to "waving to us":** Swett, "Floreana."

189     **"look of fury":** Ibid.

190     **"in a moment of rage":** Diary of Ziesenhenne, Jan. 19, 1934.

190     **"watch the Baroness, and try":** Ibid.

190     **he lined up the last:** Margret Wittmer, "Velero III Drops Anchor," in "What Happened on Galapagos?"

190     **"Mr. Hancock was the very soul of tact" to "dissension later": Ibid.**

190     **"started to accuse the Baroness":** Diary of Ziesenhenne, Jan. 19, 1934.

190     **It ended, finally, with:** Ibid.

190     **"The nine people" to "do murder":** *Nebraska State Journal*, Dec. 16, 1934.

190     **Margret asked Harry:** Margret Wittmer, "Peaceful Island," in "What Happened on Galapagos?"

191     **Friedrich insulted her with such cruelty:** Wittmer, "Death over Galapagos."

191     **"She began telling me" to "embarrassing":** Ibid.

191     **The *Stella Polaris* had listed:** Strauch, *Satan Came to Eden*, 249.

191     **Dore realized, with pleasure:** Ibid.

191     **"America currently doesn't know" to "are mistaken":** Ritter, "Yacht Velero," *Als Robinson auf Galapagos*.

192     **"a most peculiar costume" to "did not suit her":** Strauch, *Satan Came to Eden*, 250.

192     **". . . miss the theater?" to "wonderful revue":** Ibid.

192     **thoughts "were riveted":** Ibid.

192  "Do play a waltz": Ibid.

192  The conductor glanced: Ibid.

192  The Baroness's cheerful confidence: Ibid.

192  She made up her mind: Ibid.


### Thirty-One: A Woman's Natural Instinct to Play with Fire

193  "She acted the spoiled": Ritter to Hancock, Jan. 25, 1934, box 6, folder 13, Collection no. 0257, Special Collections, USC Libraries.

194  The temperature registered: Strauch, *Satan Came to Eden*, 253.

194  "a real wild creature": Margret Wittmer, "Five Months Without Rain," in "What Happened on Galapagos?"

194  "green stuff": Ibid.

194  "The solution": Ibid.

194  Heinz and Harry made: Ibid.

194  The sun's strength scared Dore: Strauch, *Satan Came to Eden*, 253.

195  "invisible fire": Ibid.

195  "We were alone": Ibid.

195  "prolonged drought is hard": Ibid., 254.

195  "some strange strength" to "extraordinary": Ibid.

195  He spoke of daily fights: Ibid.

195  the money was nearly gone: Ibid., 255.

195  "Get out of my sight" to "all I care": Ibid.

196  Rudolph was seized with rage: Ibid.

196  When Rudolph awakened: Ibid., 256.

196  He also begged for Hancock's address: Ritter to Hancock, April 1934, box 6, folder 13, Hancock Foundation Archive.

196  the "truth" of his relationship: Ibid.

196  "something had changed" to "in madness": Strauch, *Satan Came to Eden*, 256.

196  "Philippson's threatened to kill me": Wittmer, *Floreana*, 79.

196  Margret would later report: Margret Wittmer, "Lorenz Moves In," in "What Happened on Galapagos?"

196  Dore would say that Rudolph: Strauch, *Satan Came to Eden*, 256.

196  Margret, too, worried: Wittmer, *Floreana*, 79.

197  "Reich Festival Week": *Cincinnati Enquirer*, March 25, 1934.

197  "Things are not going so good" to "back to Germany": Quoted in Treherne, *The Galapagos Affair*, 153.

197  "Please help me" to "with Philippson": *New York Times*, Dec. 13, 1934.

197  "I left your wife" to "a divorce": *Los Angeles Tribune*, Nov. 21, 1935.

197  "The Baroness and her 'husband'" to "chief victim": Wittmer, *Floreana*, 79.

197  She found it difficult: Ibid.

197  "Lori" to "say to you": Ibid.

197  At first he seemed to be: Ibid.

197  Nothing she did or said: Ibid., 80.

198  waiting for a human sacrifice: Strauch, *Satan Came to Eden*, 256.

198  "No one knows what the future" to "these islands": *El Universo*, Dec. 4, 1934.

198  "more than anything": Ibid.

198    "One day," she said: Blomberg, *Underliga Mäniskor.*

198    Along the trail to Post Office Bay: *Miami News,* July 7, 1935.


## Thirty-Two: And Then There Were Seven

199    At noon on March 19, 1934: Strauch, *Satan Came to Eden,* 257.

199    "weighted upon": Ibid.

199    "It was an outcry" to "for a moment": Ibid.

199    "playing havoc": Ibid.

200    Instead, on March 21, Dore claimed that Rudolph: Ibid., 257–59.

200    gone was the defeated: Ibid.

200    "Have you made it": Ibid., 258.

200    "Not this time": Ibid.

200    "Oh, then you're staying": Ibid.

200    "Yes, I am" to "gets off": Ibid.

200    "Will she": Ibid.

200    "I think": Ibid.

200    "Why won't you" to "from here": Ibid., 259.

200    "I wish you'd" to "as a baker!": Ibid.

200    She delivered these words: Ibid.

200    "If you give me" to "had enough": Ibid.

201    "At any rate": Ibid.

201    "She'll be back" to "come around again": Ibid.

201    Dore did not believe: Ibid.

201    "This is for you": Ibid., 260.

201    "Antoinette, Robert, Lorenz": Ibid., 261.

201    Dore felt disgusted: Ibid., 261.

201    "The only thing I'd like to know": Ibid.

201    "got them off the table": Ibid.

201    "It is an outrage" to "here on Floreana!": Ibid.

202    "Judge not" to "That is enough": Ibid.

202    posed pointed questions: Ibid., 262.

202    Two days later, on March 27: Wittmer, *Floreana,* 80.

202    She wore her riding costume: Ibid.

202    The Baroness appraised Margret: Ibid.

202    "Then please tell him" to "my plans": Wittmer, *Floreana,* 80.

202    "Then I wish you": Ibid.

202    *I can hardly believe my ears* to *a reality:* Wittmer, "Our Wish Becomes Reality."

202    "Thank you" to "perhaps goodbye": Wittmer, *Floreana,* 80.

203    "It's a trap to lure me" to "about her": Ibid.

203    already dug a grave: *New York Daily News,* Dec. 29, 1924.

203    Rudolph was gone: Wittmer, *Floreana,* 80.

203    But he returned with a strange story: Ibid., 80–81.

203    Dore and Friedrich were surprised: For Margret and Rudolph's visit to Friedo, see
        Strauch, *Satan Came to Eden,* 262–65.

203    that made Dore suspect: Ibid.

203    a "set" story: Ibid., 263.

203 "It's rather strange" to "things direct": Ibid., 264.

204 "I hope they both": Ibid., 265.

204 He wondered if Dore might: Ibid.

204 "What are you thinking": Ibid., 266.

204 "You played your part": Ibid.

204 "My part?" to "What part?": Ibid.

204 "My dear child" to "is very clear": Ibid.

204 "Tell me" to "really gone?": Ibid.

204 Friedrich took her hand: Ibid.

204 "Yes" to "so has Philippson": Ibid.

204 "great pity": Ibid., 267.

204 "While she lived": Ibid.

204 "unspeakable hideousness": Ibid., 266.

205 "I thought a murderess": Ibid., 266–67.

205 "Somehow I knew" to "stained with blood": Ibid., 267.

205 She took them to: Ibid.

205 Margret told a different version: Wittmer, *Floreana*, 81.

205 "The Baroness" to "you know?": Ibid.

205 Friedrich shook his head: Ibid.

205 "You don't believe it?": Ibid.

205 "I've not seen" to "come out here": Ibid.

205 danced in celebration: Ibid.

205 "strikingly silent": Ibid.

205 "spared all philosophical discourse": Ibid.

205 "The sooner you get away": Ibid.

205 Friedrich also insisted: Ibid.

205 "he merely shook" to "word for it": Ibid.

206 That Sunday, April 1: Strauch, *Satan Came to Eden*, 267.

206 It had been another morning: Ibid.

206 The noise sounded like: Ibid., 271.

206 if Friedrich had not been: Ibid.

206 The Baroness and Robert had not taken: Ibid., 271–72.

206 "Perhaps after all it will be better" to "come back?": Ibid., 272.

206 "Don't worry" to "danger of that": Ibid.

206 Dore noticed one more item: Ibid.

## Thirty-Three: The Feeling of Tragedy

207 studying English and Spanish: Wittmer, *Floreana*, 82.

207 "On the heath": Garth, "Personal Recollections."

207 "This woman wrecked my youth" to "mental wreck": Ibid.

207 "feeble and tubercular": Ibid.

207 "fever spots on his cheeks": Margret Wittmer, "Stealing in the Bay," in "What Happened on Galapagos?"

207 "Hours on end he sits" to "were gone": Ibid.

207 She even trusted: Ibid.

208   Dore thought constantly about the disappearance: Strauch, *Satan Came to Eden*, 273.

208   "removed by violence": Ibid.

208   Two persistent fears: Ibid.

208   "We said to each other": Ibid.

208   Dore did not search for the bodies, but wondered: Ibid., 274.

208   Day after day, she waited: Ibid.

208   On April 20: *Miami News*, July 7, 1935.

208   "the leader of the grain pit": *Windsor Star*, Oct. 2, 1931.

208   "A young man on this island": Treherne, *The Galapagos Affair*, 164.

209   "pawed up": *Miami News*, July 7, 1935.

209   They went on, passing: Ibid.

209   Howell's German-speaking cook: Ibid.

209   Margret served: Ibid.

209   When Howell asked: Margret Wittmer, "Before Lorenz's Departure," in "What Happened on Galapagos?"

209   "It was one of the most weird trips" to "bright moonlight": *Miami News*, Nov. 20, 1934.

209   changed his mind: Ibid.

209   "Half for you": Wittmer, "Before Lorenz's Departure."

209   She had wept: *Miami News*, Nov. 20, 1934.

210   "Why didn't Howell": Wittmer, "Before Lorenz's Departure."

210   "have nothing to do with": Ibid.

210   "This is the same" to "enemies": Ibid.

210   "blood upon his hands?": Strauch, *Satan Came to Eden*, 275.

210   "Very honored Captain Hancock": Mrs. M. Strauch to Hancock, box 6, folder 13, Collection no. 0257, Special Collections, USC Libraries.

## Thirty-Four: And Then There Were Six

212   "Why Paradise Is Lost": Dore Strauch, "Why Paradise Is Lost," box 6, folder 12, Hancock Foundation Archives.

213   Margret noticed that Rudolph's condition: Wittmer, "Death over Galapagos."

213   Occasionally he slept there: Margret Wittmer, "Dryness and Dampness," in "What Happened on Galapagos?"

213   His shoes had worn: Ibid.

213   "Tuxedo, dress suit, dress shirts" to "really is": Ibid.

213   "building, thereby, a veritable well": Wittmer, "Stealing in the Bay."

213   "Should it ever be announced": Ritter, "Yacht Velero," *Als Robinson auf Galapagos*, July 1934.

213   On July 10: Ibid.

213   Rolf Blomberg: For Blomberg's visit to Floreana, see Blomberg, *Underliga Mäniskor*, 92–113.

213   "Nuggen": Ibid.

214   he "walked about": Ibid.

214   "I promised long ago" to "the latest": Ibid.

214 "what looked like": Ibid.
214 Blomberg was so intrigued: Ibid.
214 "wonderful time": Latorre, *The Curse*, 176.
214 "Oh well," he said, waving: *Los Angeles Times*, Nov. 21, 1934.
214 "had something unreal" to "in the dark!": Blomberg, *Underliga Mäniskor.*
215 "New Eden": Ibid.
215 "Maybe she is": Ibid.
215 "Ah, Sie haben": Ibid.
215 "was emaciated": Ibid.
215 "a true Galapagonian": Ibid.
215 "Where is the Baroness?": Ibid.
215 "Disappeared": Ibid.
215 Blomberg had trouble: Ibid.
215 "The Kaiserin of the Galapagos": *San Francisco Examiner*, Nov. 22, 1934.
215 "a sensation-hungry and sadistic": Blomberg, *Underliga Mäniskor.*
216 "often walked about" to "teeth in place": Ibid.
216 "We got another impression" to "photographed": Ibid.
216 "trained to agree": Ibid.
216 "We brought some coffee plants" to "want them?": Ibid.
216 "Oh," Dore said, and clapped: Ibid.
216 "No, thank you" to "alcohol": Ibid.
216 "completely out" to "funny thought": Ibid.
216 "I valued his culinary diet": Ibid.
216 "What do you make": Ibid.
216 "very happy": Ibid.
217 "Well" to "from the island": Ibid.
217 "But how do you": Ibid.
217 "I have my own theory": Ibid.
217 "When it became obvious" to "natural explanation": Ibid.
217 Dore thought of her long-ago luncheon: Strauch, *Satan Came to Eden*, 275.
218 "Don't be sad" to "dreamed it": Ibid.
218 "I'm afraid" to "this trip": Ibid., 276.
218 "Why?": Ibid.
218 "extremely heavy": *Paris-Soir*, Feb. 10, 1935.

## Thirty-Five: Scoundrelism, Rascality, and Faking

219 He included a letter: Ritter to Hancock, July 16, 1934, box 6, folder 12, Hancock Foundation Archive.
219 "vanished to the South Seas": Ibid.
219 "WITTMERS AND WE": Ibid.
219 "You would have got" to "we are told": Ritter to Hancock, July 24, 1934, box 6, folder 12, Collection no. 0257, Special Collections, USC Libraries.
220 "The woman who had been": Ibid.
220 "desperate haste": Ibid., 277.
220 He whipped her, and any remaining love: Ibid.

220    **"We had found perfect harmony" to "achieved perfection":** Strauch, *Satan Came to Eden,* 277–78.

221    **three Germans arrived:** Heinz Wittmer, "The Hunt for Non-existent Animals," in "What Happened on Galapagos?"

221    **"the globetrotters":** Ibid.

221    **"because," Heinz wrote, "he has nothing":** Ibid.

221    **"not merely a small sphere":** Heinz Wittmer, "Dr. Ritter's Writings," in "What Happened on Galapagos?"

221    **the "point-curvature and zero":** Ibid.

221    **a surprise guest arrived:** Ibid.

221    **"Who has not seen" to "can account for":** Reprinted in *El Telégrafo,* Nov. 16, 1934.

222    **"numerous traces of blood":** *Der Tag,* Nov. 25, 1934.

222    **"It is out of the question" to "at another person":** *Der Morgen: Wiener Montagblatt,* Nov. 26, 1934.

222    **"Find the Baroness":** *Boston Globe,* Nov. 23, 1934.

222    **Taylor, the Rhode Island businessman, told the gathering:** *St. Louis Post-Dispatch,* Nov. 27, 1934.

222    **"When we broached the question" to "name of the yacht":** Ibid.

222    **When they asked Heinz:** Ibid.

223    **"are making the situation":** Ritter, "The Last Letter of Dr. Knight," *Als Robinson auf Galapagos,* Sept. 1934.

223    **Heinz and Margret became alarmed:** Heinz Wittmer, "Dr. Ritter Ailing," in "What Happened on Galapagos?"

223    **"nothing definite":** Ibid.

223    **"broken and old":** Ibid.

223    **"The island has not given me":** Wittmer, *Floreana,* 84.

223    **"gradually getting worse":** Wittmer, "Death over Galapagos."

223    **"extremely difficult":** Wittmer, *Floreana,* 84.

223    **"let her tongue loose":** Wittmer, "Death over Galapagos."

223    **"shut her mouth":** Ibid.

223    **"But it's three months":** Wittmer, *Floreana,* 84.

223    **"You never know what":** Ibid., 98.

224    **"Dear Sir":** Philippson to Hancock, box 6, folder 12, Hancock Foundation Archive.

224    **a journey of eighty days:** *Los Angeles Times,* Nov. 23, 1934.

225    **"The meat of some of the species" to "for airplanes":** *Reno Gazette,* Dec. 8, 1934.

225    **Four days before:** *Los Angeles Times,* Nov. 23, 1934.

225    **a series of fragmented:** *San Francisco Examiner,* Nov. 19, 1934.

225    **"Passing Marchena Island" to "near man":** *Oakland Tribune,* Nov. 19, 1934.

225    **"I don't know what he means" to "this mystery":** Ibid.

## *Thirty-Six: And Then There Were Five*

226    **ten million listeners:** *New York Times,* Oct. 20, 1975.

226    **22 percent unemployment:** www.historic-newspapers.co.uk/blog/great-depression -timeline/#1934.

226    **"The characters were just":** *New York Times,* Oct. 20, 1975.

226    **Yet a backlash was building:** Jerry Berg, "Setting Sail on the Seth Parker World Cruise," ontheshortwaves.com.

226    **He had lost his lone sponsor:** Jim Harmon, *The Great Radio Heroes*, 32.

226    **bedbugs and cockroaches:** Berg, "Setting Sail on the Seth Parker World Cruise."

227    **lingering, low-grade illness:** Ibid.

227    **"handsome":** Strauch, *Satan Came to Eden*, 278.

227    **"a projection in our physical minds" to "mainly run by women":** Anderson, *Zigzagging the South Seas*, 73.

227    **"Now you'll hear how long":** Strauch, *Satan Came to Eden*, 278.

227    **whose expression, in an instant:** Ibid.

227    **"Oh sure I'll tell her":** Ibid.

227    **said he'd be ready:** Ibid.

227    **"stank":** Olshausen, "Galapagos Lure and Lore."

228    **"strange and dark":** Strauch, *Satan Came to Eden*, 279.

228    **"Nor can we really" to "punished for":** Ibid.

228    **Silently, Dore decided:** Ibid.

228    **The occasion was particularly:** Wittmer, *Floreana*, 85.

228    **She and Heinz gave Lord:** Heinz Wittmer, "No Trace of Lorenz and Nuggerud," in "What Happened on Galapagos?"

228    **"All Dr. Ritter's chickens" to "meat-poisoning":** Wittmer, *Floreana*, 85–86.

228    **"Always thought":** Ibid.

228    **"Well, he's not" to "they're dead":** Ibid.

228    **"And there you are":** Ibid.

229    **"a medically qualified man":** Ibid.

229    **"But will they be":** Ibid., 86.

229    **"Oh yes" and "It's not as bad":** Ibid.

229    **"Thanks very much," Heinz said, "but":** Ibid.

229    **Lying in bed that night:** Strauch, *Satan Came to Eden*, 280.

229    **"that strange, dead, truncated remnant":** Swett, "Floreana."

229    **It had the distinction:** Schmitt, Hancock-Galapagos Expedition.

229    **Unlike Floreana:** Ibid.

229    **No tortoises:** Ibid.

229    **"An arrow of gray dry brush":** Swett, "Floreana."

229    **They were determined:** Report of Kraft.

229    **"seals lying on the beach":** Garth, "Personal Recollections."

230    **suffered from engine trouble:** *St. Louis Post-Dispatch*, Nov. 24, 1934.

230    **Some wondered if, instead of a shipwreck:** Mielche, *Let's See*, 122.

230    **He lay on his side:** Swett, "Floreana."

230    **He was hatless and barefoot and wore blue:** Ibid.

230    **her trademark embroidery stitch:** Schmitt, Hancock-Galapagos Expedition.

230    **Baby clothes were piled:** *Los Angeles Times*, Nov. 21, 1934.

230    **His passport was found nearby:** *Los Angeles Times*, Nov. 21, 1934.

230    **"The poor devils"; "Lorenz, if murderer":** Schmitt, Hancock-Galapagos Expedition.

230    **"As I gazed on the body" to "horrible death":** Garth, "Personal Recollections."

230    **"Ritter-wards":** Schmitt, Hancock-Galapagos Expedition.

231    **the heliographic flash:** Ibid.

231   stumbling with her crude cane: Swett, "Floreana."

231   "act of Providence": Ibid.

231   She had dashed off a letter: Strauch, *Satan Came to Eden*, 283.

231   "instantly alarmed": Ibid., 280.

231   "It may be something": Ibid.

231   "My tongue feels heavy": Ibid.

231   She peered inside his mouth: Heinz Wittmer, "Meat Poisoning," in "What Happened on Galapagos?"

231   Dore rummaged through his medical bag: Strauch, *Satan Came to Eden*, 280.

231   As a chaser: Ibid.

231   "the sweat of death": Ibid.

231   "only look on": Ibid.

232   "Mark these lines, Dore": Ibid.

232   "Despair surged over me": Ibid.

232   She asked herself: Ibid.

232   she walked back over: Ibid.

232   "What if he did not die" to "my help": Ibid., 280–81.

232   She told him she was thinking: Ibid., 281.

232   Don't go to the Wittmers' house: Ibid.

232   "Why didn't you come": Wittmer, *Floreana*, 86.

232   "Something terrible's happened" to "dying": Ibid.

233   Margret was stunned: Ibid.

233   "The day before yesterday" to "quite safe": Ibid.

233   "And you ate some of that?"; "You both did?": Ibid.

233   "Yes, I had some too": Ibid.

233   "How long has he been ill?": Ibid.

233   "He didn't feel well": Ibid.

233   "And you didn't have any": Ibid.

233   "Oh yes" to "worse and worse": Ibid.

233   "sensed evil": Olshausen, "Galapagos Lure and Lore."

233   "During this morning" to "would make one": Wittmer, *Floreana*, 86–87.

233   Dore would recall: Strauch, *Satan Came to Eden*, 281.

233   while Margret said they walked: Wittmer, *Floreana*, 87.

234   a knot of mucus: Heinz Wittmer, "The Death," in "What Happened on Galapagos?"

234   Dore came at him: Ibid.

234   "This is choking me" to "my gun": Strauch, *Satan Came to Eden*, 281.

234   "Die in a manner": Unmarked clipping of an interview with Strauch aboard the *Velero III*, Dec. 1934, box 8, DeStefano collection.

234   Their cats had also eaten: Wittmer, "Meat Poisoning."

234   "vomited thoroughly": Ibid.

234   "stomach rinse": Ibid.

234   "became distorted with maniacal rage": Strauch, *Satan Came to Eden*, 282.

234   Margret would remember a disquieting: Schmitt, Hancock-Galapagos Expedition.

234   "I curse you": Wittmer, *Floreana*, 87.

234   "gleaming with hate": Ibid.

234   "Here were two people" to "the other": Ibid.

234   she pretended not to notice: Ibid.

234   "hate-filled eyes": Ibid.

234   If Dore came close: Ibid.

235   "Eden in the wilderness": Strauch, *Satan Came to Eden*, 282.

235   "You want to pray?": Wittmer, *Floreana*, 88.

235   with both arms: Strauch, *Satan Came to Eden*, 282. Here Dore contradicted herself;
      on page 281 she wrote that paralysis had set in and Friedrich could "no longer
      move" his arms.

235   "All trace of pain" to "a miracle": Ibid.

235   "Looking like a ghost": Wittmer, *Floreana*, 88.

235   "He seemed to actually say" to "with him": Strauch, *Satan Came to Eden* (1935 ed.).

235   "His eyes flashed with a wild" to "in horror": Wittmer, *Floreana*, 88.

235   "Then he sank back" to "quite still": Strauch, *Satan Came to Eden* (1935 ed.).

235   "Then he collapsed": Wittmer, *Floreana*, 88.

235   "And that was death": Strauch, *Satan Came to Eden* (1935 ed.).

235   "He had gone": Wittmer, *Floreana*, 88.

236   Heinz checked Friedrich's pulse: Ibid.

236   Dore found a linen: Strauch, *Satan Came to Eden*, 282.

236   "something about a secret": Wittmer, *Floreana*, 88.

236   "Why did": Ibid.

236   "He was begging": Ibid.

236   "What for?": Ibid.

236   "I don't know" to "meant": Ibid.

236   "What did he think": Ibid.

236   "I don't know": Ibid.

236   "I shall be" and "I must get": Ibid.

236   "Come now" to "get some sleep": Ibid.

236   "No, no" to "that they are": Ibid.

236   "that bungalow of death": Ibid., 88–89.

237   words Margret believed: Ibid., 89.

237   "Perhaps" to "return": Ibid., 90.

237   "Yes" to "somewhere": Ibid.

237   They decided: Ibid.

237   Dore chose his favorite: Strauch, *Satan Came to Eden*, 282.

237   A ribbon of congealed blood: Wittmer, "Death over Galapagos."

237   Margret picked flowers: Wittmer, *Floreana*, 89.

237   Dore, according to Margret: Ibid., 90.

## Thirty-Seven: And Then There Were Four

238   "half hysterical": Swett, "Floreana."

238   "Where are your menfolk?": Wittmer, *Floreana*, 90.

238   "The doctor is dead": Swett, "Floreana."

238   "My God!" to "on the island": Wittmer, *Floreana*, 90–91.

238   "small English sailing boat": *Brooklyn Times Union*, Dec. 11, 1934.

238   "He told me": Ibid.

239    **"more birds than ever"**: Garth, "Personal Recollections," Dec. 5, 1934.

239    **"a hundred years old"**: Schmitt, Hancock-Galapagos Expedition.

239    **One of the women nearly fainted**: Garth, "Personal Recollections," Dec. 5, 1934.

239    **"out of her mind"**: Swett, "Floreana."

239    **"What am I going"**: Ibid.

239    **He had grown impressively**: Ibid.

240    **"Yes, I loved the doctor" to "Eden will vanish"**: Ibid.

240    **The water hole**: Video from Hancock expedition, 1934–1935, Hancock Foundation Archive.

240    **Dore led the men**: Swett, "Floreana."

240    **She sat down on it**: Photograph of Dore, Hancock Foundation Archive.

240    **"The island is an island" to "try"**: Ibid.

240    **Soon enough, he thought**: Ibid.

240    **At her request, Margret stayed**: Heinz Wittmer, "Lorenz and Nuggerud Also Dead," in "What Happened on Galapagos?"

240    **filming the scene**: Video from Hancock expedition, 1934–1935, Hancock Foundation Archive.

240    **"I said goodbye" to "through me"**: Strauch, *Satan Came to Eden*, 285.

241    **"merciful mist"**: Video from Hancock expedition, 1934–1935.

241    **On the walk to Black Beach**: Ibid.

241    **She listed and stumbled**: *El Universo*, Dec. 10, 1934.

241    **"We and the Wittmers"**: Strauch, *Satan Came to Eden*, 285.

241    **"Dore leaving Charles Island"**: *Sacramento Bee*, Dec. 8, 1934.

241    **"I am deeply sorry"**: *El Universo*, Dec. 4, 1934.

241    **"There was no ship anywhere" to "Heinz Wittmer"**: Wittmer, *Floreana*, 93.

242    **an apology for defiling**: Ibid., 94–95.

242    **"a great assortment of trash"**: Garth, "Personal Recollections."

242    **"old garments"**: Schmitt, Hancock-Galapagos Expedition.

242    **"the darndest junk" to "impedimenta"**: Ibid.

242    **"visit acquaintances of former years"**: Ibid.

242    **"a few punk ones"**: Ibid.

242    **"Everyone is convinced"**: Ibid.

242    **"enough rocks were added"**: Treherne, *The Galapagos Affair*, 206.

242    **"Dr. Ritter would" to "leave Charles Island"**: Ibid.

243    **"one crippled leg"**: Ibid.

243    **eventually told Ziesenhenne**: Ibid.

243    **Ziesenhenne was surprised**: Ibid.

243    **Waldo Schmitt was dubbed Sherlock Holmes**: Garth, "Personal Recollections," Dec. 14, 1934.

243    **"We know nothing"**: Joint statement by Heinz and Margret Wittmer and Dore Strauch as given to Captain Hancock of the *Velero III* on Dec. 14, 1934, box 6, "Letters 1933/34/35/Depositions" folder, Collection no. 0257, Special Collections, USC Libraries.

243    **Heinz was confused**: Heinz Wittmer, "Floreana in Pictures," in "What Happened on Galapagos?"

244    **"Governor's Tin Palace"**: Garth, "Personal Recollections," Dec. 15, 1934.

244   "due to suffocation": *El Universo*, Dec. 20, 1934.

244   "left out a good deal" to "impossible situation": Garth, "Personal Recollections,"
      Dec. 15, 1934.

245   "several books on the subject": *Washington Post*, Dec. 31, 1934.

245   "entirely dispassionate": *Daily Mail*, Dec. 28, 1934.

245   "Pots and pans lie around" to "complete upsetting": Heinz Wittmer, "Tragic
      Balance," in "What Happened on Galapagos?"

245   Casa de la Paz: Heinz Wittmer, "Suspicion," in "What Happened on Galapagos?"

245   she saw a group of soldiers: Wittmer, *Floreana*, 92–93.

245   "What do you want": Ibid.

245   "Tell me exactly": Ibid.

246   "You're hiding" to "at last": Ibid.

246   "Your husband killed": Ibid., 93.

246   "What?"; "Who on earth": Ibid.

246   "Dr. Ritter": Ibid.

246   "superhuman hearing": Ibid.

246   "no stain": Ibid.

246   "fruits and eggs": Wittmer, "Tragic Balance."

246   "It is basically" to "in them": Ibid.

247   Heinz considered: Ibid.

247   "do good to those": Ibid.

247   He erected a plain wooden cross: Ibid.

## Thirty-Eight: Thus Spake Floreana

248   "WE ARE ALIVE": Wittmer, *Floreana*, 94.

248   "find out what the people": Margret Wittmer, "Vacation Trip to Germany," in
      "What Happened on Galapagos?"

248   "putting out stories": Wittmer, *Floreana*, 97.

248   "Prince Charles": *New York Times*, Nov. 20, 1934.

248   "When was the last time" to "one money per word": *El Telégrafo*, March 13, 1935.

249   "Racial kinship to the German people" to "who fly flags": *Baltimore Sun*, April 28,
      1935.

249   very uneasy: Wittmer, *Floreana*, 99.

249   "When we left the country" to "island": Ibid.

249   "With Wittmer at Galapagos": Margret Wittmer to Hakon Mielche, April 15, 1934,
      box 1, DeStefano collection.

249   "dried up": Wittmer, *Floreana*, 98.

249   "scarcely dispute": Ibid.

250   "My father was ashamed": Mayer, *Widerspruch*, 39.

250   "there was still a crowd": Treherne, *The Galapagos Affair*, 196.

250   "Papa, Papa": Wittmer, *Floreana*, 103.

250   "a minor stir"; "was not very": Ibid., 99.

250   "bodiless Friedrich": Strauch to Hancock, 1935, box 6, "Letters 1933/34/35/
      Depositions" folder, Hancock Foundation Archive.

251   "I could give you" to "decided": Ibid.

251 **"I know that among"; "impossible":** Oskar Hieber to Hancock, July 31, 1935, box 6, "Letters 1933/34/35/Depositions" folder, Hancock Foundation Archive.

251 **"Do you know" to "in comparison":** Strauch to Hancock, "Before Christmas 35," box 6, "Letters 1933/34/35/Depositions" folder, Hancock Foundation Archive.

251 **"Although I never got an answer" to "tropics":** Strauch to Hancock, May 12, 1938, box 6, "Letters 1933/34/35/Depositions" folder, Hancock Foundation Archive.

252 **"menopausal bleeding":** Dore Strauch's death certificate, document number 2315, Standesamt Berlin.

252 **"the last person":** Wittmer, *Floreana*, 99.

252 **"latest knowledge":** *Miami News*, Nov. 25, 1934.

252 **Another report claimed:** Ibid.

252 **An even wilder tale:** *Tampa Tribune*, March 15, 1935.

252 **"Stop" to "I don't like you. Go":** Ibid.

252 **"We hunted for the Baroness" to "on to us":** *Reading Times*, March 21, 1935.

253 **"The official news report" to "four years":** *Time*, Aug. 8, 1938.

253 **On Baltra Island:** Roslyn Cameron, email message to author, June 23, 2023.

253 **the *Velero* crew discovered:** libraries.usc.edu/locations/special-collections/allan-hancock-foundation-pacific-expeditions.

253 **male genitalia of noctuid moths:** Ibid.

253 **"It was the general understanding":** George Myers to Lorenzo DeStefano, Jan. 27, 1978, box 2, DeStefano collection.

254 **"When Ritter and the Baroness":** Mielche, *Let's See*, 119.

254 **In December 1938:** A record of Heinz and Margret's marriage: Acc. 429 (Personalamt (PA)), A412), Stadt Köln—Die Oberbürgermeisterin, Historisches Archiv.

254 **it wasn't until 1939:** Heinrich Wittmer and Anna Ebel divorce trial proceedings and decision housed in Landesarchiv Nordrhein-Westfalen, Abteilung Rheinland, Duisburg.

254 **The ground floor:** Author visit to Floreana, May 2022.

254 **rumors began to circulate:** Moore, *Galápagos: An Encyclopedia*, 222.

255 **Both Frances and Ainslie had read:** Conway, *The Enchanted Islands*, 147.

255 **The Path of the Dead:** Ibid.

255 **"The garden was as quiet" to "now and then":** Ibid., 149–50.

255 **In 1940, soon after:** Moore, *Galápagos: An Encyclopedia*, 222.

255 **Having heard a rumor:** Woram, *Charles Darwin*, 298.

256 **his body was never recovered:** Moore, *Galápagos: An Encyclopedia*, 33.

256 **"I remembered bitterly":** Wittmer, *Floreana*, 207.

256 **rather, it belonged to one:** *Miami Herald*, Nov. 27, 1935.

256 **Despite extensive searching:** Elian Ehrenreich, "The Dark Secret of the Galapagos Island of Floreana," *Welt*, Jan. 19, 2015, welt.de.

256 **"Mario, he was sick":** *Cincinnati Enquirer*, Oct. 11, 1970.

256 **"On the Galapagos":** Ibid.

256 **a cerebral hemorrhage:** Moore, *Galápagos: An Encyclopedia*, 356.

256 **Doctors didn't arrive:** Ibid.

257 **A group of tourists:** Roslyn Cameron, email message to author, Nov. 5, 2021.

257 **"something"; They asked Margret:** Ibid.

257 **"God helps those":** *Cincinnati Enquirer,* Oct. 11, 1970.

257 **"Everything is exaggerated":** Ibid.

257 **she dredged up old memories:** Olshausen, "Galapagos Lure and Lore."

257 **"The Baroness" to "with holes":** Ibid.

257 **"She was always":** Ibid.

257 **"Dr. Ritter" and "He couldn't stomach":** Ibid.

257 **"Ritter was uncouth":** Ibid.

257 **"The last note":** Ibid.

258 **"Everybody knows":** *Cincinnati Enquirer,* Oct. 11, 1970.

258 **"It is all an inexplicable mystery":** Olshausen, "Galapagos Lure and Lore."

258 **"En boca cerrada":** *The Galapagos Affair: Satan Came to Eden,* zeitgeistfilms.com /userFiles/uploads/films/242/galapagosaffair-presskit.pdf.

258 **"Do you think I did it?":** Moore, *Galápagos: An Encyclopedia,* 33.

# BIBLIOGRAPHY

## Archival Sources

Allan Hancock Foundation Archive, Collection no. 0257, Special Collections, USC
   Libraries, University of Southern California.
Lorenzo DeStefano collection on the Hancock Pacific Expeditions, Collection no. 6215,
   Special Collections, USC Libraries, University of Southern California.
Private collection of Jane Brennan.
Smithsonian Institution Archives, Record Unit 7231, Waldo L. Schmitt Papers.

## Books, Essays, and Manuscripts

Baarslag, Karl. *Islands of Adventure*. London: Robert Hale, 1941.
Barlow, Nora, ed. *The Works of Charles Darwin: Diary of the Voyage of H.M.S. Beagle*. New
   York: New York University Press, 1987.
Beebe, William. *Galápagos: World's End*. New York: G. P. Putnam's Sons, 1924.
Blackwelder, Richard E. *The Zest for Life: Or, Waldo Had a Pretty Good Run*. Lawrence,
   Kans.: Allen Press, 1979.
Blomberg, Rolf. *Underliga människor och underliga djur*. Stockholm: Hugo Gebers, 1936.
Brittain, Vera. *Testament of Youth: An Autobiographical Study of the Years 1900–1925*. 1933.
   New York: Penguin Classics, 2005.
Bryant, John H., and Harold N. Cones. *The Zenith Trans-Oceanic: The Royalty of Radios*.
   Atglen, Pa.: Schiffer Publishing, 1995.
Cassidy, Mike. *Biological Evolution: An Introduction*. Cambridge, U.K.: Cambridge University
   Press, 2020.
Clover, Sam T. *A Pioneer Heritage*. Los Angeles: Saturday Night Publishing, 1932.
Conway, Ainslie, and Frances Conway. *The Enchanted Islands*. New York: G. P. Putnam's
   Sons, 1947.
Coolidge, Amory. *A Visit to the Cocos and Galapagos Islands on Board the* Blue Dolphin.
   Privately published, 1933.
Darwin, Charles. *The Voyage of the* Beagle. 1839. New York: Penguin Classics, 1989.
Dearborn, Lynne M., and Abbilyn Harmon. "Hoovervilles." In *The Encyclopedia of Housing*,
   edited by Andrew T. Carswell. 2nd ed. Thousand Oaks, Calif.: SAGE Publications, 2012.
D'Orso, Michael. *Plundering Paradise: The Hand of Man on the Galápagos Islands*. New York:
   HarperCollins, 2002.
Eichler, Arturo. *Ecuador: Snow Peaks and Jungles*. Quito: Edicion del Autor, 1970.
Finsen, Walter. "Debunking the Baroness." Unpublished manuscript, 1944, Puerto Ayora,
   Galápagos.

Friedrich, Otto. *Before the Deluge: A Portrait of Berlin in the 1920s.* New York: Harper & Row, 1972.

Gibbs, James, Linda Cayot, and Washington Tapia, eds. *Galapagos Giant Tortoises.* Amsterdam: Elsevier, 2020.

Gordon, Mel. *Voluptuous Panic: The Erotic World of Weimar Berlin.* Port Townsend, Wash.: Feral House, 2008.

Guadalupi, Gianni, and Antony Shugaar. *Latitude Zero: Tales of the Equator.* New York: Carroll & Graf, 2001.

Hancock, Eleanor. *Ernst Röhm.* New York: Palgrave Macmillan, 2008.

Harmon, Jim. *The Great Radio Heroes.* 1967. Jefferson, N.C.: McFarland, 2001.

Hoffmann, Dieter. *Einstein's Berlin: In the Footsteps of a Genius.* Baltimore: Johns Hopkins University Press, 2013.

Hurt, Douglas R. *The Dust Bowl: An Agricultural and Social History.* Lanham, Md.: Rowman & Littlefield, 1981.

Jackson, Michael Hume. *Galápagos: A Natural History Guide.* Calgary, Canada: University of Calgary Press, 1985.

Johnson, Irving. *Westward Bound in the Schooner* Yankee. New York: W. W. Norton, 1936.

Keynes, Richard Darwin, ed. *Charles Darwin's* Beagle *Diary.* Cambridge, U.K.: Cambridge University Press, 1988.

Kricher, John, and Kevin Loughlin. *Galápagos: A Natural History.* 2nd ed. Princeton, N.J.: Princeton University Press, 2022.

Lange, Vernon. "The Wittmers of Floreana." Unpublished manuscript, 1983, Sacramento, Calif.

Larson, Edward. *Evolution's Workshop: God and Science on the Galápagos Islands.* New York: Basic Books, 2001.

Latorre, Octavio. *The Curse of the Giant Tortoise.* Quito, Ecuador: Latorre Torres, 2015.

Lundh, Jacob P. "Floreana." In *Notes on the Galapagos Islands,* edited by Edgardo Civallero. Santa Cruz, Galápagos: Charles Darwin Foundation, 2023.

———. "The Last Days of a Paradise." Unpublished manuscript, Oslo, Norway.

Madsen, Axel. *John Jacob Astor: America's First Multimillionaire.* New York: Wiley, 2001.

Marhoefer, Laurie. *Sex and the Weimar Republic.* Toronto: University of Toronto Press, 2015.

Maury, Richard. *The Saga of Cimba.* Tuckahoe, N.Y.: J. de Graff, 1973.

Mayer, Elisabeth. *Widerspruch: Erinnerungen, 1925–1945.* Stadthagen: Booksfactory, 2019.

Melville, Herman. *The Encantadas, or Enchanted Isles,* edited by Victor Wolfgang Von Hagen. San Francisco: Grabhorn Press, 1940.

Mielche, Hakon. *Let's See if the World Is Round.* New York: G. P. Putnam's Sons, 1938.

Moore, Gwen. *Destination Galápagos.* Norland, Wash.: Turtle Press, 1998.

Moore, Randy. *Galápagos: An Encyclopedia of Geography, History, and Culture.* London: Bloomsbury, 2021.

Moore, Randy, and Roslyn Cameron. *Galápagos Revealed.* Galápagos Islands: Galápagos Conservancy, 2019.

Mulford, Prentice. *Thoughts Are Things.* 1889. Reprint, Radford, Va.: Wilder Publications, 2008.

Nicholls, Henry. *The Galápagos: A Natural History.* New York: Basic Books, 2014.

Otterman, Lillian. *Clinker Islands: The Mysterious Galápagos.* Burbank, Calif.: Great Western Publishing, 1983.

Palmer, Edwin O. *Third Galapagos Trip of the* Velero III *in the Winter of 1933–1934: From the Log Book of the "Medicine Man" of the Trip*. Privately printed, 1934.

Pinchot, Gifford. *To the South Seas: The Cruise of the Schooner* Mary Pinchot *to the Galápagos, the Marquesas, and the Tuamotu Islands, and Tahiti*. Philadelphia: John C. Winston, 1930.

Porter, David Dixon. *Memoir of Commodore David Porter, of the United States Navy*. 1875. London: Forgotten Books, 2018.

Ritter, Friedrich. *Als Robinson auf Galapagos*. Leipzig: Frethlein, 1935.

Robinson, William Albert. *Voyage to Galápagos*. New York: Harcourt, Brace, 1936.

Schopenhauer, Arthur. "Prize Essay on the Basis of Morals" (1839). In *The Two Fundamental Problems of Ethics*, translated by David E. Cartwright and Edward E. Erdmann. London: Oxford University Press, 2010.

Sterling, Christopher H., and Cary O'Dell, eds. *The Concise Encyclopedia of American Radio*. New York: Routledge, 2011.

Stewart, Paul D. *Galápagos: The Islands That Changed the World*. New Haven, Conn.: Yale University Press, 2007.

Strauch, Dore. *Satan Came to Eden*. London: Jarrolds, 1935.

———. *Satan Came to Eden*. New York: Harper & Brothers, 1936.

Straumann, Tobias. *1931: Debt, Crisis, and the Rise of Hitler*. Oxford: Oxford University Press, 2019.

Sur, Ernesto [Fritz Hieber]. *Tod am Äquator: Die Wahrheit über die Galápagos-Affäre*. Privately published, 2012.

Thornton, Ian. *Darwin's Islands: A Natural History of the Galápagos*. Garden City, N.Y.: Natural History Press, 1971.

Treherne, John. *The Galapagos Affair*. New York: Random House, 1983.

Vanderbilt, William K. *To Galápagos on the* Ara: *1926*. Privately printed, 1927.

Von Hagen, Victor Wolfgang. *Ecuador the Unknown: Two and a Half Years' Travels in the Republic of Ecuador and Galapagos Islands*. New York: Oxford University Press, 1940.

Vonnegut, Kurt. *Galápagos*. New York: Delacorte Press/Seymour Lawrence, 1985.

Weiner, Jonathan. *The Beak of the Finch: A Story of Evolution in Our Time*. New York: Knopf, 1994.

Wilde, Oscar. *The Picture of Dorian Gray*. 1890. London: Penguin Books, 2020.

Wittmer, Margret. *Floreana: A Woman's Pilgrimage to the Galápagos*. 1961. London: Moyer Bell, 2013.

Wittmer, Margret, and Heinz Wittmer. "What Happened on Galapagos?" Unpublished English translation of German manuscript. Box 6, folder 10, Collection no. 0257, Special Collections, USC Libraries.

Woram, John. *Charles Darwin Slept Here*. Rockville Centre, N.Y.: Rockville Press, 2005.

Worster, Donald. *Dust Bowl: The Southern Plains in the 1930s*. New York: Oxford University Press, 2004.

Young, Julian. *Friedrich Nietzsche: A Philosophical Biography*. Cambridge, U.K.: Cambridge University Press, 2010.

# PHOTO INSERT
# CREDITS

# INDEX

# ABOUT THE AUTHOR

ABBOTT KAHLER, formerly writing as Karen Abbott, is the *New York Times* bestselling author of *Sin in the Second City; American Rose; Liar, Temptress, Soldier, Spy; The Ghosts of Eden Park* (an Edgar Award finalist for Best Fact Crime); and a novel, *Where You End.* A native of Philadelphia, she lives in New York City and in Greenport, New York.